Refining the Imagination:
Tradition, Collecting,
and the Vassar Education

The exhibition, *Refining the Imagination:
Tradition, Collecting, and the Vassar Education,*
has been generously supported by
The Friends of the Frances Lehman Loeb Art Center

Refining the Imagination: Tradition, Collecting, and the Vassar Education

THE FRANCES LEHMAN LOEB ART CENTER

VASSAR COLLEGE

EXHIBITION SCHEDULE

The Frances Lehman Loeb Art Center,
Vassar College, Poughkeepsie, New York
23 April—19 September 1999

Library of Congress Catalog Card Number: 98-74016
ISBN 0-9644263-2-3

This book has been published in conjunction with
an exhibition entitled, *Refining the Imagination:
Tradition, Collecting, and the Vassar Education*,
organized by The Frances Lehman Loeb Art Center.

Design: Vassar College Office of Publications
Editing: Peduzzi Editorial Services, Poughkeepsie, New York
Printing: Judith A. Zimmer, Thames Printing Company, Inc.,
    Norwich, Connecticut
Binding: Acme Bookbinding, Charlestown, Massachusetts

Cover/Jacket Illustration: *Mary Cassatt at the Louvre, the Etruscan Gallery*
(ca.1879-80), softground etching, acquatint, drypoint, and etching,
cat. no. 60

This publication has been supported by
The Friends of the Frances Lehman Loeb Art Center.

CONTENTS

Frances Beatty Adler and Allen Adler
  (Frances Beatty, class of 1970)
Anonymous, class of 1953
Mr. and Mrs. Henry A. Ashforth, Jr. (Georgia M. Perkins,
  class of 1954)
Joyce and Michael Axelrod (Joyce Jacobson, class of 1961)
Anne Hendricks Bass, class of 1963
Joan and Robert Bernhard (Joan E. Mack, class of 1953)
Hilda Bijur, class of 1940
Frances L. Brody, class of 1937
Peggy Brooks, class of 1940
Mary Sharp Cronson, class of 1947
Virginia Herrick Deknatel, class of 1929
Leon M. and Marian H. Despres (Marian H. Alschuler,
  class of 1930)
Alessandra Manning Dolnier, class of 1982, and
  Kurt A. Dolnier, class of 1981
June and Jack Dunbar (Janet S. Coan, class of 1948)
Barbara Doyle Duncan, class of 1943
Elizabeth L. Eisenstein, class of 1945-4
Mrs. Carolyn P. Farris, class of 1953
Frances D. Fergusson and Michael Moohr
Gerry Gewirtz Friedman, class of 1941
John H. Friedman and Jane H. Furse
Maryann K. and Alvin Friedman (Maryann Kallison, class of 1955)
Dr. Mary Weitzel Gibbons, class of 1951
Elizabeth Gosnell, class of 1984
The Greenberg Rohatyn Collection, New York, N.Y.
  (Jeanne Greenberg, class of 1989)
Nancy G. Harrison, class of 1974
Sue Peirce Hartshorn, class of 1962
Eugenie Aiguier Havemeyer, class of 1951
Mary Pick Hines, class of 1953
Steven R. and Susan Hirsch (Steven R. Hirsch, class of 1971)
Nancy and Tom Hoving (Nancy M. Bell, class of 1953)
Anne Hoene Hoy, class of 1963

Isabelle and Jerome E. Hyman (Isabelle Miller, class of 1951)
Anne Keating Jones, class of 1943
Virginia Lewisohn Kahn, class of 1949
Meg Newhouse Kirkpatrick, class of 1974
Diana Klemin, class of 1944
Phyllis Lambert, class of 1948, Montréal
John Post Lee, class of 1981, and Karin Bravin, New York
Thomas Krasne Levine, class of 1982
Stephen Mazoh
Thomas and Margaret McCormick
Bannon McHenry, class of 1952
Mary McLaughlin in memory of Pamela Askew, class of 1946
Alice Pack Melly, class of 1956
Ellen G. and Leonard Milberg (Ellen D. Gordon, class of 1960)
Mr. and Mrs. Kenneth Lane Miron (Andrea Leeds Miron,
  class of 1975)
Priscilla Morgan, class of 1941
Ann L. Balis Morse, class of 1959
Marian Phelps Pawlick, class of 1948
Marjorie and Arnold Z. Pfeffer (Marjorie P. Fingerhood,
  class of 1941)
Joan Quigley, class of 1946
Belle K. Ribicoff, class of 1945
Norma Honig Schlesinger, class of 1952
The Schloss Collection
Dorothy Seiberling, class of 1943
Dixie Sheridan, class of 1965
Georgia Sims, class of 1952, and William C. Carson
Philip and Lynn Straus (Lynn R. Gross, class of 1946)
Evan and Mary Tawil, New York (Evan Tawil, class of 1989)
Christopher Tunnard
Anne H. and Frederick Vogel III (Anne M. Henoch, class of 1963)
Lissa Cabot von Wentzel, class of 1964
Drs. Alvin and Lenore Weseley (Lenore S. Levine, class of 1954)
Alan Wintermute, class of 1981, and Colin Baily, New York
And two Anonymous collectors

ACKNOWLEDGMENTS

This exhibition is, itself, a gigantic acknowledgment of an institution comprised of many individuals and interests that have helped weave for generations, and that continue to weave, a fabric that adorns its students. This fabric is woven of the carefully balanced warp of sensibility and the woof of thought. *Refining the Imagination: Tradition, Collecting, and the Vassar Education*, as a finished product, owes its realization to the very great efforts of a large number of people. First of all, the generous financial support of the Friends of the Frances Lehman Loeb Art Center is acknowledged with respect and appreciation. This group has performed an essential service since its founding twenty-five years ago and is the envy of many of our peer institutions as a support group with the knowledge and dedication to make things of importance happen. This exhibition is gratefully dedicated to their quarter century of steadfast commitment. Harriet Drake, class of 1952 and Chair of the Friends, and her officers, have been enthusiastic in their support of this project. While the leadership of the Friends is acknowledged in the roster on the opposing page, I would like to single out several individuals whose particular dedication helped fashion this project. My greatest thanks go to Anne Keating Jones, class of 1943 and Co-Chair of the twenty-fifth anniversary committee, whose very diligent work has kept this project growing and achieving its goals. Not only has Anne, with her Co-Chair Andrea Leeds Miron, class of 1975, worked to organize the many events that led up to this exhibition, she also led the committee that helped identify many of the potential lenders to the show.

Next, I would like to thank the many generous lenders to the exhibition, who have kindly consented to be without some very beloved works of art for a period of seven months, so that the quality of the exhibition could be as high as possible. I would particularly like to single out those generous individuals who have designated their works as promised gifts: Joyce and Michael Axelrod; Peggy Brooks; Virginia Deknatel; Leon and Marian Despres; Jack and June Dunbar; Carolyn Peck Farris; Frances Fergusson and Michael Moohr; Nancy G. Harrison; Eugenie Havemeyer; Mary Pick Hines; Stephen and Susan Hirsch; Anne Hoene Hoy; Virginia Kahn; Diana Klemin; Thomas McCormick; Mary McLaughlin; Ellen and Leonard Milberg; Joan Quigley; and Lissa Cabot von Wentzel. Thanks to their remarkable commitment, nearly one-third of the objects in the exhibition are promised gifts to Vassar—this is a truly exceptional ratio.

This catalogue, too, is a work of art formed by committee. A number of authors and researchers have participated and helped us elucidate the essence of everything from Chinese funerary art to contemporary African painting. The largest bulk of the text has been composed by the Loeb Art Center's two curators, Rebecca Lawton, the Emily Hargroves Fisher '57 and Richard Fisher Curator, and Francesca Consagra, the Philip and Lynn Straus Curator of Prints and Drawings. Their considerable work on this project has tested the range of their art historical interests in writing so many fine entries. Additional entries have been written by Vassar faculty: Karen Lucic, Associate Professor; Lisa Gail Collins, Visiting Assistant Professor; and Carol Thompson, Instructor in the art department; and Vassar alumnæ, Candace Jenks Lewis, class of 1966; and Frances Prindle Taft, class of 1942. Andrew Watsky, Assistant Professor in the art department, offered indispensible advice on the single Japanese object in the exhibition. Finally, Ingrid Schaffner and Justin Spring of New York helped us greatly by contributing a number of entries in the twentieth-century section. I am greatly indebted to Elizabeth Daniels, class of 1941, Professor Emerita and Vassar College historian, for her excellent summary of the Friends' first quarter century. My thanks also go to Mary McLaughlin for permission to edit and publish the excerpt from Pamela Askew's history of the art department and art museum at Vassar. The research for the catalogue entries was assisted greatly by a number of student assistants, particularly our two Ford Scholars, Allison Bren and Hei Yeon Kim; as well as the efforts of research assistants, Hannah Ries, Tyler Rowland, and Margarita Luna. All are members of the class of 2000, which is appropriate for an exhibition about the future of Vassar as well as a celebration of its past.

In most respects, this exhibition, its catalogue, and its installation is of unprecedented size for Vassar College and the staff of its art museum. In addition to the curators mentioned above, I would like to express my wholehearted thanks to the other members of the Art Center staff who have worked so hard to make this project happen. Joann Potter, Registrar/Collections Manager, and Karen Casey, Assistant Registrar, have been assiduous in organizing the myriad details of loans, photography, and shipping—a complicated enough task when working with several lenders, but exceptional given the more than sixty collections represented by this exhibition. Bruce Bundock, Preparator, has excelled in presenting the works on loan within the context of the permanent collection of the Art Center in a manner that sets the loaned works apart but stresses their rational coherence in the presentation of the history of art. Francine Williams, Administrative Assistant, has taken on many different tasks from manuscript preparation to the tracking of expenses on this large project. The professional staff of the Friends of the Frances Lehman Loeb Art Center, Maureen Andola, Executive Administrator, and Beverly Doppel, Membership Secretary, have kept the Friends and the Art Center integrated throughout the research and development of this exhibition in honor of the Friends' milestone anniversary. Thanks also go to Vassar College President, Frances Fergusson, and Dean of Faculty, Norman Fainstein, for permitting us to organize this project, and to Karin George, Vice-President for Development, for her support and helpful suggestions as we developed the list of lenders. John Mihaly, also of the Vassar development office, played an important role in designing and organizing a number of regional events that led up to this exhibition. Finally, the look and legibility of the catalogue are owing to George Laws, Graphic Designer and Publications Manager, and Kelli Peduzzi, Editor. Susan DeKrey, Director of College Relations, and Diane Zucker, Associate Director of College Relations, worked to promote this project to the broader public. It is the significant contributions of the many individuals involved in this milestone project that have enabled us to celebrate the important and lasting role of the Friends of the Frances Lehman Loeb Art Center.

James Mundy, class of 1974
The Anne Hendricks Bass Director

REFINING THE IMAGINATION: A PROMISE DELIVERED

JAMES MUNDY, class of 1974
The Anne Hendricks Bass Director, Frances Lehman Loeb Art Center

The exhibition, *Refining the Imagination: Tradition, Collecting, and the Vassar Education*, attempts to demonstrate in an empirical fashion what many people have known intuitively—that the emphasis on honing a student's abilities to discern quality in the world of ideas or the world of art has built a network of perceptive art collectors with something in common—a Vassar education forms the foundation of their connoisseurship. The assemblage of almost one hundred and fifty works of art borrowed from private Vassar collections indicates that the impetus to collect art with such a knowledgeable foundation is a Vassar tradition that will continue into the next century. What has helped shape the excellent Vassar College art collection for one hundred thirty five years—the perspicacity of its alumni—promises to increase the quality of the collection in the foreseeable future. One cannot help but recognize, owing to the installation of this exhibition where the works are placed within the context of the permanent collection, the impact on the already superb Vassar collection were any portion of these fine works ultimately to reside at Vassar; indeed, some are planned gifts.

The exhibition takes its title from a report written by founding Vassar trustee, the Reverend Elias L. Magoon on behalf of the Committee on the Art Gallery, to the trustees in 1864. This report, a highly colorful and quotable rhetorical *tour de force*, presents the argument for instructing the young women of Vassar with the aid of original works of art to be housed in a space for this purpose. What follows are some excerpts from this important document:

> Art is diviner than science; the latter discovers, this creates. It is the highest sagacity and purest exertion of human nature. The study of it possesses this great and peculiar charm—that it is absolutely detached from the disgraceful contests of sordid ambition. Above and beyond all petty strifes, mankind are most attracted and united by a taste for beautiful art—*a taste at once the most engrossing and ennobling, refining the imagination and fortifying the judgement,* elevating emotion to the loftiest enthusiasm, and, at the same time, perfecting the critical faculty, under the joint influence of subjugated sense and sovereign reason.[1]

Or, later:

> Take the gem of your prospective college, under the full sway of legitimate education. Draped in enraptured unconsciousness, her bosom swells, cheeks flush, eyes sparkle, and thrilling inspiration gleams on her brow, as all that is receptive and immortal within responds to the living words of a competent teacher expounding facts in the presence of things....You may double your expenditure in monumental structures, or in lifeless apparatus, and yet not attain an iota of educating force. That is not a medicinal bath—something soaked in—but latent ability educated forth. When all other tools of inert erudition are at hand, give them to a substratum of LL.D's, with a substratum of D.D.'s, and all you will thereby accomplish is the dignified extinguishment of what little capacity for excellence yet remains in American youth, as you might smother a swarm of young bees under a cart-load of autumnal leaves.

> On the contrary, lay your material foundation deep and broad; cumulate languages, sciences, and art, in as huge an aggregate as possible; but, in God's name, send to the centre—fire! From at least one chair let positive electricity neutralize the prostrating influences of all the rest. For that purpose, collect an ample and diversified gallery of actualities in artistic elegance—forms, tints, tone, true to every kingdom of nature, and which shall at once illustrate the loftiest principles and refine the most delighted hearts.[2]

The board of trustees heeded Magoon's appeal, and the Art Gallery in Main Building opened with a collection of original paintings,

The Reverend Elias Lyman Magoon. (Courtesy of Vassar College Libraries, Special Collections)

drawings, and prints to complement the core curriculum. Within ten years would be added a large collection of plaster casts of famous sculptures and the first collection of some two thousand study photographs.

Over the next one hundred thirty years, the collection and curriculum grew in tandem and constantly returned to the need for the real to supplement the theoretical. The late Vassar professor emerita of art, Pamela Askew, in her essay that follows, focuses on the dramatic changes in world view and, hence, curriculum, brought about by a "galaxy of stars" who joined the art faculty at Vassar during the 1920s and 1930s, a time when the College itself was entering into its early maturity. How far the curriculum had traveled from the first "Art Studies" course listed simply in the college catalogue for 1867-68 as the "history of art illustrated by the works and lives of the great artists."(!) The catalogue also advertised that the College owned "400-500" works of art "embracing specimens of the contemporary masters," a fact suggestive of the persistent influence of Elias Magoon's vision for artistic "literacy" and the importance of the original object in his thinking. In 1867, those specimens would have included works by Frederic Church, Asher Durand, and other members of the Hudson River School, as well as works on paper by various British landscape artists. By 1875, the College had added a large collection of plaster casts of many of the great sculptures from the history of art as well as a collection of over two thousand photographs of European monuments from the studio of Adolph Braun. In 1880, the photo collection was supplemented by a collection of stereoscopic views.

By 1886, a loan collection of Japanese art entered the Art Gallery, now in Avery Hall, signaling a fashion in collecting that was current during the so-called Gilded Age. In 1892, the art department expanded it offerings to four courses that provided traditional fare of the masters, including not only the expected names of Donatello, Michelangelo, Rubens, Poussin, and Millet, but also names more indicative of the tastes of the age, such as Flaxman, Thorwaldsen, and della Robbia. As the nineteenth became the twentieth century, Vassar announced with pride that its students

went regularly to the Metropolitan Museum of Art in New York to study from originals. It was also the moment when a new course on "structural aesthetics and constructive art criticism" was offered.

The combination of the real and the theoretical in art could take the form of bringing a number of temporary exhibitions to the College, as well as lectures by artists and historians. Thus, a review of the College catalogues and other records document early exhibits of the work of Gustave Courbet (1890), Anton Mauve (1894), Edward Hopper and Diego Rivera (1917), Childe Hassam (1919), members of the *Société Anonyme* (1923), Henri Matisse (1925), contemporary Russian art (1934), Piet Mondrian (1934), Jacob Lawrence (1942), and Florine Stettheimer (1948). In addition, the students heard from artists and architects such as William Merritt Chase, who spoke about "Whistler—the Man and His Art," Kenyon Cox on "Venetian Painters," Ralph Adams Cram on Gothic architecture, also from Le Corbusier, Philip Johnson, Yasuo Kuniyoshi, and Alexander Calder, as well as the most accomplished art historical scholars, many—after 1935—refugees from Nazi oppression.

For many Vassar students, this combination of pedagogy, original work, and human exempla made deep and lasting impressions. Among the most important was a continuing emphasis on the relevance of quality, whether in ideas or works of art. The Vassar collectors represented in *Refining the Imagination* came to collecting in various ways—through inheritance, travel, relationships— acquiring the soon-to-be-famous artists at opportune moments, or, means permitting, at the top of the market. Whatever the individual circumstances, the recognition of the ineffable nuances between what is "good," "better," and "best" had been reinforced by a succession of demanding faculty, from the *pince-nez-* and frock-coated Professors Van Ingen and Tonks, through émigrés Krautheimer and Katzenellenbogen, to the stately role models of Rindge, Barber, and Askew. Each lender to the exhibition will have her or his own interpretation of the configuration of the path that led from the education to the art, but the sheer volume of knowledgeable collectors with Vassar in their pasts represents more than just coincidence.

Many of us came to Vassar not necessarily aware of the deep-seated relevance of such a tradition that existed at the institution. When we were sent into the then Art Gallery on the second floor of Taylor Hall to write a description (not an interpretation or an appreciation) of an original painting or sculpture, how many of us realized then that it was intended to take us beyond the mere apprehension of descriptive prose? How frustrated some of us were with the

Vassar College Art Gallery in Main Building around 1865-75. (Courtesy of Vassar College Libraries, Special Collections)

seeming futility of describing the obvious. The idea that the
professor could grade us on such an exercise was startling. Was the
instructor not interested in our insights into the artist's motivations
and thoughts? How constrained some of us felt at not being allowed
to show off our comprehensive intellects just a bit! Little did we
then realize that this was a baptism of sorts for us—the introduction
to a method that would place the object first before our eyes in a
purposeful manner, thereby making the next such experience a
moment relative to this, and so the next and the next…. At the end
of this concatenation might lie a sense of comfort rather than
intimidation before the work of art that might later allow us to live
among such things and continue to learn from them.

Today, as I welcome the students of my museum studies seminar
into the galleries, I am aware of several things. First, that so many of
the works of art there once belonged to women and men who
started their life-long love affairs with art in a similar Vassar environment, and who understood the museum's mission so as to make
their important gifts. Second, that so many of the works of art not
given by alumnae/i were actually selected and purchased by the Art
Gallery or Art Center by directors, curators, and faculty who were
Vassar-trained or trainers. Finally, I'm aware that when I pose
whatever question occurs before this or that painting, that I—who
was taught by Professors Askew and Nochlin, who themselves
studied under Barber and Rindge, who learned in turn from Tonks
and Chatterton—perpetuate and acknowledge the wisdom of a
nineteenth-century visionary in Elias Magoon, who saw a clear
means to "refine the imagination" and "at the same time, perfect
the critical faculty." Thus, in this exhibition, we pay homage to this
concept and lay the foundation for the its further growth in the next
century.

---

[1] *Report of the Committee on the Art Gallery of Vassar Female College* (Poughkeepsie,
1864), reprinted in *Vassar College Art Gallery: Selections from the Permanent Collection*
(Poughkeepsie, 1967), xii.

[2] Ibid.

A GALAXY OF STARS

PAMELA ASKEW, class of 1946
Professor Emerita of Art, Vassar College

The advent of Hyatt Mayor, along with the arrival of Agnes Rindge in the second semester of 1922-23, introduced into the Vassar art department a succession of bright, enterprising, and pioneering young shapers of the field who, in time, became leading proponents of their various specialties. They were the liberated moderns of the twenties and, quite unlike Professor Oliver Tonks, they were advocates and promoters of modern art. Because of their universal distinction in their various endeavors, they comprise, as I call them, "a galaxy of stars."

The world was an oyster for the youth of the twenties, and there were plenty of new pearl divers who found it fun. The profession of art history, like others at the time, was increasing in seriousness of purpose and sought to put itself on a more equal footing with other disciplines. It endeavored to formulate a scientific structure that would replace a more anecdotal and descriptive approach to the history of art.

The twenties were exciting, innovative, and defining years for art history—at Vassar and elsewhere—though perhaps especially at Vassar owing to its proximity to the New York cultural scene. Vassar, after all, had never been a part of the grand old New England tradition, but over the years had associated itself primarily with the business, institutional, and cultural life of New York. As Ann Douglas has pointed out, by 1920 New York had become the world's most powerful and cosmopolitan city. Not least was this owing to its reception of a vast black population emigrating to New York during the war years. America was alive with change. In its culture and entertainment was reflected an enjoyment of a particularly American heritage that paralleled a social liberation taking place within a larger American emancipation from a European cultural standard. New York was the center for the new credo of the twenties, which in its rejection of sentimentalism and falseness in favor of truthfulness and a facing of facts no matter how painful, has been called a "terrible honesty."[1] This was the credo of the moderns, and it is not too far wide of the mark to say that it informed the approach to both art and art history.

At Vassar, the academic year of 1923-24 opened with an art department consisting of Oliver Tonks, Clarence Chatterton, Mary McGehee, and the successor to Hyatt Mayor, his classmate Alfred Hamilton Barr (1902-81). Subsequently identified with the founding and mission of the Museum of Modern Art, and as such, one of the most influential figures in the arts, he needs no introduction. Vassar President Henry Noble MacCracken had written to Tonks at the end of the previous academic year asking why the art department had recommended for instructorships people with less graduate training and teaching experience than any other department in the college. Among applicants now unknown, he must also have had in mind both Hyatt Mayor and Agnes Rindge. Tonks explained that it was difficult to find candidates and that those available were recent graduates who lacked experience. Further, he noted that it was "practically impossible to get even a well-trained bachelor of arts to come at a salary less than that of instructor because of the many opportunities that present themselves....The only well-trained candidate left," he protested, "is Mr. Barr...."[2] Had Tonks deliberately left him to the last because of his professed interest in modern art? Alfred Barr *was* well-trained. He had received his B.A. at Princeton in 1922, and his M.A. in 1923, also at Princeton, for which he had written a thesis on Piero de Cosimo. At Vassar, Barr shared, as Hyatt had done, the teaching of the courses in Italian painting, Northern painting, and Venetian painting. He also shared the course in Italian sculpture with Kate McKnight, and joined Tonks and Chatterton in teaching modern painting.

Barr, whom Tonks had found to be "a man of gentlemanly instincts," was twenty-one when he taught at Vassar.[3] The students called him "Mr. Mixed-Suits," because, quite unconventionally, he wore jackets that didn't match his trousers.[4] An apparently intense, responsive, yet judicious young man, he was, I believe, an inspiring scholar and teacher; in a certain sense he remained long after he had left the classroom behind. He was kept busy at Vassar, writing home to his mother, Annie Wilson Barr (Vassar ex-1891), "I am intoxicated with work—imagine it, never have I been so utterly busied....I have completely rearranged the Modern Painting course. It took eight and a half hours to plan it. A continuous urge to learn more, to understand what before was woefully superficial—and then I have no energy for anything and I am far behind in sleep."[5]

How lasting an effect Barr's revision of the modern painting course had is highly dubious, for inevitably he found Tonks "insufficiently sympathetic to the arts of the twentieth century."[6] Whatever Barr chose to say to Tonks on the subject, he had, I believe, an effect upon his superior—not in the sense of a conversion but, I suspect, in the form of a backlash. As soon as Barr had moved on, in the very next year, Tonks wrote an article on modern art which he inimically called, "The Creed of Abstract Art."[7] Had he felt Barr to have been its apostle? In it, Tonks instructs the reader that emotion, not representation, is the basis of art, and assesses the viewpoint of modern artists as "distinctly personal and selfish if you wish."

In 1929 Barr was appointed director of the then-new Museum of Modern Art, through which he became the most influential crusader for modern art in this country. During the short time he was at Vassar, he arranged for two exhibitions of modern art; with the exception of the exhibition of expressionists the year before, both were radically different from what had been shown until that time. The first was an exhibition of twelve works by Kandinsky, which he procured from Katherine Dreier's *Société Anonyme,* founded in 1920,[8] and in certain respects a precursor of the Museum of Modern Art. Vassar's exhibition of his work in the fall of 1923 was preceded by Dreier's presentation of his first one-man show in America the previous spring.[9] Since the exhibition took place in America, it must have been hastily acquired, unfortunately leaving no time to print the checklist brochure that usually accompanied each exhibition.[10] The other exhibition for which Alfred Barr was responsible was an international gathering of works by modern artists borrowed from New York galleries, private collections, and in great part from the *Société Anonyme.* Among the sixty-one works loaned were those by Arp, Derain, Matisse, Ernst, Moholy-Nagy, Severini, DeChirico, Lissitzsky, Kandinsky, Gris, and Picasso.[11]

In 1924-25, the Vassar art department had two new members replacing Kate McKnight and Alfred Barr. They were Agnes Rindge who had been studying for the M.A. degree at Radcliffe, and Arthur McComb, who had come with a Harvard B.A. 1918, and M.A. 1922. Agnes Rindge, it will be recalled, had taught in the art department the second term of 1922-23, and had shared an office with Hyatt Mayor.

On her return to Vassar, Rindge taught ancient art, a course in Renaissance and modern sculpture, which expanded the earlier Italian sculpture course taught by McKnight and Barr, and shared in the modern painting course with Tonks, Clarence Chatterton, and McComb. Something she never mentioned in later years was that she taught with Chatterton a semester course in interior decoration. Interior decoration was a subject undoubtedly thought to be too easily centered on the domestic instincts of young females. Agnes preferred to equip them for a more worldly stage. The course was described as "a study of the problems of artistic house furnishing," included a review of the domestic furniture of Assyrian, Egyptian, Greek, Roman, Medieval, Renaissance, Georgian, and modern times. These were considered from the point of view of handicraft, environmental influence, and the effect of one style upon another. This course was not counted toward the number of courses required in sequential study in the department, and so was in essence down-graded. As an academic subject, interior decoration was spoken of with considerable disdain by Rindge; she never referred to its having been offered at Vassar,

much less having taught it herself! Quite different was the story it amused her to tell of herself in connection with teaching the course on ancient art: "I put the Coliseum right up there on the Acropolis!" Her class was never boring!

She also participated in what was an entirely new course, offering a one-term "General Introduction to Art" taught by the department. The catalogue described it as "a study of the past periods of artistic activity with reference to the problems of technique, the effect of environment, national temperament and the sequential development of art throughout historical times." This landmark addition to the curriculum, required of all the students taking art, was the incipient survey course best known today as Art 105.

Vassar, however, was late in offering a chronological course in the field. Smith had first established such a course in 1914, and the number of such courses had steadily increased, with the chronological type of survey remaining dominant in 1925.[12] The mid-twenties, in fact, saw a sudden burst of writing on art history as an academic subject. The courses generated by this explosion were marked by the imbalance between a demand for staff and a lack of qualified persons trained in the new field to supply the universities and colleges. Not least in this growth was the purpose and value of the survey course. It laid the groundwork, by definition, for a historical treatment of the subject. "In short, instruction in art in the colleges should be, in the broader and most delicate sense, historical," wrote Princeton's Frank Jewett Mather in 1923. With Princeton and Harvard advocating the historical survey, the die was cast for its becoming the norm in institutions of the Northeast. It bore the seal of approval.[13]

At Vassar, there were four introductory courses. The introductory survey was now called Art 105a, and its description significantly reversed the previous one by placing "the effect of environmental and national temperament," and "the sequential development of art throughout historic times," before consideration of technique.

McComb and Rindge stayed in the department for two years, their second year under the chairmanship of Leicester B. Holland, who served as acting head of the department during Tonks's leave of absence for the academic year 1925-26. In this year they shared curatorial duties, of which more will be said in connection with the gallery. Central Italian Painting of the Renaissance was a course introduced by McComb in his second year, which established a more concentrated focus than the general history of Italian painting, which was given as usual. This was entirely in keeping with his Harvard training and subsequent Berensonian orientation acquired during a prolonged stay in Florence in 1922-23.[14] In 1926-27, the Vassar art department instituted a course cross-listed with the zoology department, Anatomy for Art Students. It was taught by Miss Cora Beckwith, and included the study of the human skeleton and muscles, with special attention to the influence of muscular action on form. It was given in the zoology laboratory and was intended to be beneficial for those taking applied art as well as students taking sequential courses in art history. It was not dropped from the curriculum until 1932-33.

The greatest weight of teaching in 1925-26 fell upon the other appointment for the year—another star, as it were, in the male galaxy of the twenties—Arthur Kilgore McComb (1896-1968).[15] At Vassar, he taught Ancient Architecture; Medieval Art, a new course that was devoted exclusively to the architecture and sculpture of the Middle Ages; and Renaissance and Modern Architecture. He taught as well with Tonks in the courses on Northern painting and Venetian painting, and with Tonks, Chatterton, and Rindge in the course on modern painting, not to mention the semester survey course. It is for his work on Italian painting that McComb became known and most particularly for having pioneered the reinstitution of an interest in Italian painting of the Baroque period in this country. (The term "Baroque" encompassed both the seventeenth and eighteenth centuries). Italian Baroque painting had been marginalized by an infatuation with early Italian painting in this country.

More will be said of McComb's role in the rehabilitation of the Baroque within the Vassar Art Gallery, and, as will be seen, he was influential for the Vassar art department in several ways long after his departure from it. Not least important, in a scholarly sense, was his publication in 1934 of the first book in English, *The Baroque Painters of Italy: An Introductory Historical Survey*, a text that was generally in use until the surge of new scholarship on the Baroque took place in the 1950s.[16] In promoting Italian painting of the seventeenth and eighteenth centuries, McComb had moved in a direction quite opposed to the aesthetic preferences sustained by Harvard at the time, as well as the derogatory view of the Baroque held by Berenson.

Both Agnes Rindge and Arthur McComb left Vassar at the end of the academic year 1925-26. According to Rindge, during her two years at Vassar, she "could see clearly the writing on the wall: you get a degree if you want to get ahead."[17] She went to Harvard to earn it. It was in 1926-27 that she first met, as she put it, "all those bright young men."[18] In that year, also enrolled in Paul Sachs's museum course that Agnes took, were Alfred Barr (who was at Wellesley but was taking the course), Kirk Askew, Arthur Everett ("Chick") Austin, Henry Russell Hitchcock, and James Rorimer.[19] Agnes's lifelong friendships with the first four of them proved of crucial importance for the department, and especially for the gallery, as will be seen.

James Thrall Soby, *Portrait of Henry Russell Hitchcock* (ca. 1938). (Collection of Pamela Askew)

Agnes Rindge was replaced in 1926-27 by Elizabeth Baily Lawrence, who had graduated from Bryn Mawr. She felt herself to be especially well-grounded in the ancient and modern fields, and was pursuing graduate work in Rome under the direction of Professor Charles Rufus Morey.[20] It is possible that she married and continued her career under a married name, or she might have abandoned an academic career altogether; in any event, the usual channels have not yielded any further trace of her.

The next star in the galaxy of brilliant young men was Henry Russell Hitchcock (1903-72), who taught in the department in 1927-28. He came as an assistant professor, having received his M.A. (1927), and B.A. (1924) from Harvard. He had already started to publish, having been asked by Lincoln Kirstein to write for *The Hound & Horn*, a magazine of the arts started by Kirstein as a freshman at Harvard. It trumpeted change and sought out what was innovative and exciting, announcing that it took as its point of departure what was at once a valediction and a call to action. In the mood of Plato it bade farewell to a land where long-familiar contours have ceased to stir creative thought: it bade farewell—and sounded the hunting horn.[21] Its advance issue and first number in September 1927 carried Hitchcock's "The Decline of Architecture." It dealt with the limitations imposed by, and the freedoms taken in, the modern techniques of building. Hitchcock from the start was a "modern," and soon became a pivotal figure in that group responsible for both energizing and redirecting the arts in this country during the next decades.

In 1927 Tonks published *A History of Italian Painting*. It was written for beginning students, and attempted to present them with a clear "consecutive statement," devoid of the kind of scholarly detail or extended discussion that he believed suitable for more advanced students. Tonks's book was accepted at the time as sensible and readable, and it was judged to be "not as detailed as Crowe and Cavalcaselle's *History of Painting*, not as brilliant as Mather's *History of Italian Painting*, but a good book for the college student."[22]

Two years earlier there had come to Vassar from Rome a student assistant in the Italian department, Margaret Scolari (1901-87). While here, she spent a good deal of time in the art library, where she came to know Agnes Rindge, Arthur McComb, and in 1927-28, Russell Hitchcock. The following year, still teaching in Vassar's Italian department, she again commuted to New York for graduate work at New York University, leaving at the end of the year to live in New York as a full-time graduate student. In late November of 1929, Agnes Rindge had returned to Vassar. She went with Margaret Scolari to the Museum of Modern Art, which had just opened that month with Alfred Barr as director. Agnes introduced her to Alfred Barr, whom Scolari married a few months later (May 1930) in Paris.[23] Russell Hitchcock was best man, having helped the bride shop for a dress and hat for the occasion.[24]

While at Vassar, Hitchcock taught the courses in Medieval and Renaissance architecture, and Venetian painting. He shared in the teaching of Tonks's modern painting, and taught Italian painting with both Tonks and Chatterton. He also participated in the introductory survey. His scholarly output remained prolific all his life, as did his teaching activities, the greater part of which were centered first at Wesleyan and then at Smith College, where from 1949 to 1955 he was also director of the Smith College Museum of Art. Vassar can lay small claim to him, but it was characteristic of the College and department at the time to have nabbed him as a young man of exceptional energy, breadth of interest, and singular promise.

More than any other American architectural historian, he changed the perception of the architecture in this country, primarily through the analytic approach to modern architecture, in such works as his Modern *Architecture, Romanticism and Reinterpretation* (1928), and *The International Style, Architecture Since 1922*, written in collaboration with Philip Johnson, with a foreword by Alfred Barr (1932). An exhibition on this theme at the Museum of Modern Art in 1932, of which Hitchcock and Johnson were curators, put the International Style, which they had themselves named, definitively on the map, and for its importance in changing the course of architecture in this country, it has been deemed as important as the exhibition of the Crystal Palace in London in 1851.[25] Hitchcock has justly been called "the father of modern architectural history in the United States."[26] Although Russell Hitchcock and Agnes Rindge did not teach in the Vassar art department at the same time, they had forged a lifelong friendship at Harvard in 1926, which meant that Russell remained in indirect contact with the department for the rest of his life.

The department in 1928-29, consisting of Tonks, Chatterton, and McGehee, saw the return of Agnes Rindge at the rank of associate professor. She had earned an M.A. at Radcliffe in 1927, and the Ph.D. was conferred on 20 June 1928. "They just shoved me through, like that, or didn't pay too much attention," she said, "and in the meantime there were all these fascinating people around."[27] In addition to her friends, Barr, Russell Hitchcock, and Rorimer, also at Harvard in 1926-27 were Jane Abbott, Kirk Askew, and A. E. Austin.[28] Her participation in their dynamics with respect both to the creation and advocacy of modern art, as well as to the establishment of new trends in the marketplace, affected collectors and bestowed a distinguishing character upon the Vassar art department, as will be seen.

George Platt Lynes, *Agnes Rindge*. (Frances Lehman Loeb Art Center)

Taught by Rindge in 1928-29 was Introduction to Architecture in place of a course entitled Northern Painting, which was extended to two terms; Renaissance and Modern Sculpture; a share of the course on Italian painting, taught with Tonks and Chatterton; not to mention participating in Art 105. Apparently not given by her until the following year was an advanced course in Spanish art, for which the ability to read French and German or Spanish and German was required.

For the changes that would bring the department to the forefront and its students to the attention of those in the field, Rindge worked sedulously and perseveringly. Bright students were not only specially noted, but if possible, were put forward in ways befitting their gifts. A vehicle for bringing the intellectually talented to notice was the *Vassar Journal of Undergraduate Studies*, which had been founded in December 1925 by President MacCracken and certain members of the faculty, and whose first issue appeared in 1926. Its purpose was to publish student papers, written in connection with course work, in order to demonstrate that recent criticisms of college ideals and methods, alleging superficiality and evasion of broad concepts of scholarship, were not based on valid evidence.[29] The *Journal* represented the best scholarly work produced by undergraduates, and acquired, in fact, a reputation beyond the walls of Vassar in which for many years the college took pride. It was not until 1929, however, that papers written in connection with course work in the history of art entered the *Journal*; when they did, it was with two prepared for Agnes's course, Renaissance and Modern Sculpture.

Consistently, Agnes submitted the work of her students to the *Journal*, and just as regularly the *Journal* published them. Throughout its history, by far the greatest representation in the field of art history came from courses taught by Agnes.[30] She had an unerring eye for potential as well as achievement, and she exercised it for the benefit of the student but also as a means of demonstrating the kind of undergraduate work that, as teacher, she both elicited and judged worthy of recognition. She had a cause, and the *Journal* papers demonstrated in a tangible way the efficacy of its pursuit.

By the early 1930s, change was, indeed, taking place, with the history of art occupying a larger place in colleges and universities, leading to a greater awareness and attention on the part of a wider range of students. The historical was replacing the aesthetic as an approach to the teaching of art.[31] Agnes Rindge, implying its separation from classical studies, put it thus, "The fine arts are being more and more recognized as concrete blocks of historical and archaeological endeavor." She was also quoted as saying that "this recognition of the cogency of the matter of fine arts is almost sufficient to insure the status of the field in the liberal arts college." In short, she concluded, "the subject is no longer a cause."[32]

What were some of the core motives expressed by institutions offering art as a course of study at the turn of the decade? Many are familiar, surprisingly: the cultivation of taste in fine and industrial art, the supplementation of a knowledge of civilization and the provision of a general background for courses in other disciplines, and the enlargement and enrichment of aesthetic experience. A newer direction was expressed in such purposes as preprofessional

training, and the provision for students of "the methods and basic facts of the history of art in general and (secondly) the beginning of a genuine mastery (connoisseurship) of some one restricted field of art."[33] The latter implies a degree of specialization which the Vassar department did not offer and which the college had not yet institutionalized. It soon would.

The next major curricular changes came in 1930-31, and both were initiated by Agnes, who had extended her Renaissance and Modern Sculpture course into two terms. This no doubt was a corollary of the appearance of her book on sculpture. This publication also put her in demand on the reviewing circuit, an activity that reached its peak in 1930 and 1931.[34] In addition to reviews that reinforced her identification with sculpture, there appeared an article on the sculptor, Charles Despiau (1874-1946). Revealing, perhaps, is the feeling his sculpture gave her of a "genial atmosphere of a small room holding the customary gathering of congenial persons, where people live and understand one another without introspective analysis.[sic]"

As will be seen in another context, Agnes enjoyed a good deal of time in such rooms in New York and Harvard, where she had many congenial friends who likewise eschewed introspective analysis as a mode of communication. They were especially the Harvard crowd, the friends she had made in Cambridge and continued to see after they had all moved into their respective positions in the workplace. At this time, 1930-31, they were all more or less starting on and forging those careers that sparked new life in the American art world.

Principal among them were Kirk Askew (1903-74), who had married Constance Atwood in 1929, himself a dealer in Old Masters at Durlacher Brothers, an old London family firm with a New York branch; and Chick (Arthur Everett) Austin (1900-1957), who had been appointed acting director of the Wadsworth Atheneum, Hartford in 1927.[35] He, too, married in 1929, the daughter of the president of the board of trustees, Helen Goodwin; Alfred and Margaret Barr; Henry Russell Hitchcock, who was teaching at Wesleyan; Julien Levy, Harvard, class of 1926, and a protégé of Paul Sachs. Levy had married Joella, daughter of Mina Loy, in 1927, and in 1930 decided to open a gallery of modern art in New York. The novelty of its first exhibition in 1931-32 was twofold: photographs and surrealism were introduced to the American public for the first time.[36] Julien's secretary, Allen Porter, a charmer who seemed always to be on the verge of bubbling over with amusement, and whose enjoyment of people and sense of fun was contagious, became a new friend of Agnes; dancing the Charleston was a favored way of kicking up their heels.[37]

The circle was continually expanding, but this was the core group of the early thirties directly connected with the fine arts. All play a part in Vassar's history, directly or indirectly, and it is not an exaggeration to say that Agnes's personal identification with the pioneering museum outlook advanced by the group conditioned her teaching and informed her educational mission. Unlike Tonks, she was not content to be immured, for the most part, in the "ivory tower," but was a woman who enjoyed the world's stage, and fostered an interaction with it. This was evident in her teaching and in her many related enterprises, such as the gallery, in which she sought to bring to the college and students the excitement of new ideas and directions. Her affiliation with the group, moreover, denoted a point of view that, I believe, put its stamp on the character and content of the Vassar art department, and served to distinguish it from art departments with which it might reasonably be compared.

The 1930s proved to be a decade of continuing growth and hard-earned academic stabilization for the Vassar department. Totally new, however, was Agnes's institution of Art 350, Studies in Italian Baroque Art. The course was described as "a consideration of the origins and character of Baroque art in Italy, in which the study of seventeenth- and eighteenth-century painting is supplemented by that of architecture and sculpture." The Italian Baroque was at that time commanding art-historical attention, and Agnes's introduction of it was part and parcel of the recent efforts towards its revival promoted and advanced by the Harvard circle. Overlooked, though by no means totally avoided, Italian Baroque painting became a tantalizing cause for Agnes's generation. Sympathetic to its dynamic variety and merits, the Harvard group set about putting it before the public and reinstating it as worthy of scholarly investigation.[38]

Of seminal importance in reestablishing Italian Baroque painting was Arthur McComb, author of *The Baroque Painters of Italy*, the first historical survey of the period in English. Starting research on his book, McComb taught a course on Italian Baroque painting at the Fogg Museum of Harvard in 1928, on the very terrain that had generated prejudice. Early in 1929 an exhibition of Italian seventeenth- and eighteenth-century paintings and drawings accompanied his lectures;[39] it was noted to be the first exhibition of its kind in the United States.[40] Agnes was wholly aware of this departure from the *status quo*,[41] as she was also of Chick Austin's follow-up Baroque exhibition at the Wadsworth Atheneum in 1930.[42] Agnes's introduction of an advanced course in Italian seventeenth- and eighteenth-century painting, as well as her acquisitions for the Vassar Gallery, as will be seen, demonstrated her position in the forefront of the reevaluation of this neglected area of art. As Hitchcock observed, in his review of the Hartford exhibition, "the field is now established as

one worthy of the attention of collectors and scholars...." The continuous effort it required, however, paid off in roughly twenty years' time in an avalanche of scholarly activity. Vassar's historical part as an academic leader in this movement lent a particular prestige to the department. Art 350, despite several mutations both of content and instructor, remained intact until very recently.

Another person in the Harvard group, who was intimately involved in promoting the Baroque, was Kirk Askew. His role in arranging exhibitions, lending pictures to Vassar, and of furnishing Baroque paintings for the market, and, therefore, museums, including the Vassar Gallery, must be taken up in another context. Worth observing here, however, is that Agnes's circle was itself of a novel constitution. Now a group of scholars, specialists of one kind or another, it consisted of friends functioning within different frameworks—museum, gallery, college and university, and studio. It was, therefore, a different kind of circle, perhaps, than had existed previously in the fine arts. Its reach extended to those directly engaged in the arts as academics, producers, writers, and artists.

In 1931, Agnes was promoted to full professorship.[43] Owing, no doubt, to her newly attained rank, a larger pool of potential candidates for hire, as well as contacts and recommendations from Harvard, Tonks seems to have left the next departmental appointment to her. A replacement needed to be found for McGehee. Agnes seems to have considered all the arrangements, curricular and otherwise, involving the person of her choice, Leila Cook Barber (1903-84). Tall and stately, Leila was also strikingly good-looking. This, combined with her manner of speech in which key words were emphatically accentuated in a range of tones from sonorous to honeyed, made for an imposing, authoritative, and awe-inspiring lecturer. Her style, I'm told, had its source in Bryn Mawr from which she had received her B.A. in 1925. After a year at home, Leila had returned to do graduate work with Georgiana Goddard King in 1926-27. At that time Bryn Mawr was the only independent women's college to offer the Ph.D. in art history, as distinguished from archaeology.[44] As a graduate student, Leila would have taken "G.G.'s" course in Spanish art. The next year, Leila enrolled as a graduate student at Radcliffe, earning her M.A. in 1928. She undertook a dissertation on the Italian sixteenth-century painter, Dosso Dossi. She was never to finish this thesis, but on coming to Vassar from Radcliffe in 1931, she was to remain one of the department's most valuable and valued members until her retirement in 1968.

Ancient art was taught by Barber in 1931-32, and the reason why Agnes believed it could be regarded as a temporary course was that other courses in ancient art offered by the classics department were cross-listed in the art department. Greek sculpture and an advanced course in Hellenistic art were taught by Grace McCurdy, and Inez Scott Ryberg of the Latin department offered a course in Roman sculpture. Conversely, Tonks had for years offered a course in Greek vases for the Greek department, and Agnes thought that Tonks would take over the art department course in ancient art. That, however, did not immediately occur. The cross-listings with the classics department continued until 1936-37, with Barber teaching ancient art until that time. Medieval art also became her province, expanding to two terms in 1933, and continuing through 1942-43.

By 1932, Vassar's was also a department that, according to Tonks's statistics, already offered more hours in the study of art than any other of the seven women's colleges, except Smith. He listed Smith as having 100; Vassar 91; Wellesley 83; Radcliffe 66; Bryn Mawr 66; Mount Holyoke 63; and Barnard 54.[45] But it was Leila's induction into the introductory course that amounted to an immersion. With Tonks, she taught the entire course in her first years, beginning in 1931-32. She also taught an inordinate number of conference sections, averaging fifteen students each. She used to recall that she taught eleven sections, and, indeed, Tonks wrote to MacCracken that Miss Barber "meets one hundred and fifty students for Art 105 every week in conference groups."[46] At the same time that he informed MacCracken of this phenomenon, he requested that the money that had been used for the interior decoration course now be allocated to the hiring of a teacher who would take over some of the conference work and "give a year's course in the history of architecture, and possibly develop a course in the Art of the Far East—a subject which should appear in a well-organized art curriculum...."

The appointment made on the strength of this proposal was that of John McAndrew (1903-78). McAndrew had graduated in 1924 with a B.S. from Harvard, where he had been a classmate of Russell Hitchcock, and had spent the next three years as a student in its School of Architecture. He had spent a year abroad where (quite by chance) in a gallery in Mannheim he fell into conversation with a young fellow Harvardian who was visiting museums, looking at buildings, and seeking out modern architecture on the advice of Alfred Barr.[47] This was Philip Johnson. They decided to join forces in a minute's time, and they traveled all over Germany looking, at the architecture of Le Corbusier, Gropius, and others. McAndrew became secretary to Julien Levy in 1931, the year of the Levy Gallery's opening.[48] He was already a friend of the Barrs, the Askews, and therefore, Agnes Rindge, when he joined the Vassar art department in 1932.

McAndrew's architectural training and Bauhaus orientation were exactly what could move the curriculum into encompassing the modern without impinging on Tonks's preserve. Agnes recom-

George Platt Lynes, *Mildred Akin Lynes*. (Frances Lehman Loeb Art Center)

mended him to President MacCracken, who asked Tonks to look into his qualifications. MacCracken was greatly impressed with McAndrew, writing that he was "obviously a thorough gentleman," with a "very agreeable manner and appearance."[49] His appointment specified that he was to teach one course in architecture, another in domestic architecture and interior decoration, and contribute to the introductory course, which inevitably carried in its wake a number of conference sections.[50]

Apart from exempting herself from teaching the history of architecture, it was Agnes's thought to promote future architectural studies, through a course with one hour of practice in architectural drawing and two hours of theoretical and historical study. Vassar, as far as I know, was the first women's college to offer architectural drafting. The course was described as "a study of the design and construction of the historic styles of architecture." Interior decoration was more of a lark. "I understand you think you can run up interior decoration," MacCracken wrote to John. He tried to soften the blow by suggesting that Ruth Adams, a Vassar graduate who designed the Dean's House, then under construction, and who was the official decorative consultant to the college, be worked into the second semester. Miss Adams, he explained, was rather conservative, mostly concerned with authoritative models in various periods, but his idea was that she could supplement this with "the more modern point of view."[51]

Not only does this suggestion not seem to have been put into effect, but McAndrew had other ideas. The course he introduced was Theory and Practice of Contemporary Architecture, Interiors, and Furniture. This was clearly a course in modern architecture that encompassed a historical perspective on interiors and furniture no doubt largely designed by architects themselves. Architecture was now fully represented in the departmental curriculum, both as practice and as theory and history. Taught by an architect/architectural historian, it functioned as a feature of Vassar's art history program that has lasted, with only slight variation, to the present day. Reliable sources have it that he was a splendid lecturer, and I have heard tell that on one Monday morning McAndrew arrived from New York to give an Art 105 lecture in white tie and tails. The advent of McAndrew, a young bachelor, in the department perked things up for both Agnes and Leila, for, as Russell Lynes has written, he had "a tremendous capacity for enjoyment."[52] He was also, as Alfred Barr was later to write, "a person of courage, integrity, and conscience...charming and excellent company...brilliant... sensitive and energetic."[53]

George Platt Lynes, *President Henry Noble MacCracken.* (Frances Lehman Loeb Art Center)

Complementary to this strengthening of architecture within the department was the introduction in the same year of the study of landscape architecture. This was taught by a second addition to the department in 1932-33, Elizabeth Meade (1905-93), a Vassar alumna of the class of 1927. Betty Meade was a seemingly conventional woman of strong character and human impulse. Tweed suits, sensible shoes, and hat up and off the face suited her outdoor activity. Her stride was purposeful and she had agreeable, well-proportioned features. She rather mistrusted, I think, any dazzling form of brilliance and scarcely gave the arrogance of youth the time of day.

The last new member of the department in this period was Mildred Akin Lynes (1909-), a Vassar graduate of 1932, whose import for the department, through her close association with many of its

members and friends over the years, far exceeded the single year she taught in it, 1936-37. The fact that Mildred was not just a former student, but a friend of both Agnes and John McAndrew, was also important, for she represented the kind of highly intelligent, open-minded, yet critically discerning person with whom they would have felt most in accord. Mildred was, moreover, a paradigm of Agnes's vision for the future of the department, which she hoped would have its share of lively minds that were engaged in scholarship, teaching, and the furthering of art, whether through writing, work in museums, or contact with artists themselves. Agnes had a strong awareness of the present. The past was a touchstone, reminder, and measure, but at this point in the department's history, direction was the issue.

In 1934, Mildred married Russell Lynes, then working at the publishing house of Harper and Brothers.[54] Russell was already a frequenter of Agnes's New York world. In 1932, Julien Levy had exhibited the photographs of George Platt Lynes, Russell's brother, whom he had met through John McAndrew. This was followed by a one-man show of fifty of G. P. Lynes's photographs in 1934-35 at the Levy Gallery.[55] Russell, in turn, had been an occasional attendee of the Askews' Sunday-afternoon salon, while still an undergraduate at Yale, from which he graduated in 1932.[56] The many connections amounted to an armature of friendship, which bound together this generation of movers and shakers in the arts of America, of which the Lyneses, about ten years younger than most, were the newest and youngest members. When Mildred came to Vassar in 1936, so did Russell as director of the Bureau of Publications. With respect to the bureau, he held that it should act not as a publicity agency but as a clearing house for Vassar information.[57]

In these years, the College also enjoyed a connection also with George Platt Lynes. Although best known for his highly composed and dramatically lit photographs of writers, artists, choreographers, and, in general, for being a style-setter of the thirties and forties, he had also photographed the Vassar classes of 1934-36 for the *Vassarion,* the senior yearbook. He found that the class of 1936 was neater, cleaner, and pleasanter than the previous two classes, and had "an awful lot of long necks." Struck too by the prevalence of tweed skirts and cashmere sweaters, he thought it "perfectly absurd that all the girls think they have to look exactly alike....I can't understand the craze for the pearl and sweater combination."[58] This was not the more aesthetically inventive Lynes's cup of tea.[59]

During his sessions at Vassar, however, he also photographed members of the art department, Agnes Rindge, John McAndrew, and, of course, Mildred Lynes. Agnes even tried to persuade President MacCracken to be photographed by Lynes.

I am really writing to make the suggestion that you avail yourself of
the last occasion for being photographed by George Lynes whose
prints I collect with avidity—not only for their technical splendour,
but for the distinction of the subjects (I'm not referring to the senior
class, but putting in a request for a print if you should follow the
suggestion.) After all, even M. Carey Thomas has fallen beneath his
lens and the last one of you is in the neo-Genthe* fuzzy style. You
deserve a better fate with posterity, don't you think? Of course it's
none of my affair.[60]

This letter, signed "intrepidly yours," resulted in an image of
MacCracken, and is certainly revealing of Agnes's gift for projecting
herself as a woman with something to offer, by seeming diffidence
and wit, and confident of her operational power. It also reveals that
she was quite seriously a booster of creative talents, by whatever
means were at her disposal.

The changes detailed above that took place in the art department
faculty during this period, as well as the many innovations in the art
department curriculum, led to its signal reputation by the 1930s.
This was not least manifested in the approbation of Walter Cook,
director of the Institute of Fine Arts in New York, who was so
pleased with the Vassar students doing graduate work that he made
a blanket offer of full-tuition scholarships at the Institute for any
students the department recommended.[61] This discussion does
not, however, complete a picture of the larger changes introduced
within the college as a whole that had an impact on the department
in the thirties. Neither does it convey all the enterprises undertaken in the interests of the department, nor the particular achieve-
ments of the individual members during these years.

Editors' Note: We are grateful to Mary McLaughlin, Pamela Askew's
literary executor, for her kind permission to publish the essay, "A
Galaxy of Stars," in its current form, which has been derived from
Professor Askew's manuscript on the entire history of the Vassar
College Department of Art, the publication of which is forthcom-
ing. We would also like to thank Katherine Smith, class of 1998, for
her typing of Professor Askew's handwritten, posthumous manuscript.

Gathering at the house of James Thrall Soby in Hartford, Connecticut, in the
1930s. From left to right: Iris Barry, Dick Abbott, Agnes Rindge, Helen Austin,
Allen Porter, Henry Russell Hitchcock, Nellie Soby, Constance Askew, James
Soby. (Collection of Pamela Askew)

1   For an excellent and lively account of the twenties, see Ann Douglas, *Terrible
Honesty: Mongrel Manhattan in the Twenties* (New York, 1995), passim, especially 3-62.

2   Tonks to MacCracken, 24 May 1923 (MacCracken, box 29, VCSC).

3   Request for Appointment, 22 May 1923 (MacCracken, box 29, VCSC).

4   Russell Lynes, *Good Old Modern, An Intimate Portrait of the Museum of Modern Art*
(New York, 1973), 21; Avis Berman, "An interview with Katharine Kuh," Archives
of *America Art Journal* 27, no. 3 (1987): 3.

5   Quoted in Rone Roob, "Alfred H. Barr, Jr.: A Chronicle of the Years 1902-1929,"
The New Criterion (Summer 1987): 5.

6   Roob, "Alfred H. Barr, Jr.," 3. For the situation with respect to modern art before
the founding of the Museum of Modern Art, see Lynes, *Good Old Modern*, 35-46.

7   Oliver S. Tonks, "The Creed of Abstract Art," *The Arts* 7, no. 4 (April, 1925): 215-
18.

8   See Roob, "Alfred H. Barr, Jr.," 12.

9   For the *Société Anonyme*, see Ibid., 1-52. For Kandinsky's exhibition schedule, see
also Gail Levin and Marianne Lopez, *Theme and Improvisations: Kandinsky & the
American Avant-Garde, 1912-1950* (Dayton, 1992), 228.

10   The exhibition probably included both paintings and prints from the
Kandinskys in the *Société Anonyme*; see Robert L. Herbert et al., eds., *The Société
Anonyme and the Dreier Bequest at Yale University: A Catalogue Raisonné* (New Haven
and London, 1984), 354-65.

11   For others, see Ibid.

12   Robert John Goldwater, *The Teaching of Art in the Colleges of the United States* (n.c.,
1943), 7-11. Harvard had introduced a two-semester survey in 1912-13; see Samuel
Eliot Morison, *The Development of Harvard University since the inauguration of President
Eliot, 1869-1929* (Cambridge, Mass., 1930), 137.

13   As pointed out at the time, "of institutions having their instruction on the
history of art, the most influential are Princeton and Harvard." See Laura Beacon,
"The Place of Art in the Liberal College," *Association of American Colleges Bulletin* 13
(1927): 268.

14   It was in this year, I believe, that he wrote a mini-monograph, "The Life and
Works of Francesco di Giorgio," Art Studies 2 (1924): 3-31. The issue did not,
however, come out until 1925. His list of persons to whom he expresses thanks
includes Berenson, and concludes with, "To Mr. and Mrs. Berenson every serious
student of Italian art is, of course, deeply indebted and I especially for numerous
favors and valuable suggestions." He remained in touch with Berenson and
eventually edited *The Selected Letters of Bernard Berenson with an epilogue by Nicky
Mariano* (Boston, 1964).

15   Arthur McComb was the biological father of the present writer, who was born in
Poughkeepsie in 1925.

[16]   On the characters and significance of this book, see Eric Zafran, "A History of Italian Baroque Painting in America," in *Botticelli to Tiepolo: Three Centuries of Italian Paintings from Bob Jones University* (Philbrook Museum of Art, 1994), 50.

[17]   Agnes Rindge Claflin, interview by Jill Silverman, 22 October 1974 (audio tape, Wadsworth Atheneum, Hartford).

[18]   Ibid.

[19]   This information was kindly furnished by Eugene Gaddis.

[20]   MacCracken to Elizabeth B. Lawrence, 9 June 1926; Appoint form, 23 May 1926. (MacCracken Papers, Box 33, SCVC).

[21]   "Announcement," *The Hound & Horn* 1, no. 1 (September 1927): 6. The title came from Ezra Pound: "Tis the white stag Fame we're hunting:/ Bid the world's hounds come to horn"; Lincoln Kirstein, *Mosaic, Memoirs* (New York, 1994), 104.

[22]   David M. Robinson, review of *History of Italian Painting* by Oliver Tonks, *American Journal of Archaeology* 33 (1929): 337-38.

[23]   Roob, "Alfred H. Barr, Jr.," 19, 24.

[24]   Ibid., 24.

[25]   For the International Style's trinity of Hitchcock-Barr-Johnson, see Irving Sandler, *Defining Modern Art, Selected Writings of Alfred H. Barr, Jr.,* ed. Irving Sandler and Amy Newman (New York, 1986), 18-22; also, Roob, "Alfred H. Barr, Jr.," 28; Franz Schulze, *Philip Johnson* (New York, 1994), 60-62, 70-86.

[26]   Roob, "Alfred H. Barr, Jr.," 13-14.

[27]   Jill Silverman, interview with Agnes Rindge Claflin, Tape 1, 22 October 1974.

[28]   Information from the Foss Archives, courtesy of Eugene Gaddis.

[29]   Statement by Christabel F. Fiske, *Vassar Journal of Undergraduate Studies* 2 (May 1926).

[30]   Among the contributors in the field of art were Lydia C. Spitzer, class of 1930; Evelyn Borchard, class of 1932; Mildred Akin [Lynes], class of 1932; Margaret D. Sloane, class of 1932; Janice Loeb, class of 1935; Esther R. Vanamee, class of 1935; Lois H. Graham, class of 1935; Alice Dunnenberg; Elizabeth Hird [Pokorney/ Rauch], class of 1937; Eleanor D. Barton, class of 1938; Clotilda A. Brokow, class of 1938; Helen Ballantine, class of 1939; Patricia Egan, class of 1939; Ellen S. Coan, class of 1942; Nancy Noland, class of 1942; Julia Cuniberti, class of 1944; Margot Landcastle, class of 1961; Susan Donahue [Kuretsky], class of 1963; Christine A. Smith, class of 1966; and Susan M. Taylor, class of 1977. Not all the papers written by the students were for Agnes's courses, but the great majority were. Nine of the above played some role later in the history of the department or the gallery.

[31]   See Frederick R. Pleasants, "Recent Art Activities at Princeton University," *Parnassus* 1, no. 4 (April 1929): 21.

[32]   Archie M. Palmer and Grace Holton, *College Instruction in Art* (New York, 1934), 6.

[33]   Arthur B. Clark et al., *Report of the Committee on Art Instruction in Colleges and Universities* (1927), 41-42.

[34]   Her reviews were: "*Orient et Occident, je recherches sur les influences byzantines et orientales en France avant les Croisades,*" by Jean Ebersolt, *American Journal of Archaeology* 34 (1930): 105-06; "*Geschichte der Russische Malerei in Mittelalter,*" by Philip Schweinfurth and Royal Bailey Franum, "*Art Education in the United States,*" *Biennial Survey of Education* 23 (1926): 523; "*Animals in Greek Sculpture,*" by Gisela M. A. Richter, *International Studio* 98 (April 1931): 56; "*Romanesque Mural Painting of Catalonia,*" by Charles L. Kuhn, *International Studio* 99 (June 1931): 64; "*French Sculpture of the Romanesque Period, xith and xiith centuries*" by Paul Deschamps, *International Studio* 99 (July 1931): 64-65; "*Estimates in Art,*" by Frank Jewett Mather, *International Studio* 99 (August 1931): 67.

[35]   On Charles Austin, see Eugene Gaddis, "The New Athens: Moments from an Era," in *Avery Memorial, Wadsworth Atheneum* (Hartford, 1984), 33-58; see also *A. Everett Austin, Jr., A Director's Taste and Achievement* (Hartford, 1958). This memorial tribute contains essays by Sir Osbert Sitwell, Edward Forbes, R. Kirk Askew, James T. Soby, Julien Levy, Henry Russell Hitchcock, Eugene Berman, T. H. Barber, Virgil Thompson, and Lincoln Kirstein. See also, Russell Lynes, "The Austin Phenomenon," in *Life in the Slow Lane* (New York, 1991), 160-67.

[36]   In fact, Levy's planned surrealism show opened in Hartford before its opening in New York because he had leant it, as a favor, to his friend Chick Austin. Its greatest impact, however, was felt in New York. See Julien Levy, *Memoir of an Art Gallery* (New York, 1977), 80; Julien Levy, "Dealing with A. Everett Austin, Jr.," in *A. Everett Austin, Jr., A Director's Taste and Achievement,* (Hartford, 1958); Eugene Gaddis, "The New Athens': Moments from an Era," in *Avery Memorial, Wadsworth Atheneum* (Hartford, 1984), 46.

[37]   Eric Zafran, "A History of Italian Baroque Painting in America," in Richard P. Townsend, *Botticelli to Tiepolo, Three Centuries of Italian Painting from Bob Jones University* (The Philbrook Museum of Art, 1994), 43-44.

[38]   The Italian Baroque was completely omitted from Tonks's *A History of Italian Painting* (1927), which leapt from Tintoretto to Piazzetta and Tiepolo, Canaletto, and Guardi. Ella S. Siple, "Art in America—Italian Baroque Painting," *The Burlington Magazine* 54 (1929): 105-06.

[39]   Jean. K. Cadogan, "Introduction: The Formation of 'A small but Distinguished Collection,'" in *Wadsworth Atheneum Paintings II, Italy and Spain, Fourteenth through Nineteenth Centuries,* ed. Jean K. Cadogan (Hartford, 1991), 13-14.

[40]   "Exhibition of Italian XVII and XVIII Century Paintings and Drawings at the Fogg Art Museum," *Parnassus* 1, no. 2 (15 February 1929): 24; drawn from nearby collections, the Fogg show consisted predominantly of eighteenth-century Venetian works.

[41]   Silverman interview with Agnes Rindge Claflin, Tape 1.

[42]   On Austin and the reappraisal of the Italian Baroque, see Zafran, "A History of Italian Baroque Painting in America," 48-50.

[43]   MacCracken notified her of this on 11 February 1931 (MacCracken Papers, Box 37, SCVC).

[44]   For Georgiana Goddard King, see Susanne Terrell Saunders, "Georgiana Goddard King (1871-1939): Educator and Pioneer in Medieval Spanish Art," in *Women as Interpreters of the Visual Arts, 1820-1979,* ed. Claire Richter Sherman with Adele Holcomb (Westport, Conn. and London, 1981), 209-38; quoted is Leila Barber's description of King's lectures as a "continuos stream of oblique, elliptical and witty references to everything under the sun about which it was assumed that you knew something, or that if you didn't, you would read up and find out," 9-10.

[45]   O. S. Tonks, Annual Report for the Department of Art, 23 May 1932 (Annual Reports—Art, 1916-1943, SCVC). Smith's lead, he explained, was owing to a course in civic planning and in Greek and Roman archaeology, and four courses to cover Italian and Northern Painting instead of the two offered at Vassar for the same periods.

[46]   Tonks to President MacCracken, 27 January 1932 (MacCracken Papers, Box 37, VCSC).

[47]   Franz Schulze, *Philip Johnson, Life and Work* (New York, 1994), 52.

[48]   Lynes, *Good Old Modern,* 178. It was Barr's recollection that Americans probably first heard of the Bauhaus after its great exhibition in 1923. (Ibid., 128). Levy, *Memoir of an Art Gallery,* 13, 86.

49   President MacCracken to Tonks, 9 March 1932 (MacCracken Papers, Box 37, SCVC).

50   MacCracken to McAndrew, 11 March 1932.

51   Lynes, *Good Old Modern*, 179.

52   Ibid.

53   Quoted by Lynes, Ibid., 221-22.

54   See the obituary of Russell Lynes, *New York Times* (16 September 1991).

55   Levy, *Memoir of an Art Gallery*, 59, 297, 298.

56   Lynes, *Good Old Modern*, vii.

57   See "Vassar Vignettes," *Vassar Alumnae Magazine 22*, no. 1 (15 October 1936): 16.

58   *Miscellany News* 21, no. 18 (December 5, 1936): 1, 5.

59   On George Platt Lynes, see Avis Berman, "George Platt Lynes Reconsidered: The Photographic Mastery of Psychology and Light," *Architectural Digest* 50 (September 1993): 60, 62, 64, 68.

60   Agnes Rindge to President MacCracken, 3 November 1935 (MacCracken Papers, Box 42, SCVC). *Arnold Genthe, pictorialist photographer (1869-1942), known for his soft-focused images.

61   John McAndrew to President MacCracken, 11 May 1936 (MacCracken Papers, Box 42, SCVC).

1974-1999: A QUARTER CENTURY IN SUPPORT OF THE ARTS
BY THE FRIENDS OF THE FRANCES LEHMAN LOEB ART CENTER

ELIZABETH A. DANIELS, class of 1941
Vassar College Historian

The year 1999 is a major milestone, as it marks the twenty-fifth anniversary of the Friends of the Frances Lehman Loeb Art Center, founded in 1974 by a group of Vassar alumnae to help support the teaching and exhibition programs of the art department and the Art Gallery. To honor this important achievement, James Mundy, class of 1974 and the Anne Hendricks Bass Director of the Frances Lehman Loeb Art Center, has created the present exhibition entitled, *Refining the Imagination: Tradition, Collecting, and the Vassar Education.* This celebratory exhibition, as he has stated, elaborates "on the continuing cyclical connection between the instruction received at Vassar and the ability of the individual to make discerning choices in the world about ideas, people, and works of art." The exhibition focuses on "the art-collecting activities of Vassar alumnae, alumni, and friends, on works promised as gifts to the collection, and on other important loans from Vassar collectors." In recent months, the Friends organization has played an especially fruitful role in helping to identify works for this anniversary exhibition, as well as continuing in its now well-established role of helping to implement the general objectives of the gallery as it carries out its mission, established in 1864, of supporting the College's teaching of art through the collection and display of fine examples of artwork.

In June 1864, Matthew Vassar purchased the art holdings of the Reverend Elias Lyman Magoon, a noted American collector and a founding Vassar trustee, as the nucleus of original works for the Vassar College Art Gallery. The preceding February 23rd, the trustees had heard the "Report of the Committee on 'The Art Gallery,'" written and delivered by Magoon, who spoke of the importance of excellent examples of original art for women's education. Magoon predicted correctly (but daringly) that "the influence for good of the Vassar gallery's collection [his own creation] would spread" until "the Great Cities of our land would send pilgrims thither perpetually; and visitors from abroad…would feel that by no means least fascinating are [Vassar's] treasures of Original Art."

From the first years when the Art Gallery was located on the topmost floor of Main Building, its walls lined with Magoon's paintings and the commissioned portrait of Matthew Vassar by Charles Elliot, to today's site in the elegant quarters of Cesar Pelli's Frances Lehman Loeb Art Center, opened in 1993, the collection has grown exponentially in size and quality. In those first years there was one professor of art, Henry Van Ingen, who presided over the development of the gallery. It was a studio gallery, with students

Henry van Ingen, the first professor of art at Vassar College, and a student. (Courtesy of Vassar College Libraries, Special Collections)

setting up easels and copying paintings, drawings, and plaster casts. But the "Rules and Regulations" of the Gallery, set forth 18 January 1867 by Cyrus Swan, College administrator, clearly indicate that the gallery was serving the College as a whole, as well as the drawing and painting students in particular. Rule 10 read: "The Gallery shall be open to pupils of the College under the direction and responsibility of the Professor of Drawing and Painting at least one half day in each week."

Upon the celebration of the College's first decade in 1875, the gallery moved from its location in Main to the new Museum of Natural History, housed on the site of the former Riding Academy. Twelve years later, in his 1887 annual report to the president, Van Ingen expressed satisfaction on the progress of the gallery. He wrote:

> The entire Art Gallery has undergone a remarkable change this year. Every picture now exhibited shows to its best advantage, the result of a careful selection of all the good works from among a large collection of miscellaneous pictures.

> The Art Gallery, as now managed, presents a creditable appearance, to which I, with considerable pride, dare to invite my fellow artists, without being obliged to resort to some excuse for the presence of many worthless pieces.

Van Ingen presented an inventory of the works in the gallery's collection in his 1894 annual report to the president. The gallery's holdings included 152 plaster casts, the Magoon collection of 130 oil paintings, an additional 21 oil paintings, the Magoon collection of 275 watercolors and prints, 14 additional watercolors, 761 lantern slides for illustrative purposes, 72 pictures "in frames around the college," 20 portraits of trustees, "various articles of artistic value," and a collection of 1,615 Braun Autotypes and photographs in portfolios in the gallery. In addition, the Art Gallery had 130 movable frames which were hung in the corridors of Main, "where they would be of the most benefit to the students." In the frames were placed pictures taken from the portfolios of the Art Gallery. The movable backs of the frames enabled the easy rotation of the pictures exhibited. In addition to these materials, there was a collection of 160 engravings "valued at 5 cents apiece." (Van Ingen valued the total collection at $33,846.10.)

Twenty-eight years later, at a Founder's Day celebration 15 May 1915, came another change in the gallery's location, with the opening of the Taylor Hall Art Gallery, presented to the College by Mary Morris Pratt, class of 1880, and Charles M. Pratt, chairman of the board of trustees, in honor of James Monroe Taylor, president of Vassar from 1886 to 1914. That event also signaled the opening of the first loan collection at Vassar, featuring a group of Italian paintings selected by Oswald Siren for Mr. Pratt. At the time of the move to Taylor Hall there were four hundred American paintings and over three thousand (primarily British) prints, drawings, and watercolors. Today, the collection contains over 13,500 works.

Even in the early days, loan exhibitions were frequently displayed in Taylor Hall. Clarence Chatterton, professor of painting, who showed his work in New York at the pioneering MacBeth Gallery on lower Fifth Avenue, mounted most of these exhibitions and borrowed works by the modern school of realist painters, including those of his teacher, Robert Henri, as well as canvases by George Luks and Edward Hopper, among others.

During the thirty-one-year administration of Henry Noble MacCracken, president of Vassar from 1915 to 1946, the Museum, as it was then called, flourished first under the direction of Professor Oliver Tonks, and then that of his successor, Professor Agnes Rindge Claflin. Claflin believed strongly in students' exposure to original works of art and characteristically emphasized this primary exposure in her teaching of such courses as Art 105, which she installed in the curriculum in 1928, and which, it is fair to say, most students at Vassar have used as their springboard to the critical study of art. From the beginning of her term, she attracted to the collection many gifts and exhibitions. Her strong cultural links drew the Vassar gallery into the periphery of the metropolitan New

Students in painting class ca. 1875. (Courtesy of Vassar College Libraries, Special Collections)

York art world, especially the Museum of Modern Art and contemporary art galleries.

By the 1930s, the loaned exhibitions at the Vassar Art Gallery, which was still operating on a shoestring, were nevertheless becoming more frequent and more significant. The College Art Association lent the gallery an exhibition of Italian Baroque paintings and drawings in 1933. During Art Week in 1934, Lincoln Kirstein, editor of *Hound & Horn*, gave a lecture. Thereafter during that period were lectures by A. E. Austin, Jr., director of the Wadsworth Athenaeum in Hartford; M. Jean Lurcat, painter; M. William Lescaze, Swiss architect; Edward M. M. Warburg, art critic, and others. In 1936 the sculpture of Alexander Calder was shown. These occasions represented the adolescence of the Art Gallery as it began to relate more intricately to the larger art community. But its quarters remained cramped and insufficient, and there was no organized effort by the College to enlarge and maintain the accumulating collection, nor were there means to do so.

Modernization of the gallery evolved slowly in the next decade. The Van Ingen Library, linking the Frederick Ferris Thompson Memorial Library to Taylor Hall, was completed in 1937, and with it, the remodeling of the South Gallery in Taylor Hall, which by then housed the permanent collection.

In May 1940 the art department exhibited Chinese paintings as part of the seventy-fifth-anniversary celebration of the College. Mrs. Felix Warburg donated over 150 etchings and engravings, mostly by Dürer and Rembrandt, in 1941. In April 1950, Marcel Breuer gave a gallery talk. In 1950, also, the estate of Paul Rosenfeld gave works to the gallery from the Alfred Stieglitz circle, including paintings by

Marsden Hartley, John Marin, Georgia O'Keefe, and Arthur Dove. Subsequently, in 1951, the Art Gallery mounted an exhibition of Picasso's drawings for *Guernica*, a traveling exhibition organized by the Museum of Modern Art. During this period, Blanchette Hooker Rockefeller, class of 1931, first began to donate a group of contemporary paintings from her collection, a magnificent gift which gave the gallery eighty works between 1952 and 1980, thus filling a void in Vassar's collection.

Under President Sarah Gibson Blanding (1946-64), the College initiated a $25-million-dollar development program in 1955, but nothing was included for the improvement of the art collection or the gallery. Blanding, however, recognized these needs as she planned for the celebration of the College's centennial in 1961. In preparation for that occasion she tapped the skills of Belle Krasne Ribicoff, class of 1945, an art major in her undergraduate years who had gone on to a career in art management. Ribicoff, a born organizer, almost single-handedly created and implemented the *Centennial Loan Exhibition* of works on paper from alumnae collections. To assist her in assembling and choosing the 155 works exhibited, Ribicoff formed a selection committee of prominent art scholars. From the present perspective, this would appear to be the initial move toward the subsequent formation of the Friends, in which she played a key role. Borrowing drawings and watercolors from alumnae and their families, the exhibition opened at Vassar in May 1961 and continued through June, then moved to the Wildenstein Galleries in Manhattan, where it remained from June to December. Through these successful ventures, the Vassar Art Gallery, as it was called, quietly began to gain recognition in a larger context.

The Centennial exhibition brought Vassar to the verge of the founding of the Friends of the Art Gallery. By the 1960s, the Vassar art department had had an impact on the lives of many students who were to engage others across the nation and subsequently make the mission of the Vassar Friends successful. At mid-century, the art department at Vassar offered an increasing number of students—majors and nonmajors alike—the opportunity to form life-long habits of scholarship, criticism, connoisseurship, and just plain educated enjoyment. Under the tutelage of Agnes Rindge Claflin, Leila Barber, Richard Krautheimer, Christine Havelock; Linda Nochlin, class of 1951; Pamela Askew, class of 1946; Eugene Carroll, Alton Pickens, Lewis Rubenstein, and others, the department expanded its curriculum, and along with this expansion came an increased reliance on the resources of the gallery for its primary sources.

Between 1969 and 1973, after the beginning of coeducation at Vassar under President Alan Simpson(1964-77), trustee Mary Villard, class of 1934, successfully chaired Vassar's first major capital campaign. As the campaign began, New York resident Carol Rothschild Noyes, class of 1939, trustee, former art major, and chair of the Special Gifts Committee for New York City, emphasized to Villard the acute material needs of the Vassar Art Gallery and the desirability of enhancing and enlarging the Vassar art collection. She also urged making available to the gallery untapped resources among alumnae and friends of the department, especially those who had proceeded from their studies at Vassar to pursue careers in the art field and to become collectors. Villard encouraged Noyes to undertake planning a suitable organization which could implement connections between the gallery, the art department, and the alumnae of the department. This, Noyes agreed to do, and she subsequently called together a selected group of art department and gallery friends to participate in a discussion of the strengths and weaknesses of the Vassar collection and the programs of the gallery. The first such meeting was held at the Cosmopolitan Club in New York. An outline for an organization to support the art department was presented and discussed.

Meanwhile, Professor Nicolai Cikovsky, who was in 1972 director of the gallery, began investigating support systems and membership groups being formed at comparable college and university museums and galleries. Among those whom he consulted were Mary Weitzel Gibbons, class of 1951, who taught at Princeton, and Constance Dimock Ellis, class of 1938, a member of the gallery staff at Smith, who urged the group to form a Friends organization.

As a result of these 1973 discussions, President Alan Simpson, declaring his enthusiastic support for the formation of a Friends group, but cautioning that funding for the organization must come from outside the operating budget of the College, asked Ribicoff and Noyes to co-chair a steering committee charged with establishing a Friends of the Vassar Art Gallery by the Spring of 1974. Simpson formally announced this new venture at a dinner held at his house on 24 October 1973. The next day the board met, with Ribicoff and Noyes at the helm of the committee.

In that first year, this twosome of Trylon and Perisphere, as the late Professor Pamela Askew dubbed them (referring to the all-embracing icons of the 1939 World's Fair), undertook the task of creating the Friends group. They drafted by-laws, formed an administrative structure, recruited a board of directors representing alumnae/i and nonalumnae/i, professionals in the art field, and others. The board of directors was structured to consist of twenty-seven members, twenty-one of whom were to be elected to three-year terms; six were appointed. Serving indefinite terms by appointment were the director of the Art Gallery and the chairman of the art department. Other appointed members were to be named by the president of the College, the director of the Art Gallery, and the chairman of the board of trustees. A student art major designated by the chairman of the department was to serve a one-year term. The first board resolved basic decisions about membership and chose an initial steering committee, which brought together the College's director of development, Herbert Shultz; Vassar Art Gallery director Peter Morrin; and art department faculty, Pamela Askew and Agnes Rindge Claflin. A $200,000 endowment was initially pledged, with pledges and contributions increasing in the following months. By-laws were further composed and adopted, a committee on membership was established, and under the leadership of New York alumna, Anne Keating Jones, class of 1943, chairman, initial

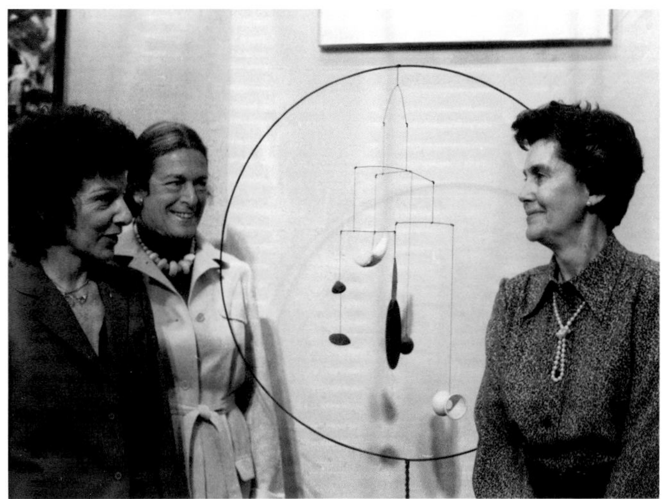

Belle Ribicoff, Carol Noyes, and Anne Jones at the *Agnes Rindge Claflin Memorial Exhibition* sponsored by the Friends in 1978. (Courtesy Friends of the Frances Lehman Loeb Art Center)

mailings were sent out in April 1975 for enrollment in the first year's membership drive, including an invitation to the first annual membership meeting in 1976. The first meeting of the Friends board was held in October 1974, and by 1 June 1975, when the Friends celebrated their first birthday, Anne Jones and her committee had enlisted 167 members.

In 1976 the Friends helped fund the first of a new series of exhibitions. This major exhibition, *Seventeenth-Century Dutch Landscape Drawings and Prints from American Collections*, conceived and executed by visiting scholar/connoisseur, Curtis O. Baer, and his advanced class in connoisseurship, opened on 28 March 1976 and set in motion a new mode of collaboration among professors and students, thus enriching the experience of the art classroom and extending it further into the professional climate of the gallery.

The main thrust of the Friends' early years was planning for the first large show, *Promised Gifts '77*, opening on 20 April 1977. Ribicoff, aided by Noyes, once again organized the exhibition. The

board created a permanent staff position to assist the codirectors in carrying out their duties, the invaluable addition of an executive administrator. A handsome 122-page, fully illustrated scholarly catalogue was issued, many of its lively essays written by Vassar graduates who had achieved prominence in the art world; the whole publication existed as a joyous tribute to the hard work and midnight labors of Ribicoff and assorted members of the art department "[whose] brains were picked…with a wrench" (according to a midnight poem created by Christine Havelock) to produce it in time. Peter Morrin, director, reported that the show generated between three- to four hundred gifts to the gallery, among them a Calder stabile, prints by Picasso, Dürer, and Ellsworth Kelly. Thus, in just two years the Friends had helped the gallery make a series of important acquisitions.

By this time, the Friends had matched a $5,000 grant from the Bowers Foundation toward the expenses of the exhibition and had applied for an additional $8,000. Other financial allocations were simultaneously made by the Friends: $5,000 (later increased to $11,000) from a newly created reserve fund for the purchase of Latin-American drawings, and $5,000 for a fund for the acquisition of outdoor sculpture. Jean Bronson Mahoney, class of 1952, established an acquisitions fund in memory of her parents, Francis Woolsey and Helen Silkman Bronson, class of 1924. A long-time donor, Suzette Morton Davidson, class of 1934, established a purchase fund, as did Blanchette Hooker Rockefeller, class of 1931.

Several other exciting smaller projects were undertaken by the Friends during these early years, among them, a Paul Strand Symposium in 1977 and a 1984 catalogue documenting Violet Oakley's role in designing the decoration of Vassar's Alumnae House, built in 1924. Latin-American expert, Barbara Doyle Duncan, class of 1943, selected drawings by one hundred artists to create the exhibit, *Latin-American Drawings (1969-1976): Lines of Vision*, and created the Duncan Fund for the gallery in early 1978. In memory of Agnes Rindge Claflin, the *Agnes Rindge Claflin Memorial Exhibition* ran from 20 April to 6 June 1978. Sponsored by the art department and the director and Friends of the Art Gallery, the exhibit, curated by Russell Lynes, included items from Claflin's own collection as well as works that she had been instrumental in acquiring for the gallery. The Friends were also responsible for raising the money for further renovations to the gallery in 1974, 1979, and 1982, and for the much-needed conservation of over two thousand works on paper in the Vassar collection.

During the late seventies and early eighties, the collections of the Vassar Art Gallery were greatly enhanced by gifts from individual donors. Donors of important contemporary works included Mr. and Mrs. Leon Arkus (Jane Callomon, class of 1950); Mr. and Mrs. Russell Lynes (Mildred Akin, class of 1932); Katherine Kuh, class of

1925; Frances Weis Pick, class of 1927; and Mr. and Mrs. Alan Stroock (Katherine Wyler, class of 1931). In addition, the Friends' purchase funds made possible the acquisition of a seventeenth-century Dutch painting by Claes Moeyaert entitled, *The Sacrifice of Noah*, and a third-century-A.D. fragment from a Roman sarcophagus.

Alumnae, many of whom were former members of the board of directors of the Friends, made regular contributions for gallery acquisitions. In addition to the aforementioned Davidson, Bronson, and Duncan funds, the Betsy Mudge Wilson (class of 1956) Memorial Fund, the Lydia Evans Tunnard (class of 1936) Fund, the Miggie Dougherty (class of 1941) Memorial Fund, and the Mary Weitzel Gibbons (class of 1951) Fund, were established. In 1980, Anne Keating Jones, class of 1943, and her husband, E. Powis Jones, established a fund for the purchase of photographs.

The years between 1977 and 1985 also saw the beginning and expansion of regional groups of Friends. Virginia Herrick Deknatel, class of 1929, launched the first group in Boston, and another followed in the mid-Hudson region, coordinated by Andrea Leeds Miron, class of 1975, and Lois Homer Graham, class of 1935. By 1998, other groups had been founded in Chicago, Westchester/ Fairfield counties, and Washington, D.C.
Roma Alessandrina, The Remapping of Rome under Alexander VII, 1655-1667, a monograph written by former Vassar Professor Richard Krautheimer, was published by the Friends in 1983, the first publication in a series honoring Agnes Rindge Claflin. The endowment for this series was established by Claflin's friends after her death in 1977 under the auspices of the Friends. The endowment was created to bring distinguished art scholars and events to the College and to preserve the proceedings of such events through publication. A European refugee and distinguished art scholar, Krautheimer had encountered Claflin in the late thirties, and she subsequently lured him from the University of Louisville to Vassar, where he stayed for fifteen years. With this monograph, the Friends published one of Krautheimer's first studies on Rome.

In 1983, a traveling exhibition, *All Seasons and Every Light, Nineteenth-Century Landscapes from the Collection of Elias Lyman Magoon*, was launched, the idea for the exhibition conceived and promoted by Friends chair, Anne Keating Jones. *All Seasons* introduced the Vassar art collection to alumnae and others across the nation. It was shown at the DeCordova Museum in Lincoln, Massachusetts; the Norton Gallery in West Palm Beach, Florida; the Mary and Leigh Block Gallery, Northwestern University, Evanston, Illinois; and the Santa Barbara Museum of Art, California. It traveled to the Carnegie Museum in Pittsburgh and also to the Taft Museum in Cincinnati. Later, it was sent on tour in South America under the auspices of the U.S. Information Agency. The visibility of the Art

Gallery was steadily enhanced during this period. By 1985, membership had multiplied from the original nucleus to 831, and membership had been broadened to include students. (At last count, in 1998, there were 1,137 members.)

During the fruitful chairmanships of Anne Keating Jones from 1979 to 1983, and of Mary Coxe Schlosser, class of 1951, from 1983 to 1987, there were many developments. Two Friends' funds were matched by the National Endowment of the Arts, enabling the publication of two illustrated handbooks—one on the gallery's sculpture (*Sculpture* [1982]) and one on its pre-twentieth-century painting collection (*Paintings 1300-1900* [1983]). Successively during this period, the Friends sponsored spring exhibitions, which opened at the time of their annual meetings: in 1980, *Selections from the Winston-Malbin Collection: Various Media and Formats*; 1981, *Blanchette Hooker Rockefeller: Gifts to the Gallery*; 1982, *Hudson River*

Student in Taylor Hall ca. 1950. (Courtesy of Vassar College Libraries, Special Collections)

People: Albany to Yonkers, 1700-1900; and 1983, *Photo-Collecting at Vassar, 100 Years +10*. From August 1983 to June 1984 there were fifteen special exhibitions, five on loan, and the others derived from the permanent collection. In each case, the Friends sponsored the publication of a catalogue for the exhibition. In June 1984, works of art given by members of reunion classes were exhibited.

Andrea Leeds Miron, class of 1975, the fourth chairman of the Friends, served from 1987 to 1990. During her tenure, many regional Friends' groups planned and hosted gala receptions for exhibition openings. As she stated in a review of her years, she "utilized the format established by [her] predecessors, Anne Jones and Mary Schlosser, and encouraged members of the community to attend lectures, receptions, seminars, and exhibits." In her words, "Taylor Hall became a 'Happening.' None of these activities incurred additional expenses; however, they did receive outstanding publicity, which enhanced our financial position and our ability to provide quality art experiences. In time, the Vassar Art Gallery achieved its true status as a center of cultural excellence on campus and throughout the Hudson Valley."

The years since 1990 have been the most exciting and fulfilling in the history of the Friends. Anne H. Bushman, class of 1944, was elected chair of the Friends at the annual meeting in 1990 and presided with distinction over these stimulating transitional years. These were the years in which the handsome Frances Lehman Loeb Art Center, funded in large part by the extraordinary gift of $7,500,000 from Frances Lehman Loeb, class of 1928, was designed by architect Cesar Pelli, constructed, and opened in October 1993. Concurrently, Taylor Hall and the art department section of Van Ingen were remodeled. The collection was removed from the Taylor gallery in preparation for the new construction and returned to the new site after the Loeb Art Center was completed.

During these years, the Friends, under Bushman's leadership, embraced many new challenges as the Art Center enlarged its role in the Vassar community and in the larger art community. The Friends' board reconfirmed the purpose of the organization as "maximizing support for the Art Center's critical needs in areas of acquisitions, communications, conservation, exhibitions, and publications, and, in conjunction with the Art Center and the art department, providing support for lectures and visiting artists." Not only were there loan exhibitions shown at Vassar, but increasingly, works from the Vassar collection were lent to other museums, both in the United States and abroad. In the mid-nineties, Katherine Sanford Deutsch, class of 1940, bequeathed an outstanding gift of paintings by Vuillard, Miró, Picasso, Pollock, and Balthus, among others, one of the major gifts by a Friend. In the nineties, membership in the Friends flourished, helping to bring interest in the Art Center to a new high.

During the last decade, most recently in the administrations of Claire Werner Henriques, class of 1952 (1993-96) and of the present chair, Harriet Bouvy Drake, class of 1952, collaboration of the Friends with the College administration has been strengthened through closer planning with the Office of Development. The board committed $233,600 to support the wish-list of James Mundy, class of 1974, director of the Art Center, including a catalogue of the twentieth-century collection, this catalogue of the twenty-fifth-anniversary exhibit, a commitment to a Friends' Annual Exhibition Fund for three consecutive years, and funds for establishing both a World Wide Web page and implementing a recorded tour of the Art Center. The Friends have also assisted with advisory support for the redesigned and secure alternative exhibition gallery in the College Center, which has greatly enhanced the experience of members of the Vassar community through frequently changing loan shows by faculty members, students, and outside artists (including local school children).

The Friends also have implemented the staffing of an information/sales desk at the Art Center with community volunteers. In this way, closer relations have been established between Vassar and those interested in art in the community at large. School groups have come with their art teachers, organizations from near and far have scheduled outings and tours, and alumnae have been drawn by openings and new shows to reinforce their interest in the College. The diversity of shows, in turn, has attracted a diverse audience. As a result, the whole community is richer, and the mission of the Art Center is extensively sustained.

Claire Henriques, retiring chair of the Friends in 1996, said in her final report to the Board:

> When the Friends were founded in 1974 by a core group of committed and visionary alumnae, the Vassar Art Gallery was a very different teaching museum from today. It has grown into the Frances Lehman Loeb Art Center, and the quality of the collection has been enhanced thanks to the support and gifts of art from alumnae/i and other Friends. Frances Lehman Loeb's and the late Katherine Sanford Deutsch's early commitment to the College resulted in the leadership gift for the Pelli building and the gift of a major twentieth-century art collection.
>
> Current Friends...have made major gifts to the Art Center both individually and as members. Through the years, the Friends' endowment and reserve funds continued to support acquisitions, conservation, exhibitions, lectures, openings, and student projects. In addition, the Claflin Fund supports art department lectures and publications.
>
> The great and ongoing legacy of the Friends to the teaching of art and the Vassar collection does not just reside in tangible gifts, but comes from that initial vision which continues to expand through those board members who serve and contribute untold time, energy, expertise, and skills to the Frances Lehman Loeb Art Center.

Wherever one pauses in time in perusing the history of the Friends, one can spot new developments and new aspects emerging. At home on Vassar's campus during the academic year 1997-98, one of the new developments was the initiative of the student Friends in involving other students with the Art Center, not only in connection with their classroom study, but also in their leisure time. (There were three hundred student members.) On 12 February 1998, Christopher Drago, class of 1998, student representative to the board of Friends of the Art Center, hosted an open house in the galleries to attract the interest of students, who, Drago felt, might be too intimidated to browse in the Art Center otherwise. "Ambient background music" was "spun" between 6 and 7 p.m. A tour was given by museum staff of the permanent collection and also, according to the *Miscellany News*, of "the guts of the museum—seeing the print room, the registrar's office, and other places behind the scenes." The student Friends also hosted a gathering in the galleries connected with the installation of a Sol LeWitt wall drawing, during which the students involved in executing the drawing spoke of their experience.

Anne Jones, whose contributions to the Friends have been seen by one of her colleagues as "the warp in its ever-strengthening fabric" and who has always kept her educated eye on both the past and the future of the organization, is now culminating her exceptional, continuous dedication by serving with Andrea Miron, class of 1975, as co-chair of the twenty-fifth-anniversary committee, which is arranging for this celebration. For two years, Mrs. Jones and Mrs. Miron and their fifty-one-member committee have been planning with the College's development office a series of events leading to the opening of the current exhibition.

These events have taken place in collaboration with five art museums of national stature, focusing on the role of a college art museum within the broader art-museum context. Vassar alumnae/i from across the country and Europe attended heavily, some in all-day seminars on art, both renewing and reaffirming their strong connection with the art education gained at Vassar. On 24 April 1997, James Mundy, class of 1974, director of the Art Center, joined Dr. Andrea Rich, president of the Los Angeles County Museum, for a "Conversation," followed by a dinner hosted by Mrs. Frances Lasker Brody, class of 1937. A similar "Two Directors" discussion took place with Robert Bergman at the Cleveland Museum of Art, with Evan Maurer at the Minneapolis Art Museum, and with Earl "Rusty" Powell at the National Gallery of Art in Washington, D.C. Following these events, on 19 September 1997, Mundy paired up with Nicholas Serota, director of the Tate Gallery of Art in London in conducting the fifth "Two Museums, Two Directors" conversation. This occasion was part of the program for a gathering of alumnae from throughout Europe. On 23 September, a reception was held at the Newhouse Gallery in New York City for the opening there of an exhibition of prints and drawings from Vassar's collection. This event was co-chaired by New York Friends, Margot Feely, class of 1952, and Phyllis Landes, class of 1950.

Students in the Taylor Hall Art Gallery in the 1950s. (Courtesy of Vassar College Libraries, Special Collections)

In most recent years the impact of the Friends' efforts on behalf of the program of the Art Center is much in evidence. The art department is using the Art Center in its teaching program now more than ever, and the Friends' efforts have been very important in bringing this about, according to Professor Susan Kuretsky, class of 1963, in an art department report to the Friends in February 1997. Art 105 now teaches "a significant number of sections a year in the museum." Ms. Kuretsky herself taught a freshman course last semester "focusing for the first time on works in the collection." To accompany his seminar for Art 262, Professor Brian Lukacher conceived of the exhibition, *No Incidents but a Ghost and a Storm: European Prints and Drawings from the Romantic Period*, with works drawn entirely from Vassar's collection. In addition, the art department considers the Christopher Wilmarth sculpture, *My Divider*, purchased with the aid of the Friends, to be a "most valuable teaching addition to the sculpture collection."

In the fall of 1997, Francesca Consagra, the Philip and Lynn Straus Curator of Prints and Drawings, created an exhibition, supported by the Smart Family Foundation, Inc., entitled, *The Lines of Battle: Images of War from the Fifteenth to the Twentieth Centuries*, to honor British historian John Keegan, the Delmas Visiting Distinguished Professor of History. Professor Keegan conducted a student seminar on the history of warfare during the first semester. The exhibition highlighted works from Vassar's collection as well as that of the United States Military Academy at West Point.

Following this exhibition, in the spring of 1998, drawings for the murals of James Daugherty, W.P.A. muralist of the 1930s, were the featured exhibition in the print gallery, an exhibition conceived, researched, and curated by Rebecca Lawton, the Emily Hargroves Fisher '57 and Richard B. Fisher Curator of the Art Center. This exhibition encapsulated the contribution of the Friends, whose sponsorship made it possible. Both exhibitions serve as prime examples of the ever-broadening use of the gallery in supporting the basic mission of the College's teaching of art.

It seems fitting to conclude this history of the Friends with a recent summarizing statement made by James Mundy, director of the Art Center:

> The past twenty-five years have been ones of tremendous growth and productivity for the Friends as they have pursued their goal of supporting the Vassar College Art Gallery and, now, the Frances Lehman Loeb Art Center. The dual milestones of this important anniversary coupled with the approach of a new millennium indicate that the potential to support the presentation of original art of high quality at Vassar is without limit. The Friends' continuing dedication to serve Vassar College and its community by fostering a love of the visual arts is reassuring. With their present broad base and secure foundation, the Friends can greet the next twenty-five years with confidence that their work up to this time has insured a measure of excellence of which we can all be proud.

Throughout the last twenty-five years, the success and growth of the Friends of the Frances Lehman Loeb Art Center has been accomplished through the excellent administration of those running the organization for the board of directors, including Mary Busch, executive director, 1975-79; Eleanor Daniels, class of 1966, acting executive secretary, 1978-79; Joan Grennan, executive director, 1979-84; Ellen Curtis, class of 1964, executive administrator, 1984-91; Janice Fischlein, executive administrator, 1991-96; and Maureen Andola, executive administrator, 1996-. Finally, the consummate imaginative energy and management talents of the successive chairpersons of the board have been the driving force behind the Friends. They are: Carol R. Noyes, class of 1939, and Belle K. Ribicoff, class of 1945, co-chairs, 1974-78; Anne Keating Jones, class of 1943, 1978-83; Mary C. Schlosser, class of 1951, 1983-87; Andrea L. Miron, class of 1975, 1987-90; Anne H. Bushman, class of 1944, 1990-93; Claire Werner Henriques, class of 1952, 1993-96; and Harriet Bouvy Drake, class of 1952, 1996-99.

Author's Note

I wish to acknowledge with gratitude the help I have received from many members of the Friends board, who have taken the time to talk with me about their activities and the development of the Friends organization and who, in some cases, have permitted me to quote them. In particular, I wish to thank Phoebe Banta, class of 1961, the tireless keeper of the organization's records, and Anne Keating Jones, Belle Ribicoff, Andrea Miron, Carol Rothschild Noyes, Ann Morse, class of 1959, and Claire Werner Henriques. I acknowledge gratefully also the help of the current administrator of the Friends, Maureen Andola, and of Beverly Doppel, her administrative assistant, as well as Ellen Curtis, class of 1964, past executive administrator. I owe thanks, also, to Anthony Stellato, vice president, and Paul Mutone, controller. James Mundy, the Anne Hendricks Bass Director of the Frances Lehman Loeb Art Center, and Rebecca Lawton, the Emily Hargroves Fisher '57 and Richard B. Fisher Curator of the Art Center, made valuable suggestions to me, for which I thank them. Professor Susan Kuretsky and Professor Emerita Christine Havelock were helpful in their assistance to me. Finally, I wish to thank President Frances Fergusson for giving me the opportunity to draw together this history: it was a chance to connect the present with the long traditions of the past.

Catalogue

1

Chinese (Western Han period, 206 B.C.-23 A.D.)

Two Tomb Figures (second century B.C.)
Pottery with applied pigments
Female figure: Height 21¼"
Male figure: Height, 24"
From The Schloss Collection

Literature: Janet Baker, *Seeking Immortality: Chinese Tomb Sculpture from The Schloss Collection* (Santa Ana, California, 1996), 59, fig. 12., pl. 31

Exhibitions: *Seeking Immortality: Chinese Tomb Sculpture from The Schloss Collection*, Bowers Museum of Cultural Art, Santa Ana, California, 1996, no. 49; *Seeking Immortality: Early Chinese Ceramics from The Schloss Collection*, Bruce Museum of Arts and Science, Greenwich, Connecticut, 19 September 1998-3 January 1999

In 1990, several large, ancient burial pits were discovered outside the modern city of Xi'an, China.[1] They were placed near the mausoleum of an early Han emperor, Han Jingdi (reigned 157-141 B.C.), and were determined to be subsidiary to the main burial mound, which remains unopened. The pottery figures found inside these pits were astonishing; they depicted male and female forms in the nude. In early Chinese art, unlike Greek art, representations of nude figures are extremely rare. The archaeologists soon revealed, however, that these figures had not been intended to be seen in the nude, but had originally been dressed for burial in cloth outfits.

The two ceramic nude figures in this exhibition are very similar to the examples found near the tomb of Han Jingdi. Both figures were manufactured in bivalve molds of red-clay pottery with added pigments. The female figure is smaller, with an overall surface covering of white slip to indicate her fairer skin shade. It probably represents a serving girl of the imperial court. The male figure is larger, with a rectangular head and strong musculature in the face, as the body would originally have been seen clothed. It represents a soldier of the court.

The discovery of these pottery figures has raised some intriguing questions about early China and early Chinese art. This excavation has been compared to the earlier discovery of over six thousand terracotta figures in burial pits near the tomb of Qin Shihuangdi (died 210 B.C.). The first emperor and unifier of all China is also credited (or maligned) for the construction of the Great Wall,

unifying weights and measures, standardizing roads and axle widths, and for the odious act of burning the books, which was an attack on Confucian values. The figures from the tomb of Qin Shihuangdi are all lifesize, whereas the figures from the tomb of Han Jingdi are about two feet tall. The effort at the later site was considerable, however, with over ten thousand figures uncovered to date. (In neither case has the main tomb of the emperor yet been excavated.)

The level of naturalism in each group of tomb sculptures has been the subject of much debate. Early on, in the 1970s, after the initial discovery of the lifesize buried figures at the Qin Shihuangdi site, several of the archaeologists made claims that the figures were true portraits, expressing the individuality of single people. Then, in the early 1990s, with the excavation of the two-foot-high figures at the tomb of Han Jingdi, the issue was raised again. More recently, a European scholar, Ladislav Kesner, has presented a convincing argument for viewing the entire grouping at each site as a portrait of the emperor's bodyguard in congregate—a kind of group portrait stressing not individual identities but the appearance of the group as a political entity.[2]

Candace J. Lewis, class of 1966

---

[1]   For an account of the site, see Wang Xueli, "*Xi Han Yangling ling yan kaogue you li da faxian*" (An important archaeological discovery in the graveyard at Yangling), in *Kaogu yu wenwu* (Archaeology and Cultural Relics) (1991): 1, 96, and no. 2.

[2]   Ladislav Kesner, "Likeness of No One: (Re)presenting the First Emperor's Army," *Art Bulletin* 75, no. 1 (March 1995): 115-32.

2

Chinese (Eastern Han period, 25-220 A.D.)

Tower with Moat (second century A.D.)
Earthenware pottery with green lead glaze
Height, 37"
From The Schloss Collection

Literature: Janet Baker, *Seeking Immortality: Chinese Tomb Sculpture from The Schloss Collection* (Santa Ana, California, 1996), 24, 56

Exhibitions: *Seeking Immortality: Chinese Tomb Sculpture from The Schloss Collection*, Bowers Museum of Cultural Art, Santa Ana, California, 1996, no. 1; *Seeking Immortality: Early Chinese Ceramics from The Schloss Collection*, Bruce Museum of Arts and Science, Greenwich, Connecticut, 19 September 1998-3 January 1999

Many green-glazed pottery towers are presently in Western museums and private collections. Coming out of China in the 1920s and 1930s, these objects immediately attracted the attention of collectors, who were taken with the large scale of the towers, the apparent naturalism of the representation, and the liveliness of the many figures, both human and animal. Since 1950, fairly extensive archaeological excavations in China have given us a more complete understanding of these objects. The towers were placed with other *mingqi* (burial objects) within the tombs of the gentry of the first century B.C. and the first and second centuries A.D. The complex of pottery tomb objects usually included pottery replicas of a well, a privy, a tower, a granary, lamps, wine vessels, and other containers. They were intended to accompany the soul of the deceased as it made the journey into the afterlife.

The towers have been studied most often for the information they could yield about the architectural practices of the Han period. This approach is understandable, since we have no surviving wooden buildings from this period. The pottery towers confirm literary accounts of the importance of the freestanding wooden tower as a major architectural development of the Han period. Before the Han, large buildings and towers were constructed with an earthen core, surrounded and surmounted by wooden rooms. The freestanding wooden tower, in contrast, allowed building for height and the construction of watchtowers and pleasure pavilions. Also important to note is that these pottery towers demonstrate how the Han wooden towers functioned as the precursors of the pagoda, as it developed along with early Buddhism in China from the second to the fifth centuries A.D.

This tower, three stories high, stands in a basin, representing a moat. In the moat are figures of ducks, geese, and a running dog. On the first balcony are men in officials' caps and robes, while on the second balcony are four younger men guarding the four

corners. At the apex, on the ridgepole, perches a large bird. The tower is comparable to a group of green-glazed towers with moats excavated from an area in the western section of modern Henan Province and nearby Shaanxi Province and is datable to the later decades of the Eastern Han dynasty (circa 150-180 A.D.).[1]

The period was marked by the decline of the central court, the rise in importance of manorial estates and great families, as well as by strife and purges. These events led to the rise of messianic utopianism in several areas of the Chinese empire, the most notable being the Yellow Turban Rebellion of 180 A.D., when the populace took to the roads proclaiming their allegiance to the Daoist leader, Zhang Jue, and their hope for a new era of *taiping* (perfect peace), a perfect world on earth.

Some of these popular utopian wishes are also expressed in the form of the green-glazed towers made for tombs. These objects were intended to represent a highly revered ritual building known as the *mingtang* (bright hall or sacred hall), which represented the structure of the cosmos and could be seen to insure harmony between earth, man, and heaven. Thus, the deceased was seen as existing in a sacred space, reborn into a perfect land after death.

Candace J. Lewis, class of 1966

---

[1] See tower from Zhangwan, Lingbao County in Henan Province in *Henan sheng bowuguan* (Henan Provincial Museum), "*Lingbao Zhangwan Han mu*" (The Han tombs at Zhangwan, Lingbao, Henan Province), *Wenwu* (Cultural Relics), no. 11 (November 1975): 75-93. See also Sanshengwan, also in Lingbao County, Henan Province in *Henan sheng bowuguan* (Henan Provincial Museum), *Henan sheng bowuguan* (Beijing, 1982), 7:no. 76. See also a tower from Xichuan County in Henan Province in Sherman Lee, *China, 5,000 Years: Innovation and Transformation in the Arts*, Howard Rogers, ed. (New York, 1998), no. 100.

3

Chinese (Tang dynasty, 618-906 A.D.)

Tomb Guardians (eighth century A.D.)
Red pottery with white slip and applied pigments
Left: Height, 23^1/$_2$"
Right: Height, 29"
From The Schloss Collection

Literature: Janet Baker, *Seeking Immortality: Chinese Tomb Sculpture from The Schloss Collection* (Santa Ana, California, 1996), 53, 59 and fig. 42

Exhibitions: *Seeking Immortality: Chinese Tomb Sculpture from The Schloss Collection*, Bowers Museum of Cultural Art, Santa Ana, California, 1996, no. 151; *Seeking Immortality: Early Chinese Ceramics from The Schloss Collection*, Bruce Museum of Arts and Science, Greenwich, Connecticut, 19 September 1998-3 January 1999

Mythical and supernatural beings were represented in the tombs of ancient China, occasionally from earliest times and frequently from the Han dynasty (206 B.C.-220 A.D.) onward. By the Six-Dynasties period (220-581 A.D.), the *mingqi* (burial objects) in the tomb often included a pair of fearsome beings known as *zhenmushou* (tomb guardian creatures), composite beings with the body of a lion, the hooves of an ox, and the wings of a bird. One of the pair possessed a human face and the other an animal face, both contorted in frightening grimaces. The figures were intended to scare evil spirits that might invade the space of the tomb and interfere with the tranquil abode of the deceased. By the Tang period (618-906 A.D.), there were often two pairs of these figures, one pair with human heads, the other with animal heads, placed in the entranceway of the tomb, guarding against malevolent intruders.

The two examples seen here, both with animal faces, probably come from different sets of guardian figures, but they share many features—the dramatic gesture with raised arm, grimacing faces, horns, and a depiction of combat between the forces of good (represented by the guardians) and the forces of darkness (represented by the lowly, evil-looking composite creatures under their feet). Presented in large scale and painted with vibrant natural pigments, these figures demonstrate their supernatural power to conquer evil.[1] The subordinate figures are derived from the iconography of Buddhism. These particular representations are similar to ones imported from India; when they entered Chinese religious art, they were shown as strange, almost inchoate earth-bound beasts, bloated and angry under the feet of the guardians. An unusual feature of the gray tomb guardian (right) is the relatively good preservation of the floral designs on the front of its garment. Floral designs, too, were imported from India with Buddhist art and textiles. They were represented often in the Tang period, usually in beautiful shades of red, green, and other colors. Here the gracefulness of the floral designs contrasts with the super-realistic depiction of the fearsome guardian.

Both of these works are datable to the first quarter of the eighth century, a period of great power for the Chinese empire and international Buddhism.

Candace J. Lewis, class of 1966

---

[1]   For another example, see the three-color glazed work in Albert Dien, *The Quest for Eternity* (Los Angeles, 1987), 38.

SHAFT-TOMB CERAMIC SCULPTURE
FROM WEST MEXICO

Nayarit, Jalisco, and Colima are modern coastal states of West Mexico. They face on the Pacific Ocean, but are also crossed by the Sierra Madre Occidental Mountains, which run from the northwest to the southeast, creating valleys and lake basins. In these highland regions, many agricultural communities formed as early as 1500 B.C. Not until the late formative period (300 B.C.-200 A.D.) did shaft-chamber tombs appear in this region. It is the ceramic tomb art of this period that is represented in this exhibition.

The names of these modern states have been given to the varied styles that are found in West Mexico. We speak of Nayarit, Jalisco, and Colima when describing styles, but quite naturally the different styles do not coincide exactly with these modern geographic boundaries. We also have more than one style represented in some tombs, indicating trade and exchange. It would appear that specialized workshops had developed in different areas and that work from these workshops might have been considered prestigious.

The funerary ceramic sculpture taken from the shaft-chamber tombs of this region is today highly sought after, but difficult to interpret, because almost all of it was looted and removed from its original context. West Mexico was for a long time considered peripheral and of little cultural consequence, in part because no large architectural remains in urban centers were found. It was a region that was neglected by serious archaeologists.

Today that has changed. Many serious scholars of different disciplines are working to retrieve and interpret the art of West Mexico, to uncover more of its past, and to better understand how this area related to other cultures in Mesoamerica. It seems clear now that this region did not live in total isolation and perhaps shared in cultural concepts that we associate with much of the rest of Mesoamerica.

Much of this modern interest comes too late. Almost all of the burial sites of the region have been looted and the original context damaged or destroyed. This, of course, occurred when these lively and expressive figures were "discovered." Figures from these tombs had been described as early as the 1890s, but there was no interest in these "primitive" and ugly pieces. By the 1920s, however, a number of artists—among them Diego Rivera, Frida Kahlo, Covarrubias, and Henry Moore—began to respond to these works as having artistic merit.

Rivera saw in these works an art of the people that suited his leftist political views. He also saw with the new eye of the twentieth century and found in these figures great expressive power and aesthetic appeal. Rivera collected vigorously and built the Anahuacalli to serve as his studio and to house his collection. At the time of his death, after the Mexican Revolution, he gave his studio-gallery to the government. Frida Kahlo's collection also was opened to the public. These early collectors stimulated great interest in these pieces and created a major market for figures that had been found in the fields and that farmers had, at one time, used for target practice.

Viewed with fresh eyes, these figures became objects of delight, amusement, and mystery. Since many of the Colima figures portrayed everyday activities, the notion grew up that West Mexican tomb sculpture was a nonreligious genre. Books and exhibitions of the 1960s showed a real interest in the formal and expressive quality of the figures, but they did not search for spiritual meaning in them.

Though there has been one spectacular discovery, in 1993 at Huitzilapa, of an undisturbed 7.6-meter-deep shaft tomb, the paucity of archaeological data has meant that it is the figures themselves that have had to tell the story. Scholars recently have begun to see in the funerary sculpture evidence of social stratification, concern with family lineage, and a desire to link the living with their ancestors. Also in the tombs were articles useful in everyday life that were consistent with the lifestyle or social position of the deceased.

Rituals and rites of passage were represented in the tombs, and much of the sculpture undoubtedly had symbolic significance. The people tied their own life/death cycle to the agricultural cycle. There is clear evidence of knowledge of the cardinal points and the position of the sun. They played the ball game for both ritual and recreation. We are coming to believe that they shared in the general belief system of all of Mesoamerica. While the exact meaning of these sculptures eludes us, we do have the fascinating forms that these artists built by hand to help us fathom their beliefs, their fears, and their aspirations.

Objects from Nayarit, Jalisco, and Colima in the exhibition contribute to our ongoing effort to understand the art and culture of West Mexico. It should be noted, however, that because there has been no scientific excavation in the region until recently, and a great many pieces came from looted shaft tombs, it is impossible to know their origins. This is true of all the West Mexican objects in this exhibition.

Frances P. Taft, class of 1942
Professor of Art History, Cleveland Institute of Art, Cleveland, Ohio

4

Mexican, Colima Style

Standing Figure with Vessel (late formative period, 200 B.C.-250 A.D.)
Terracotta with red slip
Height, 14"; width, 8$^1/_2$"; depth, 8"
Lent by June and Jack Dunbar (Janet S. Coan, class of 1948)

This standing figure, a little over a foot in height, is characteristic of the finest hollow, hand-built ceramic figures of Colima from the shaft-chamber tombs. It can be dated to between 200 B.C. and 250 A.D. in what is called the late formative period. These tombs had a vertical shaft and then one or more chambers that ran horizontally from the shaft, where the deceased was interred. The tombs were used over several generations, and exact dating is difficult since the ceramics of West Mexico do not seem to respond to the thermoluminescence dating technique. All aspects of life are represented in these ceramics, from everyday occupations to special rituals and shamanistic figures. From Colima there are also carefully observed and skillfully simplified representations of the flora and fauna from the region, and also perhaps from mythology. Many of the figures seem based on life, but may also carry some symbolic significance. All funerary art undoubtedly carried specific meaning. We are left with the forms to appreciate and possible meanings to pursue.

The Colima artists achieved a remarkable sense of life, energy, and action in their fully rounded three-dimensional forms. This figure is carrying out some specific activity. In this case, we seem to have a potter, tool in hand, engaged in shaping or burnishing the pot before firing. This polished look adds greatly to the surface appeal and the tactile quality of the object.

Typical of many Colima figures are the shoe-button eyes, the simple treatment of a lipless mouth, the prominent, but not exaggerated nose, all on a well-rounded face. The curved ears are good-sized, and each has an opening above the lobe, which perhaps was originally adorned with some object or ring that was made of transient material. The hair is indicated with a simple incised pattern. The head, as is usually the case, is a good deal larger than natural proportions, and the legs are enlarged to support the figure. The arms do not exhibit any muscles, but are rather tubular and are curved around as they grasp the vessel. This adds to the sense of movement and solves the technical problem of closing the contours. Hands and feet are treated in a summary fashion, with fingers and toes indicated by simple incised lines.

The patterning on the upper body may represent his shirt, but it also seems to be repeated on the pot itself. This may be negative or resist painting. Throughout the figure, nonessentials are eliminated. There seems to be little interest in gender or in exact anatomy. The overall sculptural quality is outstanding. The figure seems very much alive and able to function for the deceased in his journey to the beyond or to his new life in his earthen chamber.

Frances P. Taft, class of 1942

5

Mexican, Jalisco Style

Marriage Pair (late formative period, 200 B.C.-250 A.D.)
Terracotta
Height, 14$^{1}/_{2}$"; width, 14$^{1}/_{2}$"; depth, 8"
Anonymous lender

This Jalisco marriage pair indicates how well the artist was able to bring two individual figures together and make of them one integrated whole, and to express their affectionate interrelationship. He holds a small cup in one hand, while his other hand rests on his wife's shoulder. He leans forward as though he were offering her the cup. She holds a shallow bowl or shell in one hand and then gently rests her right hand on his knee. The composition is pleasing and the piece well balanced. She has her legs tucked under her, which provides a very solid base. He has one leg firmly on the ground and the other bent, which gives a sense of movement. We feel the potential movement of both figures, which is partly accomplished through their gestures.

The buff or ochre color of the clay is typically Jalisco, the use of color is very restrained, limited to a reddish-brown on the head-dresses and costumes—her skirt and his short trousers. The treatment of their heads is characteristic of this style. They are large and elongated, tapering towards a rounded skull with a very high brow. The eyes stare at us. They are very carefully delineated and the lids are accentuated. Notice the different treatment given to the eyes on the Colima figure (cat. no. 4). Here, the noses are very long and sharp, which is also characteristic of the Jalisco-Ameca

style. The cheeks are defined, and the mouth is good sized and presented with lips parted, revealing the teeth, particularly in the lower jaw. The whole face in these figures is concave and seems to swoop down from forehead to the enlarged chin. These faces are very strong and really demand our attention. He wears a rather large ear ornament, but her ears are rather plain. The long, sharp noses are surprising, since we don't think of them as typically Mexican.

One detail that is also typical of Jalisco figures is the attention paid to the finger- and toenails. This is best seen on his hand that rests on her shoulder. Each and every nail is carefully delineated. Here again is a distinctive feature, because in many West Mexico figures the hands are barely defined, much less having individual digits.

This couple is fully realized in their interactive pose and, despite distortions and exaggerations, is thoroughly believable. They may represent a man and wife enjoying some kind of ritual feast or celebration, or perhaps they relate to an archetype of man and woman and their creative possibilities.

Frances P. Taft, class of 1942

© Justin Kerr 1997

6

Mexican, Jalisco, Ameca-Etzatlan Style

Standing Warrior (late formative period, 200 B.C.-250 A.D.)
Terracotta, buff-colored clay with reddish-brown slip
Height, 18"; width, 8"; depth, 8"
Anonymous lender

Exhibition: *Ancient West Mexico*, Art Institute of Chicago, 1998

This standing warrior from Jalisco, in the Ameca-Etzatlan style, is a truly impressive piece of sculpture. It is made of buff-colored clay typical of Jalisco and enriched with a reddish-brown slip. The arms and legs are a rich brown, in contrast with the pale ochre of the rest of the figure. This warrior, standing eighteen inches in height, is remarkably lively, superbly engineered to stand in a balanced position, poised to strike or throw his large dart. This is achieved by transforming the feet into platforms large enough to support the figure as he bends at the waist. The legs are enlarged to provide stability. They are bent at the knee, but must enter the feet in the center rather than at the rear. These anatomical adjustments are so elegantly accomplished that we do not find them disturbing. The figure reads as strong, able, and ready to do his job. The distortions matter little when the whole figure achieves convincing form.

Since this is another Jalisco figure, we notice again the carefully detailed fingernails and toenails (see cat. no. 5). The stress here is on all the essentials. The legs are powerful, the hands are large and strong, the figure is enveloped in protective armor, and on his head a wonderful bell-shaped helmet shields his head.

His armor is probably deer or rabbit leather, or perhaps pounded bark or cotton. Whatever it is made of, it envelops him, it encircles his upper body, and projects above his neck and chin. His short trousers show no pattern and his head and body are unadorned. He is ready for action.

His very large and carefully rimmed eyes are white, which makes them stand out from the shadow of the helmet, and we feel he is staring directly at us. Perhaps he is a guardian of the grave or perhaps a true warrior, a figure celebrating the warrior accomplishments of the deceased, or he may be a symbolic figure from the other world, providing eternal protection for those who lie within. Perhaps he celebrates one of the rites of passage that a chieftain must go through.

We cannot determine his function, but we can certainly admire the craftsman's skill displayed here. This figure is immediately appealing, and the horizontals and verticals here are so beautifully balanced that this image stays in our minds as a wonderful solution to expressing strength, purpose, and action.

Frances P. Taft, class of 1942

7

Mexican, Jalisco Style

Mask (late formative period, 200 B.C.-250 A.D.)
Ceramic and white slip
Height, 7"; width, 6"; depth, 5"
Lent by June and Jack Dunbar (Janet S. Coan, class of 1948)

This ceramic mask from the late formative period is easily assigned to the Jalisco style, although it does not display all the characteristics of the style. It is a light-colored clay, covered with white slip, which gives it a rather ghostly appearance. It is probably a death mask, since the eye sockets are not perforated, and hence it would not be suitable for a person to wear. The very large and pointed nose, as we have seen, is typically Jalisco, as are the very distinct eyes. These eyes seem to be dead. They don't stare at us, but seem sightless. The mouth is slightly open, once again revealing the teeth of the lower jaw, as we have seen in other Jalisco figures (see cat. nos. 5 and 6). There is a ring in the nose where the septum has been pierced, and ear decorations are also apparent. The chin is relatively prominent, but what is lacking is the elaborate head turban, which on so many of the living Jalisco figures gives them such a powerful presence. If this were a mask to cover the face of a deceased person, it is quite logical that it would do nothing more than cover the face; any rendering of a headdress would be inappropriate. The angle of the face and eyes also suggests that it covered a human face. We find masks throughout Mesoamerica, but they are not as numerous, or perhaps not as popular, in West Mexican sculpture.

Frances P. Taft, class of 1942

8

Mexican, Nayarit, Lagunillas "C" Style

Seated Figure with Polychrome Face Paint (late formative period, 200 B.C.-250 A.D.)
Polychromed terracotta
Height, 14¹/₂"; width, 6"; depth, 9¹/₂"
Anonymous lender

Nayarit is the northernmost coastal state of the West Mexico states we have been considering, and it seems to have produced the widest variation in styles. Very well known and so delightful to modern audiences are the group scenes in clay from Ixtlan del Rio. Here we have ball games, weddings, festivals, funerals, and battles all enacted by miniature clay figures set up around a circular plaza, ball court, or some enclosed space. The figures are without detail, but full of animation.

This piece is over a foot tall and in a style once called "Chinesco" because of the slit eyes and little mouth. This no longer is the label of choice and a more geographically descriptive term is used. Whatever the label, these polychrome ceramic figures are quite intriguing because they seem to be so self-contained, so contemplative, and offer no hint of their meaning.

This seated male figure has his arms folded around his knees, which produces a very abstract composition of the body. The orange clay is burnished and painted with red, black, white, and yellow paint. The head is heart-shaped, with protruding ears and a tight-fitting polychrome hat. The most prominent feature of the face is the mask, worn over the eyes, which makes the figure quite mysterious and, of course, leaves us wondering about its meaning. The nose is bulbous and a nose ornament is prominent, attached to the pierced septum.

The figure is symmetrical and frontal, with little or no movement implied. The person could perhaps stay in this position through eternity. The polychrome decoration is red, black, and white and adds a great deal of vitality to the piece. The bands around ankles, knees, and wrists are quite abstract. The patterns of painted areas are rather simple, but a more complex textile waistband is differentiated from the treatment of chest and arms.

The treatment of arms and legs is well-suited to modeling with clay, keeping the contours closed, and folding the figure in on itself. The arms are essentially tubular. They are brought together over the knees, making a contained space between the large head and the lower limbs. The arms become one continuous form with no concern for details like hands.

These figures seem so real, but realistic detail has nothing to do with achieving this convincing form. These artists were masters of simplification and abstraction, and by eliminating the nonessentials they spoke about the formal essentials.

Frances P. Taft, class of 1942

9

Mexican, Nayarit, Ixtlan del Rio

Standing Male Warrior and Female Cup Bearer (late formative period, 200 B.C.-250 A.D.)
Polychromed terracotta
Height, 16"; width, 9½"; depth, 7"
Lent by June and Jack Dunbar (Janet S. Coan, class of 1948)

This pair, a male figure, clearly a warrior, and a female figure carrying a cup on her shoulder, is typical of one of the styles from the Nayarit region, in this case, Ixtlan del Rio, which is in the southeast corner of the state. This pair is striking in its brutal, archaic quality, with startling exaggerations of human features and proportions. The clay is handled in a rough way, quite different from the beautifully burnished surfaces of the Colima piece (see cat. no. 4). It is therefore problematic to lump all of these figures under a generic West Mexican label, but the reason is that they are linked by having come from the shaft tombs common to these states, and because we find in many cases that, while their forms vary widely, they served the same purpose for the journey of the deceased into and through the underworld.

This pair is presented in a frontal position; a full three-dimensional sense is not achieved. The unburnished surfaces are decorated in polychrome using black, white, red, and yellow. The distortion of proportion is much more noticeable in these figures than in those of Jalisco or Colima. Details are noticed separately rather than being integrated into one composition. The heads are very large and compelling as they stare out of their big almond-shaped eyes, with the oval pupils indicated in black. Noses are bulbous, and each figure has a nose decoration through the pierced septum. The arms are obviously diminished, but perform the essential tasks, which for the male is displaying his weapon and for the female, supporting the cup on her shoulder. In contrast to Jalisco hands, which are carefully rendered, these hands of Nayarit are not. Her cup was once possibly filled with liquid, but certainly it is symbolic sustenance.

Their gender is made clear in both cases, and both are supported by enlarged lower limbs and feet. The textiles they wear are also out of scale, and the geometric patterns are enlarged. Especially intriguing is the fact that the shirt he wears has a pattern that is rather closely related to Peruvian textiles. The possible connections between the coastal states and the west coast of South America, observed in textile patterns and in early stirrup spout vessels, would appear to have been in the early formative period.

They both wear ear ornaments, which were characteristic of Nayarit. They seem to be a series of rings put into perforations along the ear's edge. These are quite different from earrings of the other states and styles. Her headdress seems to be a simple rolled and twisted band. His head covering is more elaborate. It is conical and probably made of some kind of skin. It is fringed, but the fringe looks almost more like teeth than soft textile.

These startling, rather bizarre, figures are perhaps the furthest removed from a European-based aesthetic, but they undoubtedly function in the tomb as symbolic of a certain ritual or of exploits of the chief as a warrior.

Frances P. Taft, class of 1942

Baccio della Porta, called Fra Bartolommeo
Italian (1472-1517)
or
Paolino del Signoraccio, called Fra Paolino
Italian (1490-1547)

Virgin and Child (ca. 1500-25)
Black chalk on paper, lightly squared for transfer
10" x 6⅝"
Inscription: "from the collection of Dr. Henry Wellesley, 1791-1866" on verso
Promised Gift of Mrs. Carolyn P. Farris, class of 1953

Provenance: Dr. Henry Wellesley, Oxford (Lugt 1384); sold Sotheby's, London, 25 June-10 July 1866; William H. Schab, New York

In certain cases, the drawings of the master of the Florentine High Renaissance, Dominican monk Baccio della Porta, known as Fra Bartolommeo, are very difficult to distinguish from those of his talented student and successor at the Monastery of San Marco in Florence, Fra Paolino. The previously unpublished Farris drawing is one of these cases. Otto Benesch, on a note on the drawing's mat, considered it a "characteristic" work by Fra Bartolommeo, and the attribution of it to this artist has been traditional. However, with recent research, particularly the work of Chris Fischer, a clearer picture of the drawings of Fra Paolino is gradually emerging. The drawing cannot be connected directly with any surviving published painting by either artist, thereby making stylistic differentiation a more important aspect of its existence.

Benesch called attention to similarities between the Farris drawing and studies in the Uffizi for Fra Bartolommeo's major, yet unfinished, altarpiece, *Madonna and Child Enthroned with Saint Anne*, commissioned in 1510 to be erected in the Sala del Consiglio Maggiore in the Palazzo Vecchio, Florence. A number of these studies show an evolution of the pose of the Virgin and Child into which this drawing could, at least theoretically, be placed. The sheets were published by Fischer.[1] There, the artist explores different positions of the Child on the lap of the Virgin, turning to the left, as in this sheet, and ultimately to the right, as in the painting now in the Museo di San Marco.[2] Other analogous drawings by the master to the one under consideration are the study for a *putto* in the painting, *Salvator Mundi*, for the Billi Chapel of Santissima Annunziata[3]; and a preparatory study for *Madonna del Santuario*, in the cathedral at Lucca.[4]

Fra Paolino, who succeeded Fra Bartolommeo and inherited his studio, is represented in public and private collections with many fewer drawings than his more famous teacher. Those works which are known are, in general, more energetic black chalk studies with a hint of incipient Mannerism in some of the poses and implied psychologies of the subjects. The brisk strokes of the chalk and the torsion evident in the figure of the Child bear similarities, in general, to a number of Paolino's drawings. The habit of placing the Child in such a strong diagonal position across the body of the Virgin appears in Fra Paolino's work,[5] and in Pistoian painting in general of the period, particularly in that of his father, Bernardino del Signoraccio.[6]

Fra Paolino had a long and fruitful career after the death of Fra Bartolommeo, which included not only continuing the work of the S. Marco studio in Florence, but the establishment of a similar workshop at the convent of S. Domenico in Pistoia between 1525 and 1530. Given the fact that numerous altarpieces in Pistoia are attributed to him, it is logical to expect that more drawings will emerge, both from the ranks of known masters such as Fra Bartolommeo, as well as from anonymous drawings in public and private collections. Until that time, the Farris drawing properly inhabits an area of transition between the two artists.

James Mundy, class of 1974

---

[1] Chris Fischer, *Disegni di Fra Bartolommeo e della sua scuola, Florence* (Florence, 1986), nos. 52-57, figs. 68-74.

[2] Serena Padovani, *L'eta de Savonarola: Fra' Bartolomeo e la scuola di San Marco* (Giunta regionale toscana, 1996), 99-104.

3   See Padovani, 116, no. 27b; and the drawing of a seated *Virgin and Child* in the Louvre, inv. no. 214.

4   See Chris Fischer, *Fra Bartolommeo et son atelier: Dessins et peintures des collections françaises* (Paris, 1994), 88-89, no. 52.

5   E.g. his *Sacra Conversazione* in the church of S. Maria del Sasso near Bibbiena; see Chiara d'Afflitto et al., *L'eta di Savonarola: Fra Paolino e la pittura a Pistoia nel primo '500* (Giunta regionale toscana, 1996), 25, fig. 10.

6   Cf. d'Afflitto et al., 124-39, particularly *Sacra Conversazione*, in the church of S. Vitale, Pistoia, illus. p. 139.

11

Taddeo Zuccaro
Italian (1529-66)

Group of Figures from the Wedding Feast at Cana (1561-63)
Pen and ink over red chalk on paper
10³/₄" x 8¹/₄"
Inscription: "L no. 21" in the hand of the Earl of Spencer on original mount
Lent by Marjorie and Arnold Z. Pfeffer (Marjorie P. Fingerhood, class of 1941)

Provenance: George John, 3rd Earl of Spencer (Lugt nos. 1530 and 1532); James Wadmore, sold Christie's, London, 8 May 1854; Dr. Barry Delany, London (Lugt no. 350); Paul Oppé, London; by descent to Miss Armid and Mr. Denis Oppé, London; Helen Seiferheld, New York

This previously unpublished drawing rests seemingly at the nexus of the careers of the brothers Taddeo and Federico Zuccaro. The elder and shorter-lived brother, Taddeo, was born in S. Angelo in Vado in the Marches, but spent his short, remarkable career working in Rome and its environs. Federico, Taddeo's junior by eleven years, had a much longer career and was active in many cities in addition to Rome, including Florence, Venice, Turin, Madrid, and even London. Federico died in Rome in 1609, over forty years after his brother.

During the period 1555-63, Federico assisted his brother on a number of projects in Rome and, most certainly, received commissions on his own thanks to his brother's influence and reputation. Among these were the frescoed exterior of the house of Tizio da Spoleto in the Piazza Sant'Eustachio, dating to 1558-59, and a number of scenes from the life of Moses, painted in fresco for the Belvedere in the Vatican between 1561 and 1563. Just before his death, the great connoisseur and scholar of Zuccaro drawings, John Gere, argued that Taddeo had provided his brother with a number of drawings from which to work on these projects.[1]

While this theory is demonstrably untenable in regard to certain drawings, it does provide an intriguing explanation in the case of the drawing under discussion. The drawing depicts four figures dressed in classical costume. Two bare-shouldered figures kneel beside two vessels, the one on the left quite possibly a wine cooler and that on the right more like a vase or amphora. A bearded man in a tight-fitting soldier's jerkin gestures toward the kneeling figures who attend to him. Quickly sketched behind the bearded man is the head of an additional figure. A copy in the collection of the Santa Barbara Museum of Art (59.36), after a larger portion of the composition, indicates that the subject of the original composition is *The Wedding Feast at Cana* (fig. 1). Vasari tells us that Federico "surpassed all others" in executing, among other scenes from the life of Christ, a painting entitled *The Wedding Feast at Cana* for the

Casino of Pius IV. This is the only record of either of the Zuccari designing this theme. In a notation in his personal copy of Vasari's *Lives*, Federico writes that he did not paint the Vatican works but that they were executed from his drawings.[2] Yet, as far as we know, the specific scene was not finally executed in the Casino.[3]

The very fluid pen work, the spidery line that repeats over itself several times to define a hand or head, and the narrow pinched feet, are all convincing attributes of Taddeo Zuccaro's mature late-Mannerist style. Yet, the years 1561-63, before Federico is summoned to Venice by Cardinal Grimaldi, become the years when the two brothers are most active on collaborative projects, and Federico's style comes into closest conjunction with that of his brother. In this case the background figure with the bald head and hollow eye sockets can be read as typical of certain of Federico's figures. If we may assume that the Santa Barbara drawing is a

fig. 1

partial compositional copy of an unexecuted painting for the Casino of Pius IV, and we know that Federico maintained that he provided sketches for assistants to work from on this project, and that there is also the likelihood that his brother was, in turn, providing him with designs at this early stage of Federico's career, then a logical argument could be made for an attribution of the Pfeffer drawing to

either of the Zuccari. In the opinion of this cataloguer, the drawing is more rightly given, on the basis of style, to Taddeo.

James Mundy, class of 1974

---

[1]   See J. A. Gere, "Taddeo Zuccaro: Addenda and Corrigenda," *Master Drawings* 33, no. 3 (1995): 223-323, esp. nos. 43-A, 58-A, and 75-A; and J. A. Gere, *Taddeo Zuccari nel Gabinetto delle Stampe e dei Disegni della Galleria degli Uffizi* (San Severino, 1992), nos. 24, 45-47.

[2]   Giorgio Vasari, *Le Vite de' piu eccellenti pittori, scultori, ed Architettori scritte da Giorgio Vasari pittore Aretino con nuove annotazioni e commenti di Gaetano Milanesi* (Florence, 1906), 7:91-92.

[3]   Graham Smith, *The Casino of Pius IV* (Princeton, 1977).

12

Giuseppe Cesari, called Il Cavaliere d'Arpino
Italian (1568-1640)

St. Benedict and Totila (1589)
Red chalk and red wash with white heightening on paper
$8^3/_8$" x $16^1/_8$"
Inscription: "Giusseppino d. Passignano"
Private collection

Provenance: Purchased Sotheby's, London, July 1995, lot 212

Born in Rome in 1568, Giuseppe Cesari, known as the Cavaliere d'Arpino, worked in that city with few exceptions until his death in 1640. Trained by his father, he participated in many decorative projects in Rome, according to his seventeenth-century biographer, Giovanni Baglione. Among these commissions were projects for Popes Gregory XIII in the Vatican in the 1580s and Clement VIII in the first years of the 1600s. Seemingly a prodigy, he is credited with the decoration of a house façade at the age of thirteen. He was elected to the Accademia di S. Luca and admitted to the *Virtuosi al Pantheon* in Rome by the time he was seventeen years old. Among the Roman churches that he helped to decorate are SS. Trinità dei Monti, S. Lorenzo in Damaso, S. Pressede, S. Luigi dei Francesi, and S. Giovanni in Laterano. He was also active in the decorative schemes for a number of palaces and villas.

An exception to his Roman activity was a series of frescoes he executed for the monastery at Monte Cassino, the Benedictine abbey halfway between Rome and Naples, destroyed in World War II. Carmen Bambach has suggested that the scene of *St. Benedict and Totila* is a study for a painting executed by Cesari for the abbey in 1589.

The drawing of Totila and Benedict makes sense stylistically within the early work of Cesari. One can compare the head of the horse to those in the drawings in the Louvre (inv. 3004, thought to be related to his work in San Lorenzo in Damaso of 1588-89), and the Kupferstichkabinett, Berlin (K.d.Z. 16179 and 20873, for his battle painting in the Salone dei Conservatori in the Palazzo dei Conservatori, Rome, of 1597-1601), and find passages of strong similarity.[1] The same holds true if one compares the head of Totila with the drawing of a head of a soldier in Düsseldorf (inv. FP 7517), also a study for his work in the Salone dei Conservatori, which itself has been compared with drawings for his decorations in the Certosa di S. Martino, Naples, executed in 1589. The present sheet fits comfortably within this context of secular narrative work by the artist.

Benedict of Nursia (ca. 480-ca. 547) was founder of the monastic rule that bears his name and of Monte Cassino. The only certain date in the saint's life was the visit of the Gothic King Totila to Benedict in 542, four years before Totila sacked Rome. The present drawing illustrates that moment, when Benedict, genuflecting before the mounted king and his retinue, receives him humbly.

James Mundy, class of 1974

---

[1] These drawings are illustrated in the exhibition catalogue, *Il Cavaliere d'Arpino* (Rome, 1973), 149, 159, and 160, nos. 76, 117, and 118, respectively.

13

Luca Cambiaso
Italian (1527-85)

The Mystic Marriage of St. Catherine
Oil on canvas
47" x 40"
Lent by Alessandra Manning Dolnier, class of 1982, and Kurt A. Dolnier, class of 1981

Luca Cambiaso was born in the village of Moneglia, not far from Genoa. He received his artistic education in Genoa and became its most illustrious artist of the sixteenth century, helping to develop the late Mannerist style, imported from Rome by Perino del Vaga into Ligurian art. Cambiaso spent almost his entire life working in Genoa, except for a call to Spain by Philip II to work on the religious decorations of the Escorial. He arrived in 1583 and worked steadily with the assistance of other Genoese artists, such as his son Orazio, Lazzaro Tavarone, and Nicolas Granello. He died in Madrid two years later after having finished a number of large canvases and frescoes for the church of S. Lorenzo.

This painting, *The Mystic Marriage of Saint Catherine*, was a favored composition of the artist that he undertook on at least eight occasions. While the painting is not illustrated in a monograph of 1958 by Suida Manning and Suida, it is certainly a work by the artist and might reasonably be assigned a date of between 1565 and 1575, judging by comparisons with such works from this period as *Adoration of the Magi* in the Cappella Zoagli, church of SS. Annunziata di Portoria[1] and another *Mystic Marriage of Saint Catherine* in a Neapolitan private collection.[2]

The subject of the mystic marriage of Saint Catherine stems from two legends extant by the end of the fourteenth century, one the *Catalogus Sanctorum* by the bishop of Equilio Petrus de Natalibus and the other the *Nova quedam singularis atque rara legenda exaliis sex legendis collecta et perfecta*, written by the so-called Brother Peter in the last decade of the fourteenth century.[3] In these early legends, Catherine has a vision in which the adult Christ places a ring of betrothal on her finger. Numerous Italian images of the Quattrocento portray this moment. By the year 1500, the legend had evolved to include the Christ Child and Mary, thanks to an anonymous Dutch publication of the legend.[4] While this version of the legend was extremely popular in Italian art in the Baroque period, it is of interest to note that Cambiaso is working with a literary and artistic tradition that is still quite contemporary by the third quarter of the sixteenth century. His inclusion of the infant St. John the Baptist is more difficult to explain.

James Mundy, class of 1974

---

[1] Bertina Suida Manning and William Suida, *Luca Cambiaso, La vita e le opere* (Milan, 1958), fig. 227.

[2] Ibid., fig. 370.

[3] H. Knust, *Geschicte der Legende der Hl. Catharina von Alexandrian* (Halle, 1890), 61.

[4] For a full discussion of the shift from adult to infant Christ, see E. J. Mundy, *Gerard David Studies* (Ann Arbor, 1980), 79-84.

14

Luca Cambiaso
Italian (1527-85)

The Stoning of Saint Steven
Pen and brown ink and wash on tan paper
$8^{1}/_{2}$" x $12^{1}/_{2}$"
Promised Gift of Mrs. Carolyn P. Farris, class of 1953

Provenance: P. J. Mariette, Paris (Lugt 1852); E. Calanndo (Lugt supp. 426b); purchased by the owner from R. M. Light, Boston, 1965

This is a very fine example of the Genoese artist's draughts-manship and is one of three known preparatory drawings for the engraving by Raffaele Schiaminossi dated 1608 (fig. 1; see Bartsch 17:226, no. 57). The other drawings are an almost identical sheet in Munich (Staatliche Graphische Sammlung, inv. no. 2775) and one with certain differences denoting an earlier approach to the composition in Florence (Uffizi, inv. no. 13788). The Florentine drawing and the engraving were published by Bertina Suida Manning and William Suida.[1] When one compares the present drawing to that in Munich, the Farris sheet suggests a sharper, more confident handling of the pen in its sure outlines. The washes are also more deft and delicate. Many of Cambiaso's drawings exist in multiple variations, some by the artist's own hand and some by assistants. It is reasonable to believe that either the Farris or Munich drawing was used as the point of departure by Schiaminossi for his print, since no extant painting of the subject survives. Suida Manning and Suida suggest that the artist's source of inspiration for this subject came from the painting by Giulio Romano, *The Stoning of Saint Stephen* (ca. 1523), in the church of S. Stefano, Genoa, an opinion with which Harprath differs somewhat in the Munich catalogue.

This type of "cubist" drawing by Cambiaso, while eccentric among Old Master drawing styles, is frequent among the artist's drawings. It seems to have been a method he employed to work out questions about the fall of light and shade and the more demonstrative of gestures. Such work contributes to the general opinion that Cambiaso was much more noteworthy as a draughtsman than as a painter, a status bestowed on a number of his colleagues of the Italian Seicento.

James Mundy, class of 1974

fig. 1. Raffaele Schiaminossi, *The Stoning of Saint Stephen (after Cambiaso)*, 1608, engraving, British Museum, London.

---

[1] Bertina Suida Manning and William Suida, *Luca Cambiaso, La vita e le opere* (Milan, 1958), figs. 299 and 300. The Munich drawing was published in *Zeichnungen aus der Sammlung des Kurfürsten Carl Theodor* (Munich, 1983), 23-24, no. 10, pl. 21.

15

Antonio da Trento
Italian (ca. 1508-ca. 1550)

Martyrdom of St. Paul with St. Peter Led Away to Execution
Chiaroscuro woodcut made from three blocks; B. 28 ii/ii
$11^3/_8$" x $18^3/_4$"
Lent by Christopher Tunnard

All six of the documented chiaroscuro woodcuts by Antonio da Trento are after the drawings of Francesco Mazzola of Parma, called Il Parmigianino (1503-40), who attached much importance to the activity of printmaking and worked closely (if on a small scale) with at least three printmakers during his lifetime. Giorgio Vasari informs us that Parmigianino would discuss details of composition, technique, and printing carefully with his chosen collaborator.[1] The end product was thus not a "reproduction" of one of Parmigianino's drawings, but an amalgamation and modification of several that led to a print that stood, in its own right, as a work of art.

With Parmigianino, Vasari tells us, Antonio da Trento created *Martyrdom of St. Paul with St. Peter Led Away to Execution*, which is among the best Italian multiple-block chiaroscuros. It depicts St. Paul about to be decapitated in front of the Roman emperor, Nero. While one saint is being martyred, Nero concludes his discussion with a senator (who stands behind him) about putting the other to death. The artist depicts the moment when Nero's decision has been made, and he orders a guard to drag St. Peter away to die by crucifixion.

Popham believes that Parmigianino's original composition was intended to decorate the walls of the *Sala dei Ponitifici* in the Vatican, because Vasari writes that Pope Clement VII considered granting the commission to the artist.[2] Certainly the subject would have been appropriate for this room, once known as the *Sala dei Martiri* (Room of the martyrs). No fewer than five Parmigianino drawings survive of *Martyrdom of St. Paul with St. Peter Led Away to Execution* at the British Museum and the Louvre, and they show either the whole or a part of the composition.

Parmigianino and Antonio da Trento most likely worked on the chiaroscuro version of it in 1529, after Parmigianino escaped the Sack of Rome in 1527. He moved then to Bologna for the preparations of the coronation of Charles V. There, Vasari informs us, the artist and the printmaker lived together until, early one morning, Antonio walked away with all the engravings, woodcuts, and drawings that he could find, and was never to be seen again.

Francesca Consagra

---

[1] Giorgio Vasari, *Le vite de' piú eccellenti architetti, pittori, et scultori italiani: da Cimabue insino a' tempi nostri*, ed. Luciano Bellosi and Aldo Rossi (Florence, 1550; repr. Torino, 1986).

[2] A. E. Popham, *Catalogue of the Drawings of Parmigianino* (New Haven, 1971), 1:93, no. 190.

16

Tiziano Aspetti
Italian (ca. 1559-1606)

Mars (after 1592)
Bronze
Height, 17⅝"; width, 8"; depth, 4¾"
Lent by Dr. Mary Weitzel Gibbons, class of 1951

Tiziano Aspetti was born in Padua, descended from an artistic family. By 1577, he was in the employ of the powerful Grimani family in Venice as their resident sculptor, a position he held for sixteen years. He was responsible, among other things, for the restoration work on the family's extensive collection of antiquities. At the same time, the Grimani were involved in many important domestic and religious artistic commissions with other artists, such as Federico Zuccaro, Giovanni da Udine, and Francesco Salviati. After the death of his patron in 1592, Aspetti continued to work on religious commissions in Padua and Venice until he left the Veneto for Tuscany in 1604, where he died two years later.

Aspetti did not work in bronze until late in 1592, but it is in this medium that he made his most significant contributions, most notably narrative reliefs as well as a number of important statuettes.

The subject of Mars was a favorite of the artist. Surviving statuettes of the Roman god of war attributed to him (none are signed) are found in the Metropolitan Museum and Frick Collection, New York; Museo Correr, Venice; the Collezione Auriti in the Palazzo Venezia, Rome; and the several examples in Vienna published by Planiscig.[1] Often, such a bronze figure of Mars paired with Venus would be found to decorate the upper portion of an elaborate set of firedogs. It is possible that this is the function of this particular bronze.

James Mundy, class of 1974

---

[1] Leo Planiscig, *Die Estenisische Kunstsammlung, Band 1, Skulpturen und Plastiken des Mittelalters und der Renaissance* (Vienna, 1919), nos. 207, 208, 224, and 225. Not all these works were attributed to Aspetti, but all come from the artist's Venetian milieu.

17

Ventura Salimbeni
Italian (1568-1613)

The Feast of Herod (1601)
Pen and brown ink and wash on paper
12$\frac{1}{8}$" x 9$\frac{3}{8}$"
Inscription: inscribed on verso with name of the artist
Lent by Marjorie and Arnold Z. Pfeffer (Marjorie P. Fingerhood, class of 1941)

Provenance: Seiferheld and Co., New York

Ventura Salimbeni was born in Siena, the son of the artist, Arcangelo Salimbeni, and stepbrother of another well-known Siennese artist, Francesco Vanni. He participated as a young artist in the Roman artistic milieu of papal commissions under the pontificate of Gregory XIII, with the likes of Raffaellino da Reggio and Giovanni de'Vecchi. He left Rome in 1595 and returned to Siena to take on various commissions and was very active until 1605, after which he made sojourns of various lengths of time in Assisi, Florence, Pisa, Lucca, and Genoa in order to complete projects. Thus, he, like his contemporary, Federico Zuccaro, did much to spread the early Counter-Reformation artistic style out from Rome to other centers in Italy.

This previously unpublished drawing is most likely a preparatory study for the painting, *The Feast of Herod*, commissioned of Salimbeni by the Compagnia di San Giovannino on 22 July 1601. It was finished the next year and is presently housed in the church of S. Giovanni Battista della Staffa (also known as S. Giovaninno in Pantaneto) in Siena. The document survives and was published by Alessandro Bagnoli.[1] The relevant portion reads:

> *A ms. Ventura Salimbeni pittore per farci il banchetto di Erode con la saltatrice, secondo il disgnio mostroli, e vedendoli esare impidito e fatto fermare il pittore che non faccj tal lavoro fino a nuova disposta esendo pasato alcuni mesi e vedendo che la Conpagnia e priore di detta e fratelli intorno a tal benefizio non ci piliavano spidizione alcuna.*

The drawing is perfectly in keeping with Salimbeni's drawing style around the year 1600, as can be compared with those works illustrated by Riedl.[2]

James Mundy, class of 1974

---

[1]   Alessandro Bagnoli, *Rutilio Manetti 1571-1639* (Siena, 1978), 55, no. 3. This document is also cited in idem, *L'arte a Siena sotto i Medici 1555-1609* (Siena, 1980), 146.

[2]   Pieter Anselm Riedl, *Disegni dei barocceschi senesi* (Florence, 1976), nos. 78-99.

18

Attributed to Girolamo Buratti
Italian (1580-1654)

Figure Studies (ca. 1618)
Red chalk on paper
11¹/₄" x 8¹/₄"
Lent by Marjorie and Arnold Z. Pfeffer (Marjorie P. Fingerhood, class of 1941)

Provenance: Probably Filippo Baldinucci (Lugt 1886); Seiferheld and Co., New York

This previously unpublished drawing has been traditionally attributed to the Florentine artist, Giovanni Biliverti (1585-1644), son of a Dutchman living in Florence. Careful comparison with Biliverti's known drawings turns up a number of stylistic differences, however, which suggest tabling his name as the creator until further research can determine the authorship with clearer evidence. Miles Chappell thinks someone in the circle of Florentine artists around Biliverti, such as Giovanni Battista Vanni, is a possible author, while Jak Katalan has suggested an even more likely candidate for authorship in the hand of Girolamo Buratti (1580-1654), a workshop assistant of both Ludovico Cigoli in Rome until 1613, and then of Biliverti in Florence beginning in 1615 and remaining there until the 1630s. Biliverti's influence on Buratti was considerable even late into the latter's career.

The sheet, cut down from an even larger one, is drawn on both sides with a number of what appear to be *primo pensieri* for several religious paintings. On the recto are studies for the Fall of Man, the repentant Magdalene, a kneeling female figure, a head study, and what appears to be a second truncated figure of Eve. On the verso are three studies for David with the head of Goliath, yet another study for the Fall of Man, and the Annunciation. These sketches, all typically Baroque in temperament, thus far have not been connected with extant paintings, but the repentant Magdalene, David with the head of Goliath, and the Fall of Man resemble like themes painted by Guido Reni, the Bolognese artist of the same period. With this in mind, one might view these sketches as an artist's record of existing compositions as well as a set of first ideas for the works.

A comparable drawing by Buratti with seemingly identical strokes as the David in our sketch, in defining the head and hair, was recently on the art market (Christie's, South Kensington, 17 December 1998, lot 50). A painting of David by Buratti from around 1618 survives in the collection of the Villa Demidoff in S. Martino near Portoferraio on Elba.

James Mundy, class of 1974

recto

verso

19

Anonymous
German

The Agony in the Garden (late fifteenth- or early sixteenth century)
Walnut
Height, 32¹/₄"; width, 29¹/₂"; depth, 9¹/₄"
Promised Gift of Frances D. Fergusson and Michael Moohr

This deep relief sculpture of the moment during the Passion of Christ when he ascends the Mount of Olives to communicate with God in the company of the disciples, Peter, James, and John the Evangelist, is a test of the sculptor's powers of effecting a believable composition that requires the arrangement of four figures in an uneven landscape, and at close quarters. Besides the knitting of the three sleeping figures in a manner that retains visual interest, the artist must also contend with the textures of the trees, grass, and rock, as well as create the sense of the elevation that separates Christ physically and, by extension, psychologically from his followers.

The Agony in the Garden is rarely portrayed as an isolated scene, but would have formed part of a sequence of reliefs together with, perhaps, *The Last Supper* and *Betrayal of Christ,* such as one finds in the work of Veit Stoss in the *Volckhamer Monument,* Church of St. Sebalduskirche, Nuremberg (1499). There, this series of large reliefs are executed in sandstone beneath figures of Christ and the Virgin.[1] This type of presentation refers back to late-Medieval precedents on German church tympana. Perhaps the best-known carved sequence in German art that includes *The Agony in the Garden* is to be found in Tilman Riemenschneider's *Altar of the Holy Blood,* St. Jakobskirche, Rothenburg, carved between 1499 and 1505. There, the lindenwood relief is paired as an altar shutter with *Christ's Entry into Jerusalem.*[2]

The depth of carving in the present sculpture is, while not unprecedented in the wings of altarpieces and retables, somewhat unusual, and its purpose as part of a larger narrative in such a sculptural complex should not be discounted. The use of walnut instead of linden or oak as the medium for this carving suggests a possible origin in either northern Germany, where walnut was used sometimes as an alternative to oak; the Rhine valley, or Burgundy and other parts of France. The relief is made from one piece of the tree trunk, which has been halved vertically, as can be determined from the curvature of the sculpture and the way the artist has worked it.

Such sculptures were normally polychromed until the very end of the fifteenth century, when more were made emphasizing the wood grains and tones themselves. It is not possible to tell with certainty whether this work was once painted or not.

James Mundy, class of 1974

---

[1]   Michael Baxandall, *The Limewood Sculptors of Renaissance Germany* (New Haven, 1980), fig. 51.

[2]   Ibid., 262-63 and pl. 26.

20

Pieter de Jode the Elder
Flemish (1570-1634)

The Last Judgment (after Jean Cousin the Younger) (1615)
Engraving, H. 83, ii/ii
66" x 48¹⁄₄"
Inscriptions: at bottom left of image, "IOANNES COVSIN SENONIEN/SIS INVENIT ET PINXIT./Petrus de Iode in æs Incidit/a Paris chez P. Drevet aux Galleries"; at bottom center of image, "Vidit, examinauit, et praelo dignum censuit hoc Paradigma/Laurentius Beyerlinck St. Theologiæ Lincentiatus,/Canonicus Antuerpiensis et Censor Librorum."
Collection of Anne Keating Jones, class of 1943

Provenance: Lucien Goldschmidt, 1966

According to Anthony Blunt, the most important surviving work by the French painter, Jean Cousin the Younger, *The Last Judgment*, was "engraved under his name in 1615."[1] The engraver was actually Pieter de Jode the Elder, who reproduced the image in reverse and made significant alterations to it. The first state appears to have been published in Flanders because it was the residence of the de Jode and, more significantly, it carries the imprimatur of Laurentius Beyerlink, the Canon of Antwerp, which approved the print's sale in that city. The second state, which is exhibited here, carries the name of the publisher, P. Drevet of Paris, suggesting that de Jode sold the nine plates that comprise the image of this enormous print to Drevet, who added another three plates of engraved text at the bottom, with a dedication to King Louis XIII and a privilege to print it in the French capital.[2]

The scene is the Last Judgment, in which the gates of Heaven stand across a shallow valley from those of Hell. The entire landscape is populated by a cast of thousands—either being directed by angels with sickles to the left or devils with instruments of torture to the right. Above the hordes is Christ, also carrying a sickle, surrounded by masses of souls already entered into Heaven. On one side sit the ecclesiastical leaders of Roman Catholicism, including popes, cardinals, monks, and nuns; on the other side reside its secular leaders, including both European and foreign royalty.

The original painting, now at the Louvre, is almost exactly square (57¹⁄₈" x 56"), full of atmospheric effects, with a deep receding background that de Jode's skill with a burin could not replicate.[3] De Jode not only forces the composition into a rectangle, but also feels compelled to add figures and decorative elements (such as the escutcheon held by one of the angels at top left). He also adds text to the banderoles, and changes the gestures and poses of some of the figures from those seen in the painting.

When one considers that Cousin painted *The Last Judgment* sometime around 1585 for a Roman Catholic church in Paris, during the Protestant Reformation and the French Wars of Religion (1562-98), the imagery becomes all the more apparent and impassioned. Around 1595, de Jode took a trip to Paris and most likely reproduced the image, either on copper plates or as drawings on paper to be transferred onto plates when he got home. He then must have obtained the imprimatur to sell the print in Antwerp, where there was as much a market for prints that combated Protestantism as in Paris. It is most probable that Drevet obtained de Jode's plates sometime around 1614-15 and reissued them in Paris with a dedication to King Louis XIII, the second Bourbon king of France. Drevet appropriately places the dedication directly below the center foreground of the image, in which kings and queens, wearing only their crowns, are moving or being moved by angels towards Heaven's gates. They are also placed very close to Charon's bark that transports the damned souls into Hell, suggesting to the viewer that they too had to earn their place in Heaven and may not have made it.

Louis XIII was still a child when his father died in 1610, and his mother, Marie de Medici, was named regent until September 1614, when Louis came of age. It was soon afterward that Drevet most likely issued the second state of de Jode's print, with a dedication that proclaims Louis as the virtuous heir of his father, Henry IV (1589-1610), a promoter of Catholicism and an admirer of the arts. It would have behooved the monarchy to affirm the young king's faith at this time, because Louis's father had abjured Protestantism and converted to Roman Catholicism only in 1593, and Louis needed to assuage any doubt that he might convert to Protestantism as a way to counter his Catholic mother, who had squandered

state revenues and made humiliating concessions to rebellious nobles. This image of *The Last Judgment*, both as a painting and an engraving, thus addressed the need to ratify the same faith in different places at different times in a thirty-year period.

Francesca Consagra

1   Anthony Blunt, *Art and Architecture in France, 1500 to 1700* (London, 1957), 88.

2   The dedication reads: "D. LUDOVICO XIII. GALL ET NAVAR. REGI CHRISTIANISSIMO/D. HENRICI IV. VT REGNORVM, SIC ET VIRTVTV HÆREDI/CATHOLIC Æ RELIGIONIS PROPVGNATORI ACERR./ OMNIVMQUE ARTIVM ADMIRATORI EXIMIO/AUGUSTISS. HOC VNIVERSALIS IVDICY PARADIGMA/ A IOANNE COVSINIO FRANCO PRIMVM DELINEATVM./GVILIELMVS WITTENBROOT BELGA/ LIBENS MERITO DAT, DICAT, CONSECRATQ."

3   Illustrated in Henri Zerner, *L'art de la renaissance en France: L'invention du classicisme* (Paris, 1996), fig. 243.

21

Jacques Bellange
French (ca. 1575-1616)

The Death of Portia (ca. 1615)
Etching, W. 6, R. -D. 38
9¹/₂" x 7¹/₁₆" (plate)
Inscription: Inscribed at lower margin in burin, "Bellange Eques in incide"
Lent by Frances Beatty Adler and Allen Adler (Frances Beatty, class of 1970)

Jacques Bellange's activity as a court painter at Nancy, the capital of the independent Duchy of Lorraine, is recorded from 1602 to 1616. He is best known today for his highly individualistic etching style that employed loose hatchings and extensive stippling to render women with long necks and high waists that was based on a canon of female proportions set forth by the northern Italian painter, Francesco Mazzola of Parma, called Il Parmigianino (1503-40). The grossly affected gestures, the striking silhouetted poses, and the careful attention to facial modeling, belie Bellange's individuality and his position as one of the last great Mannerist printmakers in Europe.

Bellange's oeuvre (including at least forty-eight prints) was mostly made for a learned, courtly audience that delighted in classical literature and sumptuous details and props, like the large brazier seen here in *The Death of Portia*. The subject, uncommon in the history of art, depicts Portia, the daughter of Cato and the wife of M. Junius Brutus, at the time of her suicide. Portia's story was told by the first-century moralist, Valerius Maximus, in the widely-read *Detti e fatti memorabili* (Memorable words and deeds), where she appeared as an example of fortitude. Boccaccio, too, wrote about her heroic deeds in the fourteenth-century classic, *De claris mulieribus* (Concerning famous women).

Portia's role as a classical heroine arose because her loyalty to her husband proved stronger than her desire to live. She reportedly persuaded Brutus to divulge to her the conspiracy to kill Julius Caesar by cutting her thigh with a knife; in this manner she convinced him that she was courageous, and able to keep a secret and kill herself should the plot fail. The plot succeeded, and Brutus took possession of the province of Macedonia. After loosing a battle against Octavian and Antony, he took his own life. Upon hearing about her husband's death, Portia, too, committed suicide by swallowing burning coals. Bellange depicts her wiping her tears with a large handkerchief held between the long splayed fingers of her left hand, while her right hand extends daintily across the brazier ready to select a piece of coal. More than just desultory expressions of grief, the hand gestures, along with the silhouettes of her swanlike neck, head, and arms, all help create a wonderful circular movement within the center of the composition and tie her feelings of grief to the final act of her death.

Bellange may have conceived of *The Death of Portia* while working on his earliest documented commission at the Nancy court, or the decorations of the cabinet of Catherine de Bourbon (the sister of King Henri IV of France and wife of the future duke of Lorraine, Henri II). The cabinet was decorated with scenes from the lives of virtuous women from antiquity, and an image of Portia seems an especially well-suited model for Catherine, a Protestant noblewoman newly married into a Catholic court. Although it would be tempting to date the print sometime between 1602 (the year of the commission of the cabinet's decorations) and Catherine's death in 1604, it would be implausible in view of Bellange's own stylistic development as a printmaker. Most likely he returned to the theme of Portia, as a female role model from antiquity, sometime around 1614 or 1615, when he was entering the second phase of his career as an etcher, and relied heavily on the prints of Parmigianino and Frederico Barocci as a means to enrich his etching technique and compositions.[1]

Francesca Consagra

---

[1] See Amy N. Worthen and Sue Welsh Reed, *The etchings of Jacques Bellange* (Des Moines, Iowa, ca. 1975).

Bellange Eques in incide.

22

Hendrick Goltzius
Dutch (1558-1617)

The Adoration of the Shepherds (ca. 1599)
Engraving, H. 15, B. 21; i/v
8³⁄₈" x 6"
Inscription: top center of image, "Cum privil. Sa. Cat. Mtis/ H Goltzius Fecit/I. Matham excud."
Lent by Frances Beatty Adler and Allen Adler (Frances Beatty, class of 1970)

The Dutch artist, Hendrik Goltzius, was an important Mannerist painter, printmaker, and publisher whose technique as an engraver is considered unsurpassed. Goltzius had the ability to understand and create new compositions using the character and style of past masters to the point where he could fool connoisseurs into believing that they were looking at a newly discovered print by Albrecht Dürer or Lucas van Leyden. Goltzius himself developed a new style of engraving that emphasized volume through crosshatching and a line that tapered at both ends, which made objects appear to swell.

Goltzius was active as a printmaker and publisher in Haarlem between about 1582 and 1598. Hirshmann assigned to him no fewer than 361 prints, of which 291 were after his own designs.[1] The remainder were reproductive, or after the designs or paintings of others. In 1595, Goltzius received the coveted privilege to print from Emperor Rudolf II in Prague, barring the copy of his work for six years. Around 1598-99, Goltzius wanted to devote his entire time to painting. He stopped engraving and relinquished his publishing activities to his stepson, Jacob Mathem, who continued to use Goltzius's privilege from Rudolf II until it expired in 1601. It was then renewed under Mathem's name.[2]

The Adoration of the Shepherds, exhibited here, may well be Goltzius's last known work and, though unfinished, it is an especially tender and intimate depiction of Joseph holding a candle as he proudly shows the newly-born Christ Child to two shepherds. The faces of these three men are rustic and rendered in a deep chiaroscuro that captures the tenebrism of Dutch night scenes. Meanwhile, Goltzius sets the Virgin apart from them, not compositionally, but rather in her regal countenance and highly lit face.

Filedt Kok dates *The Adoration of the Shepherds* to around 1599[3], while Hirshmann claimed that it could not have been issued until after 1601, because the inscriptions on the top center of the image inform the viewer that it was incised by Goltzius, published by Mathem, and copyrighted in Prague.[4] Yet Hirshmann did not take into consideration that Mathem was publishing Goltzius's work as early as 1598, using Goltzius's privilege, and that the inscription could have well been incorporated in the first state of the print around that time. Hirshmann may be correct, however, to assume that Mathem, in the subsequent states, added outlines in the white space around the figures and background.[5] This impression is a rare first state of the print before Mathem altered Goltzius's design.

Francesca Consagra

[1]   Otto Hirschmann, *Verzeichnis des graphischen Werks von Hendrik Goltzius* (Leipzig, 1921).

[2]   Nadine Orenstein, *Hendrick Hondius and the Business of Prints in Seventeenth-century Holland* (Rotterdam, 1996), 19.

[3]   Jan Piet Filedt Kok, "Henrick Goltzius—Engraver, Designer, and Publisher 1582-1600," in *Netherlands Yearbook for History of Art* 42-43 (1991-92): 159-219, esp. 218.

[4]   Frederick den Broeder, *Hendrik Goltzius and the Printmakers of Haarlem*, (Storrs, Connecticut, 1972), 32.

[5]   Hirschmann, *Verzeichnis des graphischen Werks*, passim.

Cum privil. Sa. Cæ. M.tis
HGoltzius Fecit
I. Matham excud.

23

Jan Muller
Dutch (1571-1628)

The Arming of Perseus to Defeat Medusa (after Bartolomeus Spranger) (1604)
Engraving, B. 69, H. 59
22³/₈" x 15⁵/₈"
Lent by Frances Beatty Adler and Allen Adler (Frances Beatty, class of 1970)

Jan Muller was a Dutch engraver and painter who was the eldest son and heir of Harmen Jansz. Muller (1540-1617), the Amsterdam book printer, engraver, and publisher. Jan produced about a hundred engravings during his lifetime, and those done after about 1590 attest to his mastering of the engraving technique established by Hendrik Goltzius of Haarlem (see cat. no. 22), which emphasized volume and created an overall iridescence and shimmering quality to a print. It was a technique that depended on curved crosshatching and the cutting of individual lines that swelled in the middle, only to elegantly taper at their ends. This burin work was well-suited to the late-Mannerist style of painting that was developing in such courts as Emperor Rudolf II's at Prague and in artists' studios in cities such as Haarlem. Jan's career was primarily based on his brilliant reproductions of these painters' works, especially those of Bartolomeus Spranger, the principal court painter in Prague.

This wonderful engraving by Muller after a design by Spranger depicts the Greek myth of the arming of Perseus to defeat the Gorgon Medusa. The myth begins with Polydectes sending Perseus, the son of the mortal Danaë and the god Zeus, off to get the head of Medusa, knowing that no man had ever returned alive from an encounter with her or one of her sisters. The Gorgons were invincible to mortals because they had wings, claws, and enormous teeth. Medusa could also turn anyone who looked at her into stone. Perseus, however, had the help of Athena, who appeared to him and explained how to proceed unharmed, and it is at this juncture that Spranger conflates two different interpretations of the myth. In the first, Perseus must find the river nymphs who possess the right weapons: a pouch to sling over his shoulder, a pair of winged sandals to fly, and a cap of darkness to make him invisible. After they have given them to Perseus, the god Hermes appears and provides him with the last weapon, a sword. Perseus keeps his own highly-polished bronze shield and flies off to kill Medusa.

Another interpretation of the myth, however, maintains that Hermes gives Perseus the helmet and his very own sandals because he finds the youth attractive, and Athena offers him the famous shield. Spranger adheres primarily to the latter reading. Athena places the shield onto Perseus's right arm and Hermes slips his winged sandal onto Perseus's left foot, alluding to the homoerotic element in the story. The youth, too, is depicted in a twisted pose from the back with a transparent dress and armor. Meanwhile, Spranger also includes the nymphs at the top right of the composition and pays homage to the other interpretation of the story, and thereby creates a vibrant and fluid composition that Muller further brings to life with the virtuosity of his burin.

Francesca Consagra

B. Sprangers inuentor.
Ornatissimo iuxta ac Prudentissimo Viro
Henrico Sprughel I.F. studiorum bonarumq;
artium patrono.
L.M.Q.D.D. Ianus Muller Sculptor.
Quid sibi vult Perseus? sibi quid Gyllenius? addit
Alarum pedibus par, tegit ense latus.
Dia quid hic Pallas? dei munere singula. Quaenam?
Aegida Quid? celer ad Gorgonis ora volet.
I. Muller excud. Amstelodami.
cɔ ɔc. IV.

24

Attributed to Adrien de Vries
Dutch (ca. 1545-1626)

Nativity
Alabaster
Height, 13^1/$_2$"; width, 24"; depth, 2^3/$_4$"
Lent by Nancy and Tom Hoving (Nancy M. Bell, class of 1953)

This lovely carved alabaster Nativity scene has been traditionally attributed to Adrien de Vries, the Northern European Mannerist sculptor born in the Hague, best known for his works for the court of Rudolf II at Prague. It is there that he helped to spread the late Italian Mannerist style of Giambologna, whose work he knew and with whom he collaborated during his stay in Florence, Milan, and Turin in the 1580s. This is the earliest documented period in his career, and there is considerable speculation about the nature of his earlier work. It is to this period, before his departure from the Lowlands, that the present sculpture has been associated. Recent scholarship, though, has even questioned his traditional date of birth around 1545 and suggested it might have been even a decade later.[1] If this is true, the possibilities for an early Dutch career for de Vries narrow considerably.

The *Nativity* is carved out of alabaster, a material not known to have been used by de Vries, although it would reasonably be part of any sculptor's repertory of materials. De Vries was familiar with relief casting and, thus, the composing of a work in relief was a comfortable medium for the artist. The prototype for this composition is a traditional Northern European portrayal of the Virgin suckling the Christ Child in the manger while the elderly Joseph sleeps at the foot of the bed, and the ox and the ass, symbols of the Old and New Testaments, stand behind the group. Also, the broken-fluted column in front of the barnyard bed is another likely reference to the New Dispensation under Christ built on the ruins of the Old.

What is not traditional is the classically inspired and very revealing "wet" drapery of the Virgin, a detail much more in keeping with the incipient Rudolfine Mannerist inversion of convention. Also curious is the small female figure, who seems to hold the bed-clothes in a protective manner behind the Holy Pair. Is she intended to be an angel or a handmaiden? In either case, her inclusion departs from most portrayals of the Nativity.

James Mundy, class of 1974

---

[1]   Rosemarie Mulcahy, "Adriaen de Vries and Pompeo Leoni," *Apollo* 139 (February 1994): 35-38.

25

Peter Paul Rubens
Flemish (1577-1640)

Saint Catherine in the Clouds (ca. 1620-21)
Etching, H. 1
$11^5/_8$" x $7^3/_4$"
Inscription: lower left, "P. Paul Rubens fecit"
Promised Gift of Mrs. Carolyn P. Farris, class of 1953

Only one print, this etching, *St. Catherine in the Clouds*, can be directly attributed to Rubens, the most versatile and influential seventeenth-century artist in Northern Europe.[1] It commemorates his first major painting cycle, the ceiling paintings for the former Jesuit church (now St. Carlo Borromeo) in Antwerp. Dated to 1620, the cycle consisted of about forty large compositions with scenes from the Old and New Testaments and the lives of the saints, including a *di sotto in su* image of St. Catherine holding the attributes of her martyrdom: the wheel, the sword, and the palm leaf.

This etching, perhaps from a preparatory study of the composition, illustrates how skillfully Rubens rendered the robes and veils around the saint. They billow upward as if they were clouds in their own right and help give St. Catherine a countenance that expresses "an ecstasy in a highly rhetorical and even sensual manner" that characterizes the entire series at the church.[2]

A fire at the church less than a century later destroyed all of Rubens's work there, but there are many surviving preparatory sketches. Such images help historians today understand how indebted Rubens was to the style and methods of the Venetian masters of the sixteenth century, especially Titian, Tintoretto, and Veronese, who had established a vibrant and painterly style full of movement and light in their monumental ceiling decorations. The cycle thus represents Rubens's move away from the classicism of his earlier work and his embarkation upon the pinnacle of his creative activity, or the Flemish High Baroque.

Throughout his career, Rubens hired and carefully supervised many reproductive printmakers as a means of disseminating his work, and he may have employed an assistant to help him produce this etching as well. Several factors, however, have led some art historians to believe that Rubens was the sole author of *St. Catherine in the Clouds*. Firstly, the technique did not require the specialized skill of the engraver or woodcutter, only the ability to draw on a varnished plate, and then to dip the plate into an acid bath. Secondly, Rubens drew in pen on a counterproof of the etching that survives today at the Metropolitan Museum of Art, signifying that he was at least present when the plate needed reworking.[3] Perhaps the most convincing argument for his authorship, however, is that the style of the etching is so exceptionally vigorous and free, like the master's own drawings, and unlike the majority of reproductive prints that he commissioned from such reproductive engravers as Cornelis Galle and Lucas Vorsterman.

The impression of *St. Catherine in the Clouds* exhibited here is the second state, after Rubens retouched the plate using the counterproof as a guide. It is signed "P. Paul Rubens fecit." It should be noted that Hults believes the second state to have been reworked by another hand, perhaps without Rubens's knowledge.[4]

Francesca Consagra

---

[1] Hollstein attributed three etchings to Rubens. See F. W. H. Hollstein's *Dutch and Flemish Etchings, Engravings, and Woodcuts*, compiled by D. De Hoop Scheffer, ed. K. G. Boon (Amsterdam, 1978), 20:118-20.

[2] Hans Vlieghe, "Rubens," in *Dictionary of Art*, ed. Jane Turner (New York, 1996), 27:287-303, esp. 294.

[3] The counterproof is made by placing a blank sheet of paper over a print that has just been pulled from the press, with its ink still wet, and then running both through the press another time. The image of the first impression pulled is in the reverse direction of what one sees on the plate, but the counterproof creates an image that matches that on the plate, and it enables the artist to see better how to retouch the plate.

[4] Linda C. Hults, *The Print in the Western World* (Madison, Wisconsin, 1996), 280.

P.Paul Rubens fecit.

26

Willem van de Velde
Dutch (1633-1707)

A Dutch Ship at Anchor Drying Sails and a Kaag Under Sail (ca. 1660)
Oil on canvas
27" x 36¹/₄"
Signature: indistinctly on the ship's side near the stock of the anchor, "WV/Velde"
Lent by Anne H. and Frederick Vogel III (Anne M. Henoch, class of 1963)

Provenance: Sir Henry Houghton, sold 1893; P. A. B. Widener, Philadelphia, by 1900; Bachstitz Gallery, The Hague, by 1923; Ralph H. Booth, Detroit, 1925; Mrs. William D. Vogel, Milwaukee, Wisconsin; by descent to the owners

Literature: C. Hofstede de Groot and W. R. Valentiner, *Pictures in the Collection of P. A. B. Widener at Lynnewood Hall, Elkins Park, Philadelphia* (Philadelphia, 1913), reproduced; C. Hofstede de Groot, *A catalogue raisonné of the works of the most eminent Dutch painters of the seventeenth century based on the work of John Smith* (London, 1923), 7:no. 99:2; *Bulletin of the Bachstitz Gallery* (The Hague, October 1923), no. 3/4; M. S. Robinson, *Van de Velde : a catalogue of the paintings of the elder and the younger Willem van de Velde* (Greenwich, U.K., 1990), 265-66

Exhibitions: *A Loan Exhibition of Dutch Genre and Landscape Painting*, Detroit Institute of Arts, Detroit, Michigan, 1929, no. 77

The Dutch developed the genre of marine painting as a logical extension of their interest in landscape, for the sea and its estuaries composed as much of the visible panorama in much of Holland as did the land. Maritime commerce, the expansion of the Dutch economic empire, and numerous naval conflicts during the seventeenth century, contributed to the rise of this specialized genre of painting, for it fed and represented symbolically the means by which many in the Netherlands enjoyed prosperity.[1]

Willem van de Velde the Younger, and his father, Willem the Elder, were among the seventeenth century's most accomplished painters of marine subjects. Almost any discussion of the one artist invariably concerns the career of the other. Willem the Younger was baptized in Leiden, where his father had been born and married. The family moved to Amsterdam shortly thereafter, and the Elder was commissioned by the Dutch admiralty to serve as its official artist, sailing with the Dutch fleet and sketching its ships at rest and in combat. His first son, Willem, after training with Simon de Vlieger, collaborated with his father, often painting from the sketches from life the Elder made while sailing with the fleet. A painting by Michiel van Musscher in the collection of the Earl of Northbrook shows the artist seated before his easel, painting, while a number of sketches of ships (presumably those of his father) lie at his feet.[2] Both van de Veldes emigrated to London in 1672, during the invasion of the Lowlands by France, and continued to depict maritime scenes until their deaths in 1693 and 1707 respectively.

Of the two artists, Willem the Younger is considered the more accomplished painter. He preferred scenes of calm, as depicted here, but could also execute dramatic images of ships tossed about on stormy seas. This portrayal of a Dutch ship at anchor and the smaller *kaag* under sail was, according to Robinson, executed around 1660, while the artist was still in Amsterdam. He believed it to be the prime example of a composition that exists in seven related versions or copies. This opinion was bolstered by the discovery of a partial signature between the stock of the port anchor and the warp leading to it during conservation in 1990.

James Mundy, class of 1974

---

[1] George S. Keyes, *Mirror of Empire: Dutch Marine Art of the Seventeenth Century* (New York, 1990).

[2] Illustrated in *The Art of the Van de Veldes* (London, 1982), pl. 1.

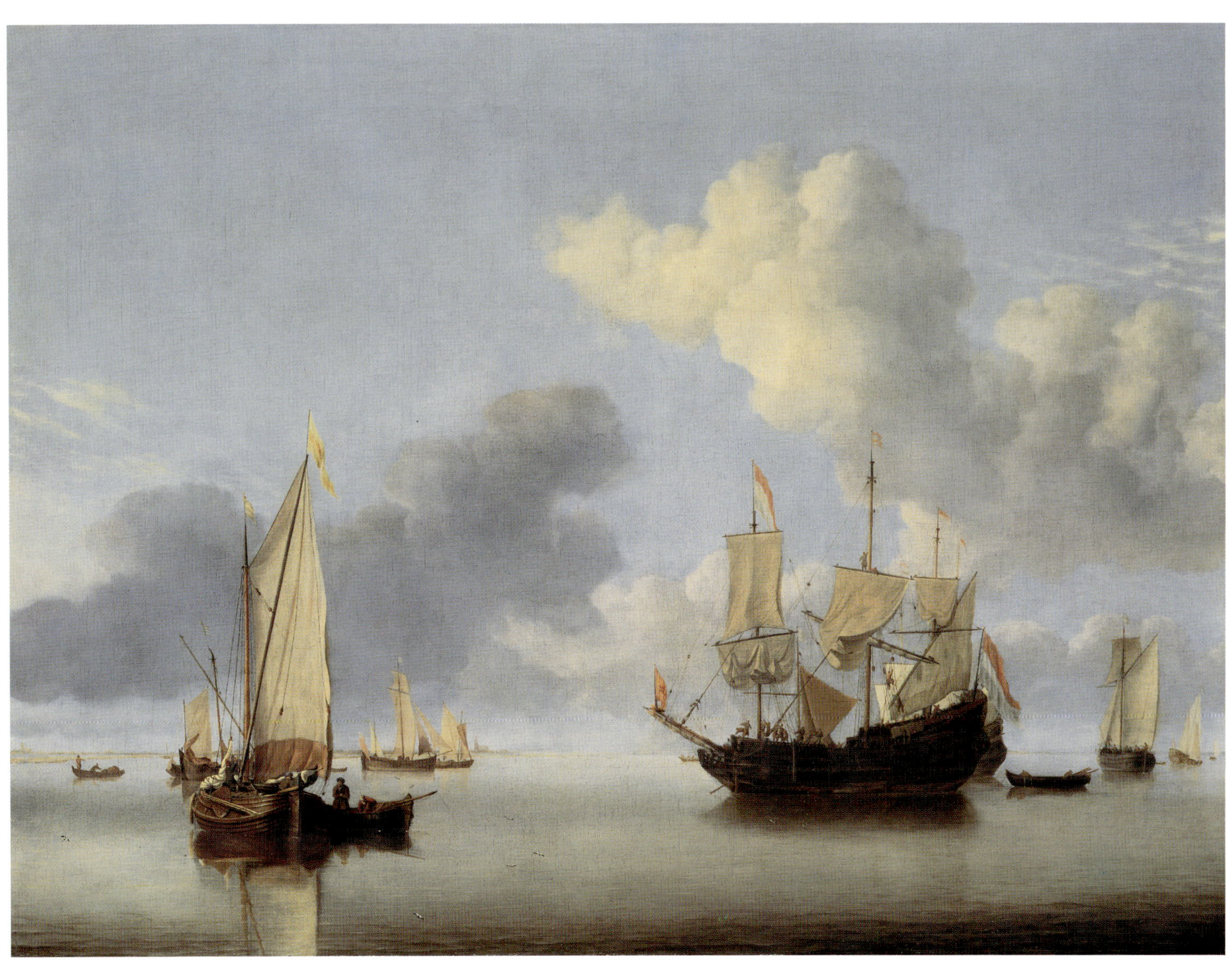

27

Cornelius Dusart
Dutch (1660-1704)

Study of a Man (1693)
Gray ink and wash on paper
9" x 8¹/₂"
Signature: "Corn: Dusart fe. 1693" on left
Lent by Frances Beatty Adler and Allen Adler (Frances Beatty, class of 1970)

Cornelius Dusart was the last and foremost student of the genre painter, Adrien van Ostade, in Haarlem. Upon the death of van Ostade in 1685, Dusart inherited the contents of his studio and also the market for the "low-life" scenes of taverns, brothels, and village fairs that were so popular among the Dutch at this time. He was a prolific inventor of such scenes and, in addition to numerous paintings in public and private collections, he produced many drawings and engravings. A number of his paintings and drawings are signed and dated, as this one is.

This drawing, while portraying a genre subject, is not based on a model. The raw and aggressively ugly physiognomy equates, in the artist's mind, the lack of physical refinement with a lack of class status. The bearded, elderly man simply dressed turns away his face, gnarled like the trunk of a van Ruisdael tree, and casts his befuddled gaze to the lower left. He is likely a stock character in Dusart's art, one found seated at a tavern table, inebriated and showing its physical effects. He is of a figural type passed down from the art of van Ostade to his student, who inherited many of the master's drawings, which he copied and interpreted for another generation.

The drawing, in spite of its ugly subject, is beautifully crafted, with supple use of medium and light washes to articulate the rugged topography of the sitter's face and the texture of his vest.

James Mundy, class of 1974

Corn: Dusart. fe
1693.

28

Eustache LeSueur
French (1616-55)

A Woman and Child Seated on a Chair (1650-55)
Black chalk heightened with white on brownish-gray paper
13" x 9"
Promised Gift of Mrs. Carolyn P. Farris, class of 1953

Provenance: William H. Schab, New York

This classical drawing of a seated woman and child has carried a traditional attribution to the Italian seventeenth-century artist, Domenichino. Jak Katalan was the first to suggest, instead, that the drawing is the work of the French Baroque classicist, Eustache LeSueur, an attribution that is completely convincing. LeSueur was born and died in Paris and, during his lifetime, never left France. He was the son of a woodworker who apprenticed in the studio of Simon Vouet between 1635 and 1637. He was strongly impressed by classicism and influenced by the work of Raphael, which he knew through his exposure to the royal collections and also by Vouet's and, possibly, Poussin's examples. It is striking that he could achieve the strong level of heroic classicism in his compositions and figures without having spent time in Rome. He was commissioned to work on religious, government, and secular projects during his abbreviated career, all located in Paris and the immediate environs.

Many drawings by LeSueur exist, with the largest assemblage of them in the Louvre, as one might expect. In his exemplary monograph on the artist, Alain Mérot arranges each known surviving painting with its preparatory drawings.[1] In most cases, LeSueur would begin with a rapid, full compositional study in pen, brush and ink, or black chalk, which he would then square for transfer. He would then make individual figure studies from studio models as he worked out the separate poses in chalks. A good example of this method can be seen in the studies for *The Allegory of Monarchy*, designed for the *apartement* of Louis XIV.[2]

No surviving painting includes our study of the seated woman and child. However, among the surviving isolated drawings by LeSueur published by Mérot is a black-chalk, squared compositional study for an enthroned *Virgin and Child Approached by an Angel* at Montpellier's Musée Fabre (inv. no. D.2211/837.1.1154).[3] This drawing seems to be the first compositional idea for the painting, for which the Farris drawing becomes an important, closely observed figural study. Mérot dates the Montpellier drawing to 1652-54 based on its "majestic composition," a description equally valid for this drawing.

James Mundy, class of 1974

---

[1] Alain Mérot, *Eustache LeSueur* (Paris, 1987).

[2] Ibid., 313, no. 180.

[3] Ibid., 333, D. 357.

29

Antoine Vestier
French (1740-1824)

Portrait of a Young Girl (1775-80)
Oil on canvas
25³/₄" x 21"
Inscription: inscribed on frame, "A. Vestier"
Collection of Mr. and Mrs. Kenneth Lane Miron (Andrea Leeds Miron, class of 1975)

Antoine Vestier was born in Avallon, where he was discovered by a local worthy and sent to Paris to study with Jean-Baptiste Marie Pierre. He painted both large oils on canvas and smaller miniatures in enamel on ivory. He was approved by the Royal Academy in 1785 and was received into it in the following year. His career as a society portraitist flourished during the period 1777-89, but the French Revolution had a negative effect on his client base and, thereby, his fortunes. Having been a perennial exhibitor at the Salon until 1791, he exhibited there only sporadically thereafter. His resulting disappointment at not receiving adequate government support for his painting led to Vestier's retiring from active painting in 1806. He died eighteen years later.

While most all of Antoine Vestier's paintings are signed, this portrait, while not signed by the artist, bears enough hallmarks of his style to be attributed to him or, at least, to a close associate. It most resembles, in style and tone, the 1781 portrait of his daughter, Marie-Nicole, in the collection of the University of Paris and the better-known portrait of Madame Hamon des Roches de Bournay, executed in 1786, and now in the private collection of the Marquis Mareschal de Bièvre, Paris.[1]

James Mundy, class of 1974

---

[1] See Anne-Marie Passez, *Antoine Vestier 1740-1824* (Paris, 1989), 124, no. 33 and 152, no. 52.

30

Jean Pierre Louis Laurent Houël
French (1735-1813)

Monument in Ruins (1763)
Wash drawing
16^1/$_2$" x 18^1/$_2$"
Signature: "J. Houël f. 1763"
Collection of Anne Keating Jones, class of 1943

Provenance: Wildenstein & Co., London, 1978

Jean Pierre Louis Laurent Houël received his earliest training in his home town of Rouen and then went to Paris, where he studied engraving with Jacques-Phillippe Le Bas in 1755. He developed an early interest in landscape painting and continued in this vein, with a close study of antique monuments, culminating in a sojourn in Rome beginning in 1769. The present work, signed and dated 1763, is of interest because it documents Houël's attraction to grand, antique, architectural fantasies in the manner of Piranesi well before the artist journeyed to Italy. Such inspiration might have come to Houël through Piranesi's prints as well as the work of vaunted countrymen such as Hubert Robert.

This drawing is executed in delicate layers of ink wash and portrays a group of workmen hoisting a large figural sculpture onto a cart with a windlass, under a loosely stretched canopy. The point of view aggrandizes the scale of the ruined, barrel-vaulted interior, supported underneath by double, gigantic, fluted columns with composite capitals and a massive entablature. The awesome scale of the structure is enhanced by the view through the colonnade of a distant extension of what seems to be the same building, whose columns disappear seemingly without end to the left and right. There is certainly a sublime and proto-Romantic quality to this image.

A number of similar drawings of actual places exist, many of them in the Louvre, and illustrated in the only monograph written on Houël.[1] The Jones drawing, however, occupies a special place as a youthful architectural fantasy of surprising sophistication.

James Mundy, class of 1974

---

[1] Maurice Vloberg, *Jean Houël, Peintre et Graveur* (Paris, 1930), 155-77.

31

Jean-Jacques Flipart
French (1719-82)

Contest for the Prize for the Study of Heads and Expressions at the French Academy in 1761 (after Charles-Nicolas Cochin fils) (1763)
Etching and engraving
17^{15}/$_{16}$" x 10^{1}/$_{4}$", sheet
Inscriptions: lower left, "Dessiné par C. N. Cochin le fils en 1763"; lower right, "Gravé par J. J. Flipart en 1763"
Lent by Alan Wintermute, class of 1981, and Colin Baily, New York

This eighteenth-century French print depicts a woman from "a sound bourgeois family" donning a laurel wreath and contemporary dress, seated on a platform, with one graceful foot propped on a cushion.[1] Her hands are folded on her lap as she casts a blank look ahead, knowing that she has committed herself to three hours of modeling in front of a group of sixty people.[2] Representing the crowd are four art students busily sketching and a group of three onlookers seated behind her to the right.

The inscriptions on the margin of the print inform us that Charles-Nicolas Cochin *fils* (1715-90) drew this scene in 1761 to commemorate the Contest for the Prize for the Study of Heads and Expressions at the Académie Royale de Peinture et de Sculpture in Paris. The comte de Caylus (1692-1765) established the annual event, for which there was a monetary prize for the most accomplished study of a specific facial expression of a live model. The look on the model's face—to an eighteenth-century audience—may well have represented *La Douceur* (Gentleness), the theme of the 1761 competition. The entrants were instructed "to draw, paint or sculpt in bas-relief a head, at least life-size, based on a model selected and posed" by the Académie Royale.[3]

The judges' identities and those of the onlookers have been well established as Caylus at the center, with the sculptor Louis-Claude Vassé (1716-72) to his right, and the painter Jean Restout II (in whose studio Cochin himself had learned drawing), seated, holding his cane and hat.

That Cochin drew this subject (and hired Jean-Jacques Flipart to reproduce it as a print for a large audience) concurs with Cochin's own pedagogical writings and concern for the use of drawing as the foundation of artistic training.[4] In France, he was extremely influential as an art theorist who represented the new trends of the Académie Royale, where he was its Secrétaire Perpétuel and entrusted with administrative oversight of the arts. Cochin strongly believed that the great artist learned from nature, such as from a live model, and then chose a style befitting only him, not those dictated by others.[5]

Cochin was a highly gifted printmaker and draughstman in his own right, but his administrative duties often forced him to commission others to reproduce his designs and help him carry out many of his outstanding projects in engraving and illustration, which included the *Histoire du roi par médailles* and Denis Diderot's *Encyclopédie*.[6] During the 1750s and 60s especially, Cochin hired for his projects Flipart, who had a technique that was all his own and for which he became famous. He etched his plates very densely to reduce as much as possible the white interstices, sometimes using as many as three bites to do so.[7] He then would use the burin to emphasize the lines already made. (A rare proof of this print at the Philadelphia Museum of Art best demonstrates this technique, especially in the shadows under the model's chair and the statue of the herm in the corner.)[8]

Although Cochin made the drawing in 1761, he commissioned Flipart to reproduce it in 1763. It was not exhibited until the Salon of 1767, the same year that the Académie Royale ended the Contest for the Prize for the Study of Heads and Expressions, that this very print commemorated.

Francesca Consagra

---

[1] For a contemporary letter describing the social status of the model of this print, see Victor Carlson and John W. Ittman, *Regency to Empire: French Printmaking 1715-1814* (Baltimore, Maryland, 1985), 146.

[2] One of the problems the organizers of the event foresaw was to find a woman who had a beautiful face and was willing to sit for three hours in the presence of sixty persons. See letter dated 10 October 1759, transcribed in E. Dacier, "A Propos d'un Dessin de Cochin, Le Concours pour le Prix d'Expression," *Académie des Beaux-Arts Bulletin* (1928): 162.

³ Carlson and Ittman, *Regency to Empire*, 146.

⁴ Carter E. Foster, "Charles-Nicolas Cochin the Younger, The Philadelphia Portfolio," *Philadelphia Museum of Art Bulletin* 90, no. 381 (1994): 18-19.

⁵ Christian Michel, "Charles-Nicolas Cochin II," in *Dictionary of Art*, ed. Jane Turner (New York, 1996), 5:495-96.

⁶ Because of Cochin's reputation as a printmaker, Hyatt Mayor wrongly assigned Cochin as the etcher of *Contest for the Prize for the Study of Heads and Expressions*

rather than Flipart. See A. Hyatt Mayor, *Prints and People* (Princeton, 1971), fig. 591.

⁷ Christian Michel, "Jean-Jacques Flipart," in *Dictionary of Art*, ed. Jane Turner (New York, 1996): 11:172.

⁸ For an illustration of the proof, see Carlson and Ittman, *Regency to Empire*, 147.

32

Carle Vanloo
French (1705-65)

Allegory of Piety (1736)
Gouache with pen and brown ink
10" in diameter
Inscription: on verso in black chalk in old hand, "La Piet"
Lent by Alan Wintermute, class of 1981, and Colin Baily, New York

Provenance: J. D. Lempereur, Paris, sold 24-28 June 1773, lot 520; Joullain, Paris; present owner since 1994

Literature: M. C. Sahut and P. Rosenberg, *Carle Vanloo, Premier peintre du roi* (Nice, 1977), no. 467

Born in Nice, Carle Vanloo became the most famous painter of his generation. By the time he was nine years old, he journeyed to Rome, where he entered the studio of Benedetto Luti and the sculptor, Pierre Legros, before returning to Rome in 1719. In 1728, he returned to Rome after winning the Grand Prix and worked there and in Savoy until 1734, when he returned again to Paris, where his career advanced rapidly with many commissions from the court of Louis XV and other notables of French society. In 1762 he was named *Premier Peintre du Roi* and the next year director of the Académie Royale. His painting style became synonymous with the decadence of royal tastes after the French Revolution, giving rise to the derisive slogan, "Vanloo, Pompadour, Rococo."

This small gouache is one of four studies executed in preparation for a suite of overdoor paintings made by Vanloo in 1736, for the royal palace of Christiansborg in Copenhagen, one year after Vanloo was received into the Royal Academy. All were allegorical figures and the others represented Equity, Marital Fidelity, and Generosity. They were destroyed in a fire that gutted the palace in 1794.

The four studies for the Copenhagen paintings were in the collection of J. D. Lempereur, and were divided and sold in two lots in 1773. Two were bought by the art dealer, Lebrun, and the other two by the art dealer, Joullain, who was one of the two organizers of the sale. Since that time, only two of the gouache studies have resurfaced, this one in 1994, and a second, which was identified by Sahut in the Musée Magnin, Dijon, in 1977, attributed at the time to Natoire.

The winged figure of Piety in this study carries on her brow the flame of faith and holds in her right arm a cornucopia from which spills Eucharistic items, such as the grapes and wheat, as well as a melon, figs, and what appear to be apples or peaches. The demure gesture of her left hand held near her heart reinforces the sense of piety, as do her eyes, closed presumably in prayer.

James Mundy, class of 1974

33

Jean-Honoré Fragonard
French (1732-1806)

The Nativity with God the Father (after G. B. Castiglione) (1760-61)
Black chalk on buff paper
4 ¹/₂" x 5 ³/₄"
Lent by Alan Wintermute, class of 1981, and Colin Baily, New York

Provenance: Ernest May

Literature: P. Rosenberg and B. Brejon de Lavergnée, *Saint-Non-Fragonard, Panopticon Italiano, Un diario di Viaggio ritrovato, 1759-1761* (Rome, 1986), no. 227; M. R. Michel, *Aspects de Fragonard* (Paris, 1987), no. 30

Jean-Honoré Fragonard, the artist whose name would become synonymous with the Rococo style in France, was educated as an artist in a very traditional manner. At the age of fifteen, Fragonard was sent from his home in Provence to the Parisian workshop of François Boucher, who in turn, finding him untrained, sent him to Chardin. The next year, 1748, Boucher agreed to allow him back in his studio. There he studied the work of the great artists of the preceding generation and century, including G. B. Tiepolo, Peter Paul Rubens, Carlo Maratta, and Rembrandt. In 1752, he was awarded the Prix de Rome and sent to prepare at the Ecole des Elèves Protégés in Paris, where he studied under Carle Vanloo. He finally arrived in Rome in December 1755 (according to Williams; 1756, according to Wildenstein). Fragonard would remain in Italy until September 1761, when he returned to Paris.

In 1760, Fragonard made the acquaintance of Jean-Claude Richard, the Abbé de Saint-Non, and made several journeys with him throughout Italy, the last on the return to Paris, stopping at Florence, Bologna, Verona, Venice, and Genoa. In Venice, Fragonard had the opportunity to study and copy from the collection of Consul Smith just before it was sold to King George III of England in 1762. In his collection were a large number of drawings by the seventeenth-century Genoese artist, Giovanni Benedetto Castiglione, called Il Grechetto. These drawings, now at Windsor Castle, include *The Nativity with God the Father* (inv. 4058).[1] Fragonard copied Castiglione with a rapid, energetic movement of the chalk that seemed to respond most readily to the peaked outlines of the drapery of the Virgin and of God the Father. His focus on the structure of the sketch indicates the influence of his years of academic training and the search to learn from other artists as his own style and artistic identity were forming.

James Mundy, class of 1974

---

[1] See Anthony Blunt, *The Drawings of G. B. Castiglione & Stefano della Bella in the collection of Her Majesty the Queen at Windsor Castle* (London, 1954), 36, no. 131.

34

Philibert Louis Debucourt
French (1755-1832)

Promenade in a Park
Black, brown, rose, and red watercolor washes
$11^7/_8$" x $18^3/_4$"
Private collection

While little-known today except among connoisseurs of prints, the painter and designer of popular colored acquatints, Philibert Louis Debucourt, was an important figure in the growth of printmaking in France during the years leading up to and just following the French Revolution. A student of Joseph-Marie Vien, Debucourt was approved by the Académie Royale in 1781. He focused on genre subjects in what was called the "Flemish" style, large and complex gatherings with much varied, anecdotal, social interaction portrayed. His collected works number over 550 paintings, drawings, and prints.

Two of his most important and successful colored acquatints were the amusing comedies of manners, *Promenade in the Gallery of the Palais-Royal*, of 1787, a work inspired by Thomas Rowlandson's *Vauxhall Gardens*, and a similar subject, *The Public Promenade*, of 1792. In the present drawing, the artist seems to have returned to a similar subject of a promenade in a public garden at a slightly later date, judging from the more Napoleonic style of the costumes and the virtual absence of powdered wigs on the gentlemen. The overall appearance of the scene could suggest almost as easily the work of an artist working just a bit later than Debucourt, such as Louis-Leopold Boilly. It is possible that this drawing, which, in general, has many points of similarity with *The Public Promenade* of 1792, is a study for *Promenade du Jardin Turc*, dating to 1810-15 and engraved later by Jean-Pierre Marie Jazet, which carries the name of the painter, "J. J. de B.", for which Bouchot recalled a drawing by Debucourt.[1] A comparison of the drawing with Boilly's painting of the same location, exhibited in the Salon of 1812, serves to confirm that Debucourt was using the popular garden café for his observation of French middle-class morés.[2] Could Debucourt have been making a punning reference to the location by his inclusion of the two men on the extreme left side of the composition, dressed, it seems, *à la turc*?

Debucourt stratifies his composition in a fairly typical manner by alternating bands of figures set in shadow and then in sunlight, a technique that underscores the activities of the main figures stretching, relieflike, across the breadth of space under a large, double-trunked shade tree. There, reading from left to right, we see a musician playing a harp, a dog relieving itself nearby, men in exotic, Eastern dress, Hussars on leave, families, children, beauties, and eligible dandies engaged in their animated activities, or simply taking in the passing parade on, presumably, a summer Sunday afternoon. Without a single dramatic focus, the drawing seems to be the continuation into the nineteenth century of the *fête galante* of the French Rococo.

James Mundy, class of 1974

---

[1] Henri Bouchot, *P.-L. Debucourt* (Paris, 1904), 80, no. 399.

[2] Illustrated in Susan L. Siegfried, *The Art of Louis-Léopold Boilly: Modern Life in Napoleonic France* (New Haven, 1995), 134.

35

Hans Jacob Oeri
Swiss (1782-1868)

A Little Girl with Her Dog (ca. 1814)
Pencil on paper
$17^3/_4$" x $14^1/_4$"
Lent by Nancy G. Harrison, class of 1974

Neoclassicism was the prevailing style of painting in Switzerland during the latter half of the eighteenth century. It continued during the reign of Napoleon I (1804-14), when Swiss artists such as Oeri went to Paris to study with Jacques-Louis David (1748-1825). The Kunsthaus, Zurich, has a large collection of Oeri's paintings, sketchbooks, and lithographs, but little has been published about the artist. He apparently traveled a great deal, particularly in Germany and Russia, and was known for the ability to capture "perfectly" the resemblance of his sitters.[1]

Oeri's drawing exhibited here depicts an idealized vision of the private life of a bourgeois girl accompanied by her pet pug. She stands near an empire chair and keeps her dog's attention by holding a chew just out of its reach. Meanwhile, she looks out directly at the viewer, carefully posed, with a contemporary hair style and ironed dress. She is the perfect embodiment of an affectionate, well-bred, obedient girl, not seen hugging or playing with her dog, but instead instructing it to stay alert for the painter.

The adult chair further reminds us that we are in a world scaled and ordered by her parents, rather than by her, which was by no means always the case in the genre. Other portraits from the 1790s to the 1820s that depict a single child alone with an animal include Jean Louis André Théodore Gericault's *Louise Vernet* (1818-19, Louvre, Paris) in which the sitter (Horace Vernet's daughter) is shown outside playing with a cat in a completely natural pose, and Antoine-Jean Gros's *Paulin des Hours Farel* (1793, Musée des Beaux-Arts, Rennes) in which a well-dressed boy captures a goldfinch joyously.

Francesca Consagra

---

[1]   E. Benezit, "Hans Jacob Oeri," *Dictionnaire critique et documentaire des Peintres, Sculpteurs, Dessinateurs et Graveurs* (Paris, 1976), 7:785.

36

Giuseppe Maria Crespi
Italian (1665-1747)

Street Musicians (1710-20)
Oil on canvas
19" x 12⅝"
Promised Gift of Mary McLaughlin in memory of Pamela Askew, class of 1946

Provenance: Painted for the Faresini of Venice; Consul Joseph Smith, Venice, sold Christie's, London, 17 May 1776, lot 29; private collection, Vienna; Agnes Rindge Claflin, Poughkeepsie, New York; Pamela Askew, Millbrook, New York

Literature: Thomas Carr Howe, Jr., "Variety in the Work of Giuseppe Maria Crespi," *Pacific Art Review* 1 (1941): 3-4; Mira Pajes Merriman, *Giuseppe Maria Crespi* (Milan, 1980), 310, no. 263; John T. Spike, *Giuseppe Maria Crespi and the Emergence of Genre Painting in Italy* (Fort Worth, Texas, 1986), 138-40, no. 16

Exhibitions: *Italienische Barockmalerei*, Galerie Sanct Lukas, Vienna, 1937, no. 31; *Exhibition of Italian Baroque Painting of the 17th and 18th Centuries*, Vassar College Art Gallery, Poughkeepsie, New York, 1940, no. 9; *Italian Baroque Painting, 17th and 18th Centuries*, Palace of the Legion of Honor, San Francisco, California, 15, no. 29; *Art of the Past*, Addison Art Gallery, Phillips Andover Academy, Andover, Massachusetts, 1944, no. 35; *Exhibition of Italian Baroque Painting of the 17th and 18th Centuries*, Smith College Museum of Art, Northampton, Massachusetts, 1947, no. 16; *Masters of the Loaded Brush*, Knoedler & Co., Inc., New York, 1967, 5-7, no. 3

The Bolognese artist, Giuseppe Maria Crespi, known also as Lo Spagnuolo, was a painter of religious, mythological, and spirited works of genre. He studied in Bologna under Angelo Michele Toni, Domenico Maria Canuti, and the academy led by Carlo Cignani. He was primarily active in northern Italy, satisfying commissions for his paintings with Bologna as his headquarters, although a brief period was spent in Florence in 1709. In regard to his genre studies, he seems to have been influenced by the Dutch and Italian genre painters of Rome known as the Bamboccianti.

This painting by Crespi has been well analyzed by Spike, as noted above (1986). The scene of a hurdy-gurdy man and a boy playing the violin next to a mother nursing her swaddled child seemed at first puzzling until Spike discovered that it is a fragment of a larger genre painting set near the wall of a church or shrine, etched in 1762 by Giacomo Leonardis (fig. 1). It was cut from a larger canvas at a later date, and one can discern a diagonal line in the lower left-hand corner indicating the point where it was separated. The discovery of the etching led Spike to connect this fragment with its remainder, a painting whose present whereabouts is unknown.[1] In this portion of the painting, one finds other activities related to the poor, such as spinning cotton by hand, tippling in public, and requesting alms. The identical rendering of the mother and child appears in paintings by Crespi in Budapest and Bologna.[2] Merriman dates the painting to 1710-15 and Spike to 1715-20.

fig. 1. Giacomo Leonardis, *Mendicants around a Shrine (after Crespi)*, 1762, etching, British Museum, London.

A second painting by Crespi, *Country Market* (location unknown or destroyed), was etched at the same time by Leonardis and together with the painting were identified as coming from the collection of the British Resident in Venice, the Consul Joseph Smith who, in turn, likely acquired them from the Faresini family, loyal patrons of Crespi.

James Mundy, class of 1974

---

[1]   Illustrated in Mira P. Merriman, *Giuseppe Maria Crespi* (Milan, 1980), no. 265; the Claflin-Askew-McLaughlin painting is no. 263.

[2]   Ibid., nos. 229 and 230.

37

Giovanni Paolo Panini
Italian (1691-1765)

A Capriccio with Alexander and Diogenes
Oil on canvas
28" x 37$^1/_2$"
Signature: "Gio: Paolo Panini" on block, lower left
Lent by Alessandra Manning Dolnier, class of 1982, and Kurt A. Dolnier, class of 1981

While not included in Ferdinando Arisi's catalogue raisonné, published in Giovanni Paolo Panini's hometown of Piacenza in 1961[1] (the three-hundredth anniversary of his birth), this signed painting fits well within a range of paintings executed regularly by the artist during the 1730s, 40s, and 50s. In his architectural caprices, Panini often included a classical or biblical subject, such as the preaching of an apostle or a scene, as in this case, from the life of Alexander the Great. This provided him with a focus around which to build an architectural fantasy drawing upon details of actual buildings or sculpture, blended with those of his imagination. Many of the elements would be recombined in new compositional solutions in other paintings.

Panini was trained in Piacenza by the stage designer, Francesco Galli-Bibiena, and the painters, Giuseppe Natali and Andrea Galluzzi. After moving to Rome in 1711, he worked with Benedetto Luti. He quickly established himself as an independent master and painted *Alexander Visiting the Tomb of Achilles* to celebrate his entry into the Accademia de San Luca in 1719. Another Alexandrian subject, *The Cutting of the Gordian Knot*, was also executed in that year. In fact, throughout his career, Panini found moments from the history of Alexander to be suitable foils for his architectural caprices. In this instance, he recounts the moment mentioned in Plutarch's life of Alexander (33:14), when the King, as a young man, sought out the Cynic philosopher, Diogenes, when the latter did not visit him. When he encountered Diogenes, the philosopher was sunning himself in front of his barrel home. Noting that the philosopher was without material possessions, Alexander asked if he could do anything for him, to which Diogenes answered that he could move out of the way of the sun. Diogenes' lack of awe for Alexander's position greatly impressed the young ruler.

The architectural and sculptural elements surrounding the scene are mostly generic "stock" types that appear, with variations, in many of Panini's paintings. The corner of the Doric temple, the vase with dancing nymphs and satyrs, the herm, bas-reliefs, and standing male figure, come close to certain Roman monuments but generally lack the specificity of detail that allows a connection with a known monument. Similar works in size, composition, and architectural elements are the pendant paintings at the National Gallery of Ireland, Dublin, portraying an apostle preaching and philosopher (or apostle) discoursing, signed and dated by Panini in 1742.[2]

James Mundy, class of 1974

---

[1] F. Arisi, *Gian Paolo Panini* (Piacenza, 1961), rev. ed. as *Gian Paolo Panini e fasti della Roma del Settecento* (Rome, 1986).

[2] Ibid. (1961 ed.), 167-68, nos. 153 and 154, figs. 201 and 202.

38

Giandomenico Tiepolo
Italian (1724-1804)

Group of Figures in a Landscape (recto); *Mother and Child* (verso) (ca. 1750)
Pen and brown ink on paper
$7^1/_2$" x $11^5/_8$"
Collection of Anne Keating Jones, class of 1943

Provenance: Wildenstein, London, 1973

This sketch of a group of figures discoursing before a tree outside of a town has been justifiably assigned to the Venetian artist, Giandomenico Tiepolo, the son and frequent collaborator of the more famous and prolific Giambattista Tiepolo (1696-1770), to whom it was originally assigned. It likely falls into a group of sketches of crowds executed in the late 1740s and early 1750s, at or around the time when both artists were called to Würzburg to decorate the Residenz. These presentation drawings, in pen only, have been published in various catalogues.[1] To this group should be added two drawings of ancient figures in the Robert Lehman Collection at the Metropolitan Museum[2], the drawing of a similar group of figures in the collection of Paul Wallraf, London[3], and a group of drawings in Trieste published by Giorgio Vigni.[4] The general composition of the drawing resembles that of Tiepolo's painting, *Christ Healing the Blind Man*, at the Wadsworth Atheneum, Hartford, signed and dated 1751.[5]

The subject of the Jones drawing is obscure. It features, as do many paintings and drawings by both Tiepolos, a hoary and bare-headed elder who is at the center of a discussion with other figures. Such figures can refer to classical subjects, such as Diogenes, or biblical ones, such as Moses or Abraham. The style is rapid and loose, with brisk evocative strokes to define the fronds of a palm or concatenations of crisply contrapuntal strokes, which define yards of drapery. The quick sketch on the verso can equally as well refer to a Madonna and Child or one of the many secular staffage figure groups that appear in Tiepolo's art.

James Mundy, class of 1974

---

[1] The analogous group is illustrated in A. Gealt and G. Knox, *Domenico Tiepolo: Master Draftsman* (Bloomington, Indiana, 1996), 150-51, nos. 71-74.

[2] Illustrated in J. B. Shaw and G. Knox, *The Robert Lehman Collection VI: Italian Eighteenth-Century Drawings* (New York, 1987), 194-95, nos. 159-160.

[3] Illustrated in J. B. Shaw, *The Drawings of Domenico Tiepolo* (London, 1962), 80, no. 44.

[4] In *Emporium* 97 (July 1943): 17ff.

[5] See Adriano Mariuz, *Giandomenico Tiepolo* (Venice, 1971), 120, and pl. 51.

recto

verso (detail)

39

Lorenzo (Baldissera) Tiepolo
Italian (1736-76)

St. Thecla Freeing Este from the Plague (after Giambattista Tiepolo) (ca. 1759)
Etching
24³/₄" x 14¹/₂" plate
Signature: lower center, "Joannes Batta. Tiepolo inv. et pin./ Laurentius Tiepolo filius del. et inc."
Lent by Frances Beatty Adler and Allen Adler (Frances Beatty, class of 1970)

Lorenzo's father was Giambattista Tiepolo (1696-1770), the most renowned painter of eighteenth-century Italy. Lorenzo and his elder brother, Giandomenico (1727-1804), became painters and assistants to their father, especially on the large fresco cycles in the Würzberg Residenz and the Palacio Real in Madrid. Both also played a role in advertising the family business by etching their father's paintings and decorations and selling them to an eager international print market interested in seeing the latest painting or fresco design by the great Venetian master. Giandomenico produced no fewer than 116 etchings after Giambattista's work[1], and Lorenzo nine.[2] Giorgio Marini recently described Lorenzo's etchings as "imbued with great feeling."[3] This etching, *St. Thecla Freeing Este from the Plague*, after his father's great altarpiece in the church of St. Thecla in Este, Italy, dated 1759, is considered his best.[4]

Lorenzo's etching style is very similar to that of his family and other eighteenth-century Venetian artists, such as Giovanni Antonio Canale, called Canaletto. It is controlled by a series of spirited lines, short or long, layered or etched more deeply for darkness, with little crosshatching, and a wonderful feeling of spontaneity—the very opposite of the linear precision found in engraving. As a reproductive method it was well suited to capturing the dazzling effects of light found in his father's dramatic paintings, often rendered in a high tonal key with subtle shadowing.

Francesca Consagra

[1]   A. Hyatt Mayor, *Prints & People: A Social History of Printed Pictures* (New York, 1971), 577.

[2]   William L. Barcham, "Tiepolo," in *Dictionary of Art*, ed. Jane Turner (New York, 1996), 30:864-65.

[3]   Giorgio Marini, "Lorenzo (Baldissera) Tiepolo," in *The Glory of Venice* (New Haven, 1995), 509.

[4]   Barcham, "Tiepolo," 30:864.

40

Giovanni Battista Piranesi
Italian (1720-78)

The Round Tower, from the series, *Invenzione Capric[ci] di Carceri all Acqua Forte* (The prisons)(etched 1749, printed 1751-60)
Etching, engraving, sulfur tint, and open bite, burnishing; i/ii (third issue of the first edition, with ink dabbing in the center of the top third of the foreground wall along right edge)
$21^7/_8$" x $16^1/_2$"
Lent by Christopher Tunnard

In 1749, Giovanni Battista Piranesi, one of the most accomplished etchers, designers, archaeologists, and theorists of his day, had begun to work on a series of fourteen plates entitled, *Invenzione Capric[ci] di Carceri all Acqua Forte* (Etchings of fantastic inventions of prisons). These images are some of the most provocative and enigmatic of his oeuvre. Before him, during the first two decades of the eighteenth century, Luigi Vanvitelli, Filippo Juvarra, and the Bibiena family of stage designers, had all created their own architectural fantasies, or *caprici*, of prisons, but none as a separate series devoted to the subject. In 1754, Piranesi incorporated a prison scene in his first published work, *Prima Parte di Architeture, e Prospettive*, which was devoted to his study of Roman architecture and architectural perspective. For this plate, entitled *Cacere oscura*, Piranesi borrowed heavily from his predecessors such motifs as the cavernous interiors filled with arches, hanging oil lamps, barred windows, and stairwells leading to unseen floors.

When Piranesi returned to the subject of prisons in 1749, he approached it with an unbounded imagination and style of etching that had hitherto had been unparalleled in the genre. Piranesi, in the first state of *The Round Tower*, as exhibited here, employed loosely etched parallel lines and playful squiggles that oppose the mood evoked by the massive architecture. Robison described *The Round Tower* as being one of the best etchings in the first state of the series.[1] He also believed that Piranesi adapted it from an earlier design, having little to do with prisons, perhaps stemming from his compositions for the *Tempio antico* in the aforementioned series,

Prima Parte. In the *Tempio antico*, a Corinthian colonnade bows outward to create a semicircular projection, which allows for the inclusion of a sweeping flight of stairs leading from foreground to middleground. In *The Round Tower*, too, staircases ascend around a large circular form, which appears more suited to an exterior space like a customs house in a shipping port or a fortification, rather than an interior tower in a prison. Indeed, the torture of prisoners is not seen, only implied by the barred windows of this image; it is the title of the series that confirms a prison interior. In the second state of *The Round Tower*, Piranesi reworked the plate extensively to create a darker, more foreboding mood than the first, more befitting to the state of mind of the incarcerated. Robert M. Adams described this versatility best: "A weighty world, this of Piranesi, one of blocks more immense than man can think of lifting, buildings more staggeringly enormous than men could envisage occupying. Yet also a world in which the impalpable, subtle enemy of all solidities looms very large; and, depending on whether he happens at the moment to be more concerned with matter or with time, Piranesi shifts character like a chameleon."[2]

Francesca Consagra

---

[1] Andrew Robison, *Piranesi: Early Architectural Fantasies* (Washington, D.C., 1986), 42.

[2] Robert M. Adams, *The Roman Stamp: Frame and Facade in Some Forms of Neo-Classicism* (Berkeley, 1974), 184.

41

Giovanni Antonio Canale, called Canaletto
Italian (1697-1768)

View of Padua from the East, with S. Francesco and the Salone (ca. 1742)
Pen and brown ink with gray wash
7^1/$_4$" x 11"
Private collection

Provenance: Benjamin West (Lugt 419) sold London, 9-13 June, 15 July 1820; Edward Speelman, London; Knoedler & Co., Inc., New York

Literature: W. G. Constable, *Canaletto: Giovanni Antonio Canale* (Oxford, 1962), 2:502, no. 681

Giovanni Antonio Canale was the foremost of eighteenth-century view painters, among whose number are included Bernardo Bellotto, Antonio Guardi, and Luca Carlevaris in Venice, and Hubert Robert and Gian Paolo Panini in Rome. Venice's many picturesque views found an active market among foreign visitors, and the English merchant, Joseph Smith, would become Canaletto's greatest single patron and promoter, selling some fifty canvases and 140 drawings to the King George III of England alone.

Canaletto started his career as a theatrical scene painter with his father Bernardo. His name appears in the lists of the painters' guild in 1720. While he worked primarily in Venice, he also traveled to and painted in Rome, and on two occasions, England.

The drawing under examination is one of two-dozen drawings Canaletto made in Padua around 1742. Many of them are fully articulated with rich detail and washes. The view was engraved in reverse by Fabio Berardi in his and Josef Wagner's *Sei Villeggi Campestri*, published around 1742. The drawing is very close in style and subject to one in the British Royal Collection at Windsor[1], which was owned by the Consul Joseph Smith in 1763, whence it joined the queen's collection. The drawing under discussion was also likely in England by the end of the eighteenth century, since it belonged at one time to Benjamin West, whose drawing collection was vast and justly famous.

Canaletto painted only a few Paduan views that survive. His greater analysis of this region was relegated to this exquisite drawing and its two-dozen related sheets.

James Mundy, class of 1974

---

[1] W. G. Constable, *Canaletto* (Oxford, 1962), 2:501, no. 680.

42

Anonymous, School of Cuzco

Virgin of the Rosary of Pomata (early eighteenth century)
Oil on canvas
45¹/₂" x 33³/₄"
Lent by Barbara Doyle Duncan, class of 1943

The image exhibited here, *Virgin of the Rosary of Pomata*, represents a cultural fusion between Andean and Christian art history. The panel dates from the first half of the eighteenth century, the height of the Cuzco Baroque period. Cuzco was the capital of the Inca empire dating from the eleventh century and a municipal center under the Spaniards from 1534. It suffered from a series of earthquakes in 1650 that caused much destruction to the buildings in the city. Hired to rebuild and decorate, the native and *mestizo* (of mixed Spanish and native blood) artists of Cuzco rebelled against the dictates of the Spanish guild system and emerged as an independent art guild in 1688. The School of Cuzco, the first indigenous organization of artists in the New World, flourished until around 1800.[1]

One of the most popular images of the school was the Virgin of the Immaculate Conception, or the Virgin standing on a crescent moon. Popular as Marian imagery with the Spanish, she was "the perfect foil for the Andean believer's devotion to the deity of the moon, who was also the queen of the Inca and consort of the sun, Inti."[2] The Cuzco artists also liked to depict the Virgin in a dress and cloak, which made her into a triangular shape of a mountain. This allied the Virgin Mary to Pachamama, the earth-mother goddess of the Inca.[3]

The form of the Virgin of the Rosary of Pomata was only one of the ways the indigenous artists of the Andes interpreted the Virgin of the Immaculate Conception. There was, for instance, the Virgin of the Candlestick, the Virgin of the Shepherds, or Our Lady of Lake Titicaca—all of which represent the Virgin and Child standing on a crescent moon, but with different attributes and ornamented dress.

The city of Cuzco especially was associated with the worship of the Virgin of the Rosary of Pomata . The dominant feature of this type of Virgin of the Immaculate Conception is the feather crowns that associate the Virgin and Child with Inca royalty, who donned plumed headdresses at ceremonial events.[4] Another Inca motif used to glorify the Virgin of the Rosary of Pomata is her elaborate brocaded dress, with garlands of pearls secured by jeweled flower brooches in a four-petal shape. These can be traced to ornaments found in tombs dating from the Moche Civilization (200 B.C. to 700 A.D.) and to Inca vessels. The swags of pearls across the Virgin's dress are not only Spanish symbols of perfection and purity but also prized decorations of Andean nobility[5]—illustrating again how the iconography of a newer Christian culture only appeared to replace that of the Inca. The Cuzco artists, working as an independent art guild, kept their own ancient symbols very much alive in such paintings as the *Virgin of the Rosary of Pomata* and may have been more defiant of conversion to Catholicism than their Spanish rulers thought.[6]

Regardless of the motives behind the Cuzco School's representations of the Virgin and Child as royal Andean deities, these artists (who had successfully fused Andean and Christian iconographies) only helped to strengthen the love that the indigenous peoples had developed for Marian imagery, especially at a time when they were undergoing significant political and social changes, as well as enduring major natural disasters such as the earthquakes of 1650.

Francesca Consagra

---

[1] See Carol Damian, *The Virgin of the Andes: Art and Ritual in Colonial Cuzco* (Miami Beach, Florida, 1995), 9.

[2] Ibid., 63.

[3] Ibid., 50.

[4] Barbara Duncan, "Statue Paintings of the Virgin," in *Gloria in Excelsis: The Virgin and Angels in Viceregal Painting of Peru and Bolivia* (New York, 1985), 53.

[5] Damian, *Virgin of the Andes*, 80.

[6] See Carol Damian, "The Survival of Inca Symbolism in Representations of The Virgin in Colonial Peru," *Athanor* 7 (1988): 21-31.

43

Thomas Cole
American, British-born (1801-48)

Sketch (ca. 1843)
Oil and pencil on academy board
10" x 13³/₄"
Promised Gift of Thomas and Margaret McCormick

Provenance: Florence Cole Vincent (artist's granddaughter); Victor Spark

Exhibitions: *Art in the Making*, Colby College, Waterville, Maine and Williams College, Williamstown, Massachusetts, 1966

Within a decade of his arrival in America, Thomas Cole, a British-born emigrant with little formal artistic training other than what he had received as an engraver's apprentice in England, had attained great promise as an artist within New York's nascent art world. He possessed keen observational skills, an imaginative mind, a love of the wilderness, and an industrious nature, all of which allowed him to elevate the art of landscape painting in America to a new level during the age of Jacksonian democracy. At the time of his death, unexpected at the age of forty-seven, his contemporaries recognized his remarkable and largely self-taught achievement by holding a memorial service with a funeral oration by the poet, William Cullen Bryant, and by mounting a memorial exhibition of eighty-three of his paintings at the recently opened American Art-Union in New York.

While learning his craft, Cole spent extensive time traveling through America's sparsely inhabited wilderness, where he sharpened his skills in sketching and painting out-of-doors. As many scholars have noted, Cole also relied upon a British painter's manual, William Oram's *Precepts and Observation of the Art of Colouring in Landscape Painting* (1810), for advice.[1] After Cole achieved recognition, sketching trips taken for days or weeks at a time, alone or with colleagues to the rugged outcrops of the Catskill Mountains, increased his prestige immeasurably, not only for the landscapes he produced, but also for the lively tales of his travel.

Cole's success lay in his approach to landscape painting as an art form in which the artist acted as the intermediary between nature and the viewer. The artist experienced nature directly and thus became both its editor and interpreter. Cole considered his paintings of the country's topographical features as truthful and accurate records of what he had seen and which he had transcribed into easel paintings in his studio. Cole's appreciation for American scenery found a receptive audience eager to "experience" it as a sublime world of natural forces, and to admire it with patriotic sentiment.

Cole's method of sketching directly from nature placed primary emphasis upon draughtsmanship. The work under discussion here, a roughly 10" x 14" unfinished oil sketch on academy board, has much to say about Cole's working method. The rapid rendering of the scene, first in pencil, is typical of the artist's compositional studies for larger and fully resolved easel paintings. Cole quickly established the middle and distant background areas with lightly-penciled skeins of circular lines shaping outlines and geomorphic features. A small building appears dashed into the middleground. Cole has already begun developing the sky into a sunset, scrambling paint to give substance to the rock and hill formations in the middleground. His brush-strokes are loosely dabbled, but handled with the assurance of an artist who knew exactly what he was doing.

Rebecca Lawton

---

[1]   Ellwood C. Parry III, "Thomas Cole's Early Drawings: In Search of a Signature Style," *Bulletin of the Detroit Institute of Arts* 66, no. 1 (1990): 13.

44

Frederic Church
American (1826-1900)

Andean Sketch (ca. 1857-59)
Oil over traces of graphite on canvas
10" x 16"
Lent by Maryann K. and Alvin Friedman (Maryann Kallison, class of 1955)

Frederic Church's artistic training took place under the most privileged of circumstances—with the encouragement of a family friend, Daniel Wadsworth, then one of the leading patrons of American art, and with the extraordinary opportunity to study for two years, 1844-46, with Thomas Cole, then the most famous landscape painter in the country (see cat. no. 43). Church was born in Hartford, Connecticut in 1826, into a prominent and wealthy mercantile family, strongly rooted in Calvinist doctrine, but not so rigid that they dispelled his artistic ambitions. Church began his apprenticeship with Cole in June 1844, and spent the summer traveling with him throughout the Catskills on sketching expeditions. He made his debut as an artist at the National Academy of Design the following year, attaining critical acclaim for his "exact" transcriptions of reality. As one of only two students of Cole, Church is considered key to the formation of the style of landscape painting commonly referred to as the Hudson River School, a group of landscape painters united by their subject matter and adherence to the doctrine of "truthfulness to nature."

Church developed his reputation by creating monumental paintings of phenomenal locations, such as *Niagara* (1857, Corcoran Gallery of Art, Washington, D.C.) and of exotic locations such as *The Heart of the Andes* (1859, Metropolitan Museum of Art, New York) and *Cotopaxi* (1872, Detroit Institute of Arts, Detroit, Michigan). The painting under discussion here, titled *Andean Sketch*, belongs to the series of small works Church executed in connection with his two astounding expeditions to South America in 1853 and 1867.[1] *The Heart of the Andes* and *Cotopaxi* are perhaps the most famous of several large and significant paintings, the so-called Great Pictures, which the artist accomplished upon his return from these trips and subsequently exhibited publicly in grandiose settings, rather than the conventional public exhibition galleries. Church undertook these arduous expeditions not only as an artist, but also as a naturalist in search of empirical knowledge of the world.

Like Church's large, imposing paintings, his small works, such as *Andean Sketch*, represent recollections of the direct observations he had made of the light, terrain, and plant life along the equator. Eleanor Jones Harvey has recently documented in *The Painted Sketch: American Impressions from Nature 1830-1880*, that Church viewed his completed oil sketches and finished work as equal in quality.[2] A comparison between this sketch and any one of his paintings reveals that they vary only in size and the degree of detail. The same motifs Church scrupulously presented in his more accomplished works, such as the jagged line of the distant mountain range, the vanishing point at the center of the picture where the sun rises or sets, the tropical fauna of the valley floor, where earth meets water, the minuscule scene of people in bright, primary-colored clothing in the foreground, and a towering palm tree on either side of the picture, are also presented accurately as motifs in minor works such as *Andean Sketch*. Church frequently exhibited such sketches in the major New York exhibitions, as well as in his studio, where the public eagerly congregated to view the world in wonderment and the American landscape as a symbol of national pride.

Rebecca Lawton

---

[1] Kevin J. Avery, *Church's Great Picture, "The Heart of the Andes"* (New York, 1993), passim.

[2] Eleanor Jones Harvey, *The Painted Sketch: American Impressions from Nature 1830-1880* (Dallas, 1998), 68.

45

Sanford Gifford
American (1823-80)

Catskill Mountain House (1862)
Oil on canvas
9⁵/₁₆" x 18¹/₂"
Signature: signed and dated, "S.R. Gifford '62"
Lent by Elizabeth Gosnell, class of 1984

Provenance: William Allen; George F. McMurray; Austin Arts Center, Trinity College, Hartford, Connecticut; Ted and Barbara Alfond, Weston, Massachusetts

Literature: Illa S. Weiss, *Sanford Robinson Gifford, 1823-1880* (New York and London, 1977)

Exhibitions: *A Memorial Catalogue of the Paintings of Sanford Robinson Gifford, N. A.*, Metropolitan Museum of Art, New York, 1881, no. 278; *American Paradise, The World of the Hudson River School*, Metropolitan Museum of Art, New York, 1987, 226-27

Sanford Robinson Gifford was born in Greenfield, New York in 1823 and studied art, after two years of college, in New York City, where he was elected to the National Academy of Design in 1851. He was an early part of the Hudson River School of landscape painting and sketched extensively in the Catskill, Berkshire, Adirondack, and Shawangunk Mountains. He traveled to Europe in the mid-1850s and returned to take a studio in the famous Tenth Street Studio Building. In 1861, he enlisted in the New York State National Guard. His later career featured more extensive traveling to Europe and the Middle East as well as to the western territories of the United States. He was honored, following his death, at a special meeting and exhibition at the Century Association, where he had been a member since 1859, and a large exhibition at the Metropolitan Museum of Art.

This painting, *Catskill Mountain House*, was made at the sublime epicenter of the Hudson River aesthetic, the picturesque hotel perched some twenty-two hundred feet above the Hudson River Valley. The hotel was the destination of many wealthy travelers from New York and elsewhere and was, by and large, too pricey and busy for artists. Thus, while it was an important landmark, it was only the occasional subject of painters such as Thomas Cole and

Jasper Cropsey. Gifford himself depicted the location in three small pictures, this one being the only one that seems to have survived to this day.[1] Avery cites three possible sketches for this painting in the collection of the Albany Institute.[2]

This small painting is a masterfully composed autumn landscape whose sophisticated diagonal countercurves take the eye from the repoussoir elements of the pine trees in the near left-hand corner to the imposing dark form of the mountain ridge behind the hotel itself. The path in between is charted by brief bursts of bright colors that evoke the pulsating autumnal colors and the awesome qualities of the site and its storied views. Without being bombastic in the manner of some artists of the day, this painting is the quintessence of the purely visual realm of the nineteenth-century American painter—controlled, varied, and indisputably lyrical.

James Mundy, class of 1974

---

[1] See Kevin J. Avery's entry in *American Paradise, The World of the Hudson River School* (New York, 1987), 226-27 and especially note 1.

[2] Ibid. and note 11.

46

William L. Sonntag
American (1822-1900)

Mill Brook near Shelburne, New Hampshire (ca. 1869)
Oil on canvas
20" x 36"
Lent by Maryann K. and Alvin Friedman (Maryann Kallison, class of 1955)

Literature: Nancy Moure, *William Louis Sonntag: Artist of the Ideal, 1822-1900*
(Los Angeles, 1980), 120, no. 293

The Reverend Elias Lyman Magoon, whose collection of Hudson River School paintings resides at Vassar College as a gift of the College's founder, Matthew Vassar, discovered William L. Sonntag's work in Cincinnati in the late 1840s. Magoon, rector of a Baptist parish in New York City, patronized Sonntag's early career, commissioning a series of four paintings, *The Progress of Civilization* (1847, location unknown), based upon William Cullen Bryant's poem, "The Ages," which was itself probably inspired by Thomas Cole's series of paintings, *The Course of the Empire* (1836, New York Historical Society).[1] Interestingly, Sonntag's allegorical works appear to have been the only American paintings Magoon purchased before he began collecting American landscape paintings in earnest in the mid-1850s.

Sonntag, born near Pittsburgh, Pennsylvania in 1822, was largely a self-taught artist. A commission to paint landscapes for the Baltimore and Ohio Railroad Company in 1852 provided Sonntag with practical training and a trip to Europe the following year with his pupil, John R. Tait, and Robert S. Duncanson provided additional experience.

Sonntag favored a horizontal format, with a sharp diagonal leading the eye into the distant space. The landscape under discussion here has several elements similar to those in the artist's *Landscape with Waterfall and Figures* (n.d., Metropolitan Museum of Art). Sonntag's biographer, Nancy Moure, has suggested that the Met's painting dates from the mid-1860s and that it might have been inspired by scenery in New Hampshire.[2] Like the Met's painting, *Mill Brook near Shelburne, New Hampshire* contains Sonntag's favored motifs, such as the central body of water surrounded by rolling hills and mountains. The artist's careful delineation of details in the foreground is characteristic of the Hudson River School style.

Rebecca Lawton

---

[1] Biographical information courtesy of Maryann K. Friedman, "Mill Brook, Near Shelburne, New Hampshire (ca. 1869), William Louis Sonntag 1822-1900," photocopy.

[2] See Natalie Spassky, *American Paintings in the Metropolitan Museum of Art*, vol. 2 of *A Catalogue of Works by Artists born Between 1816 and 1845* (New York, 1985), 163.

47

David Johnson
American (1827-1908)

Lake Placid, Adirondacks (1866)
Oil on canvas
16" x 25³/₄"
Signatures: lower left, artist's monogram, "DJ"; on verso, "David Johnson 1866"
Lent by Alice Pack Melly, class of 1956

David Johnson enjoyed a long and productive career that spanned five decades and witnessed the dramatic shift in American taste for landscape painting from the meticulous naturalism of the Hudson River School to the lush, painterly style inspired by the French Barbizon artists. Born in New York City in 1827, Johnson's career had been something of an enigma until the publication of Gwendolyn Owens's monograph on the artist in 1988 answered several questions about his career and artistic training.[1] Of primary interest was the notion that he had been a completely self-taught artist, when in fact, as Owens has documented, he had received instruction in the Antique School at the National Academy of Design for two seasons (1845-47).

While his formal training after the antique casts surely improved his skill as a draughtsman, Johnson possessed a remarkable eye for detail and the talent to paint with precision. His landscapes are thus transcriptions of the natural world, but not in the strictly topographical sense. Rather, Johnson presents a distinctly personal adaptation of nature, one that calls attention to its most intimate details, such as moss clinging to rock formations, and the quality of light illuminating and differentiating leaves on shrubs and brush. Owens notes that Johnson was interested in "the ecological relations which make each natural element a part of an intricate whole, and also the close interdependence between this natural system and the people who come to it for their livelihood, their recreation, and their spiritual renewal.[2]

In composition, *Lake Placid, Adirondacks* follows the artist's typical format of rounded hills in the distance to close off the vista, shoreline trees, and rock formations in the middleground at left and/or right, and an open expanse of water in the foreground.[3] The sun's light, with its shifts from bright- to pastel-colored shadows, is the energizing force providing a sense of movement across the canvas.

Johnson's compositional format takes the eye on a journey of this place of peace and tranquillity from a seemingly microscopic view of it beginning at left in the foreground, along a rugged, rock-embedded shoreline into the mid-distance, where there exists the most natural of human habitats, a Native American encampment. Johnson then leads the eye across the canvas along a row of majestic peaks, turned into pastel colors by the sun and backed by a nearly cloudless blue sky. Finally, the viewer travels down the terrain along Tongue Mountain to the water's edge and to a lake with a current so slight and a surface so calm that it reflects the world like a looking glass.

The artists of the Hudson River School considered Lake George, at the edge of the Adirondacks, one of the premier locations for landscape painting. They frequently painted the view with Tongue Mountain in the distance. Cole considered the "purity and transparency of the water" in upstate New York's lakes to be among the finest in America, noting that "it is a circumstance which contributes greatly to the beauty of landscape; for the reflection of surrounding objects, trees, mountains, sky, are most perfect in the clearest water; and the most perfect is the most beautiful."[4] Here, Johnson follows Cole's footprints, celebrating nature as interrelated to mankind, as shown by the Native American encampment at left and a lone tribesman canoeing across the lake, perhaps to fish or hunt game. Yet, in seeing the world as a pure, pristine place where nature and man coexist, Johnson always reminds his audience that nature is dominant.

Rebecca Lawton

---

[1] Gwendolyn Owens, *Nature Transcribed: The Landscapes and Still Lifes of David Johnson 1827-1908* (Hanover, New Hampshire and London, 1988).

[2] Ibid., 13.

[3] Ibid., 37.

[4] Thomas Cole, "Essay on American Scenery 1835," quoted in John W. McCoubrey, *American Art 1700-1960, Sources and Documents in the History of Art Series* (Englewood Cliffs, New Jersey, 1965), 103.

48 and 49

Martin Johnson Heade
American (1819-1904)

Sunset on the Newbury Marshes (ca. 1865-75)
Oil on canvas
13" x 26"
Signature: lower left, "M. J. Heade."
Lent by Alice Pack Melly, class of 1956

Northern Marsh: Sunset (ca. 1880)
Oil on canvas
8" x 16"
Lent by Maryann K. and Alvin Friedman (Maryann Kallison, class of 1955)

Martin Johnson Heade decided to become an artist at a young age, despite an apparent lack of precocious talent for a promising career. With the encouragement of his family, Heade developed into an artist, though it is clear that he never had to rely solely upon art for his livelihood. Heade's contemporaries failed to take great interest in his landscapes; his talent was recognized and his work appreciated by collectors and dealers only with the rediscovery of his paintings in the early 1940s. Unlike Thomas Cole's descendants, who treasured even his slightest sketch, Heade's family divested themselves of many of his personal effects and thus a great deal is still unknown about his life.

Heade belonged to the second generation of artists of the Hudson River School, which flourished from 1850 to 1875. The luminist style of painting Heade practiced, with its crispness and high-keyed tonal harmonies, distinguishes his work from that of his colleagues and from the earlier style of the Hudson River School. Though the two paintings discussed here are not characteristic of the artist's most luminist works, they share with them the same poetic sensibility. He favored painting the transitory moments of sunrise or sunset as if they were the timeless states more commonly experienced through visions and recollections.[1]

Heade specialized in painting views of the salt marshes along the East Coast in areas such as Newbury and Rowley on the North Shore of Massachusetts, and also in Rhode Island and New Jersey. The tidal marsh, a flat stretch of land, allowed the artist to format his canvases into horizontal bands of water, land, and sky, with the latter occupying slightly more than half the picture. Thus, the artist portrayed the earth as expansive and used the temperament of the sky as an essential feature of his work. Heade, a passionate duck hunter, would have frequented just such spots, making the subject one of convenience, as well as aesthetic interest.[2] As a hunter,

Heade needed the landscape to be a place of silence, and he no doubt took advantage of the monotony of duck hunting to hone his observational skills. The artist painted a series of marshscapes during the 1860s and returned to the theme throughout his life. After moving to Florida sometime in the 1880s, Heade painted scenes of Florida's marshlands around St. Augustine.

In each of the paintings discussed here, the line of distant hills across the horizon appears to be the same one, geographically identified as the area around Newbury, Massachusetts.[3] The cloud formations and the effects of light upon the marshland differentiate each work, as they do all of Heade's marsh scenes. The smaller canvas, without figures, captures the first stage of twilight, after the sun has set and its fading golden glow converts the marsh into a place of tranquillity. The larger canvas indicates a slightly earlier time of day, when the cows still graze in the foreground and tiny speckles of farmers dot the land in the distance. As in most of Heade's late works, the brushwork in *Northern Marsh: Sunset* is loose, lacking the precise, nearly invisible brushstrokes in his earlier, more typically luminist works. Theodore Stebbins believes that Heade intended *Northern Marsh: Sunset* and another work, *Florida Marsh: Dawn*, as pendants symbolizing Heade's past life in the Northeast and his present life in Florida, where he had settled sometime after 1884.[4]

Human activity is implied in the painting titled *Northern Marsh: Sunset*, but presented fully in *Sunset on the Newbury Marshes*. The scene in the latter work is of harvesting season, when farmers cut the marsh grass, fashioned it into conical stacks weighing one to three tons, and placed it on "staddles." It is a scene of man toiling in nature, but in harmony with it. The sun illuminates their labor in a dazzling light, while a shadow sweeps across the marsh, energizing the scene.

48

49

Heade's paintings of marshes found an appreciative audience. In 1884, critics noted that, "He has been very successful in his views of the Hoboken and Newburyport meadows, for which the demand has been so great that he has probably painted more of them than of any other class of subjects."[5]

Rebecca Lawton

---

[1] Also known as *Old Life in New England* and *Sunset: New England Marsh*. The title as given above, *Northern Marsh: Sunset*, was given to the painting by Theodore E. Stebbins, Jr. in a letter of 16 April 1977 to Island Weiss; photocopy courtesy of Maryann and Alvin Friedman.

[2] Heade did a painting of duck hunting in a marsh entitled, *Duck Hunters in a Twilight Marsh* (1866); see Theodore E. Stebbins, Jr., *The Life and Works of Martin Johnson Heade* (New Haven and London, 1975), 232, no. 101.

[3] Ibid., 50-52.

[4] Theodore E. Stebbins, Jr., letter of 16 April 1977 to Island Weiss.

[5] Stebbins, *The Life and Works*, 101.

50

Winslow Homer
American (1836-1910)

Mackerel Fishing (1884)
Charcoal and white chalk
$14^1/_2$" x $23^1/_2$" sheet
Signature: lower right, "HOMER 1884"
Private collection

Provenance: L. A. Jackson; P. H. McMahon, 1914; Annie Burr Jennings, New York, 1916; Oliver B. Jennings, New York, her nephew, by gift, before 1939; Steven Juvlis, Lynn, Massachusetts, 1963; present owner, 1964[1]

Literature: Lloyd Goodrich, *Winslow Homer* (New York, 1973), 142, no. 178

Exhibitions: *Studies in Black & White by Winslow Homer, N. A.*, Doll & Richards, Boston, 29 November-6 December 1884; *Illustrated Catalogue of Valuable Paintings by Artists of Distinction Belonging to the Estates of the Late Mr. J. R. Andrews and to Mr. P. H. McMahon and Other Private Owners*, American Art Association, New York, 27-28 January 1916, no. 125; *Winslow Homer*, Whitney Museum of American Art, New York, 3 April-3 June, 1973; Los Angeles County Museum of Art, 3 July-15 August 1973; Art Institute of Chicago, 8 September-21 October 1973, no. 178; *Winslow Homer and the New England Coast*, Whitney Museum of American Art, 9 November 1984-9 January 1985; *Winslow Homer in Monochrome*, M. Knoedler & Co., Inc., New York, 12 December 1986-9 January 1987, no. 76

With *Prisoners from the Front* (Metropolitan Museum of Art), completed in 1866 and exhibited the same year, Winslow Homer attained recognition as a major American artist. Between the painting's exhibition at the National Academy of Design and his death four decades later, Homer became America's greatest living artist, winning both popular and critical acclaim for oil painting, printmaking, and watercolor, and for his characteristically American subject matter.

Mackerel Fishing belongs to a series of drawings in charcoal and chalk that Homer executed in the fall of 1884 at Prout's Neck, Maine. Homer first visited Prout's Neck, a small spit of land along the Atlantic Ocean, ten miles south of Portland, in 1873, while his brother Arthur honeymooned there.[2] A decade later, the Homer family began acquiring oceanfront property at Prout's Neck, transforming the tiny farming and fishing community into a commodious resort of private summer homes. In late 1883 or early 1884, soon after Homer's father had built the family's seaside cottage at Prout's Neck, the artist had a small carriage house on the property moved closer to the cliffs and converted into a year-round home and studio. Thereafter, Homer used Prout's Neck as his principle place of residence until his death in 1910.

By living alone in Spartan conditions long after the summer season had ended, Homer unintentionally instigated rumors that he had become a cheerless, solitary man with little interest in society or the amusements found therein. Writing in December 1884, the *Boston Herald* romantically likened his studio at Prout's Neck to a hermitage.[3] On the contrary, Homer was involved with many local affairs, managed his family's property, and befriended the locals, whom he used as models.[4] By spending part of the fall and winter at Prout's Neck, Homer assured himself the privacy and independence he required to work.

With Homer's move to Prout's Neck, his art changed fundamentally, and although he continued to draw upon actual life, this time it was actual life on "the simplest, most elemental level."[5] His studio brought him into close proximity to the sea, and he used it as a subject because its power and drama both captivated and intrigued him.

Homer was an avid outdoorsman, who enjoyed fishing and hunting for sport nearly every year of his adult life.[6] As a sportsman, he learned to understand nature, developing a deep respect for it and the demanding technical skills needed to hunt deer and fly-fish for trout. At Prout's Neck, just as he had during his residence at Cullercoats, England in 1881-82, Homer witnessed the arduous and austere life of people who depended upon the sea, not for recreational pleasure, but for their livelihood.

The artist began his study of life at Prout's Neck in the series of monochrome drawings of the landscape and trawling, which included *Mackerel Fishing*. His choice to use only charcoal and white chalk may have been a result of his effort achieve a purer form of

expression and immediate visual sensation, but it also suggests that the climatic change in Maine, as winter approached and the sky lost its clarity and vibrancy, activated a transition towards a somber mood. Homer's vision of the rugged and dangerous life at Prout's Neck is that of a close observer. His work of the period places the viewer within the scene, as if they, too, were its witness. The monochrome drawings and etchings he accomplished in the early 1880s ushered in his greatest series of seascapes, such as *The Life Line* (1884, Philadelphia Museum of Art), *The Fog Warning* (1885, Museum of Fine Arts, Boston) and *Eight Bells* (1886, Addison Gallery of American Art, Phillips Academy, Andover, Massachusetts).

Rebecca Lawton

[1] Excerpted from the manuscript, "City University of New York/Lloyd Goodrich and Edith Havens Goodrich/Whitney Museum of American Art Record of Works by Winslow Homer." I would like to thank Abigail Booth Gerdts for providing information on the drawing's provenance.

[2] See Patty Junker, "Expression of Art and Life in The Artist's Studio in an Afternoon Fog," in *Winslow Homer in the 1890's Prout's Neck Observed* (New York, 1990), 34-65.

[3] Quoted in Charles Brock, "Chronology," in Nicolai Cikovsky, Jr. and Franklin Kelly, *Winslow Homer* (Washington, D.C., 1995), 397.

[4] Lois Graham, "The Homers and Prout's Neck," in *Winslow Homer in the 1890's Prout's Neck Observed* (New York, 1990), 30.

[5] Lloyd Goodrich, *Winslow Homer* (New York, 1973), 38.

[6] David Tatham, *Winslow Homer in the Adirondacks* (Syracuse, New York, 1996), passim.

135

51

American

Navajo Blanket (Chief style, Third Phase, ca. 1895-1905)
Woven wool
52" x 72"
Lent by Georgia Sims, class of 1952, and William C. Carson

This striking and well-preserved blanket exemplifies the Navajo mastery of textile production in the American Southwest. According to myth, the legendary Spider Woman taught the Navajo to weave in ancient times. Since then, this activity has remained sacred for the Navajo, or the Diné, as many of the people now prefer to call themselves. According to Wesley Thomas, "As a traditional weaver constructs a textile, she imbues it with part of herself through talking, singing, and/or praying as she weaves."[1] In Navajo culture, beautiful objects such as the blanket seen here are not of primary significance, even though many textiles (including this one) were made specifically for sale or display. Instead, the end product is always secondary to the creative activity and spiritual harmony that produced it.[2]

Constructed on rudimentary upright looms, Navajo textiles are traditionally made from the wool of *churro* sheep, which the Spanish introduced into the Southwest. The process of shearing, carding, spinning, and weaving is extremely time-consuming; a single blanket can take over three hundred hours to produce. Weavers are usually women, and they rarely sketch out their elaborate and precise designs on paper beforehand; instead the weaver composes the entire pattern in her head. Having learned textile making—and the properly reverential attitude toward it—at the knees of maternal elders, the weaver thoroughly internalizes the technical and aesthetic principles so that the activity becomes spiritually integrative.[3]

Navajo openness to outside influences has always kept their textile traditions fluid and dynamic, and their designs are constantly evolving. The oldest and most distinctive of Navajo textile designs is the Chief style, so named because tribal leaders among the Plains Indians eagerly sought such blankets throughout the nineteenth century. During the classic phase of Navajo weaving (approximately 1650-1868), the Chief style began as a simple alternation of tightly woven white, brown, red, and blue horizontal stripes. After 1850, some weavers added elongated rectangles to the expanded center and end stripes. A decade later, the design repertoire broadened to include a complete central diamond and eight partial ones at the edges, sometimes—as in this example—with serrated outlines inspired by Mexican serapes.[4] The residual alternating stripes (in this case white and black) act as a stable background to the assertive red lozenge shapes that appear to extend forward toward the viewer. When worn around the shoulders, the partial diamonds meet at the front of the body, and the central diamond dominates the wearer's back. Therefore, the design can only be fully appreciated when seen on the human figure.

By the 1880s, Navajo blankets and rugs ignited the Euro-American imagination as visitors poured into the Southwest via newly completed railroad lines. Collectors not only valued these objects as superlative examples of Navajo handicraft traditions, but also prized them as comforting alternatives to the increasing numbers of anonymous, mass-produced objects that threatened to banish personal associations and communal memory from everyday life. Despite the fact that most Navajo weavers lived in remote, inaccessible regions, tourists could easily buy blankets and other crafts at trading posts, such as the Fred Harvey Company's Hopi House at the south rim of the Grand Canyon. Dr. Norman Bruce Carson bought this blanket at the Hopi House shortly after it opened to the public in 1905, and it descended through family ties to the present owners.

Karen Lucic
Associate Professor of Art

---

[1] "Personification of Navajo Weaving," in Eulalie H. Bonar, ed., *Woven by the Grandmothers: Nineteenth-Century Navajo Textiles from the National Museum of the American Indian* (Washington, D.C., 1996), 33.

[2] Bonar, ed., "Foreword," in *Woven by the Grandmothers*, xi.

[3] See Kate Peck Kent, *Navajo Weaving: Three Centuries of Change* (Santa Fe, New Mexico, 1985); and Joe Ben Wheat, "Navajo Blankets," in Bonar, ed., *Woven by the Grandmothers*, passim.

[4] Nancy J. Blomberg, *Navajo Textiles: The William Randolph Hearst Collection* (Tucson, Arizona, 1988),1-4.

52

William Merritt Chase
American (1849-1916)

Boat House, Prospect Park (ca. 1887)
Oil on canvas
10¹/₄" x 16"
Signature: lower right, "Wm M. Chase"
Lent by Meg Newhouse Kirkpatrick, class of 1974

Provenance: Wilbur Peat, Indianapolis, 1967; Newhouse Galleries, Inc., New York

Literature: Ronald Pisano, *A Leading Spirit in American Art: William Merritt Chase 1849-1916 (Seattle, Washington, 1983), 159*

Exhibitions: *Chase Centennial Exhibition*, John Herron Art Museum, Indianapolis, Indiana, 1 November-11 December 1949; *William Merritt Chase, A Benefit Exhibition for the Parrish Art Museum*, Knoedler & Co., Inc., New York, 1976, no. 36; *A Leading Spirit in American Art: William Merritt Chase 1849-1916*, Henry Art Gallery, University of Washington, Seattle, Washington, 1983; *Impressionism in America*, Jordan-Volpe Gallery, New York, 18 May-June 1991

The American painter, William Merritt Chase, is known for his distinguished career as an artist and for his devotion to teaching, a concomitant career that lasted thirty-seven years and brought him into contact with scores of American art students. Born in Williamsburg, Indiana in 1849, Chase lived just long enough to see the legendary Armory Show of 1913, which introduced American audiences to European modernism. His early colleagues, fellow academicians such as Frederic Church (see cat. no. 44), Sanford Robinson Gifford (see cat. no. 45), and Jervis McEntee, upheld the Hudson River School style, while his students, artists such as Charles Sheeler, Morton Schamberg, and James Daugherty, became America's first modernists.

As a young man, Chase evidenced a proclivity for art that brought his work to the attention of a cartel of St. Louis businessmen who helped finance his six years of study, from 1872 to 1878, at the Royal Academy in Munich, in exchange for a painting for each. Upon his return to America, Chase settled in New York and began teaching at the newly established Art Students League. He joined a succession of artist's societies and organizations, from the convivial Tile Club to an unofficial group known as "The Ten" that placed him at the center of the art world at the turn of the century.

As a student in Munich, Chase adopted the fashion of energetic brushwork and gradually developed a remarkable facility to handle paint with dazzling assurance. He spent the summer of 1884 in Holland, studying *plein-air* landscape painting. His subsequent decisions to change from a dark to a high-keyed palette, and to fill his pictures with natural light, helped define the style known as American Impressionism. By 1891, Chase had achieved such success painting directly out-of-doors that he formed a summer art school in Shinnecock Hills, Long Island, to teach his method to American artists.

In *Boat House, Prospect Park*, Chase comes close to the French style of Impressionism. In its subject matter, treatment of light, and application of paint—using dabs of pure color to create the trees in the background, as well as touches of brilliant, unadulterated white to create highlights—Chase achieves the effect sought after by the French Impressionists of creating a first "impression." The air seems to vibrate and the objects appear to shimmer in the intense heat of the noon-day sun. Unlike the French artists, particularly Monet, Pissarro, and Sisley, Chase retreated from allowing his compositions to dissolve completely under natural light. He retained the solid sense of materiality preferred by American painters.

Chase's favorite subject matter were gardens, the seashore, and people engaged in leisurely activities therein. In this work, he takes full advantage of the sun's position directly overhead to create startling reflections of light off the water and the canopies on the boats. The result is a magnificent display of vibrant, saturated color. His figures, as evident in paintings such as this one, are part of the scene, blending into their surroundings as if they were a part of its beauty. Here Chase presents man-made nature for idle pleasure, and a glorious feast for the senses.

During his life, Chase had transformed himself from a small-town Midwestern boy into the consummate, urbane artist, a dapper figure, who moved with facility within international art circles. His enormous studio in the Tenth Street Studio Building in New York epitomized the artistic milieu of his day.[1] It was a sumptuous place

brimming with artistic clutter and curiosities, where society met to socialize, and Chase displayed his sense of refinement and talent while marketing his paintings.

Rebecca Lawton

---

[1]   Annette Blaugraund, *The Tenth Street Studio Building: Artist-Entrepreneurs from the Hudson River School to the American Impressionists* (Southampton, New York, 1997), 105-26.

53

Antonio Jacobsen
American (1850-1921)

The Governor Dingley (1900)
Oil on canvas
22" x 36"
Collection of Mr. and Mrs. Kenneth Lane Miron (Andrea Leeds Miron, class of 1975)

Literature: Harold S. Sniffen, *Antonio Jacobsen—The Checklist Addenda List Number 2, Paintings and Sketches by Antonio N. G. Jacobsen (1850-1921)* (Newport News, Virginia, 1994), 29, and nos. 21 and 22

Son of a violin maker, Antonio Nicolo Gasparo Jacobsen was born in Copenhagen in 1850. To avoid conscription into the Franco-Prussian War, Jacobsen immigrated to the United States in 1873, and moved his family to America sometime after 1880.

Working in New York City, Jacobsen initially received commissions for decorating iron safes and painting ship portraits for the Old Dominion Steamship Line. The latter activity proved lucrative and made good use of his artistic talent. Jacobsen thus became one of the most accomplished and prolific marine painters in America in the late nineteenth and early twentieth centuries. Shipping lines avidly commissioned him to paint portraits of their ships for their offices, in part to promote their vessels, but also for clients to admire their ships' beauty, especially ocean-going schooners under full sail. It is estimated that Jacobsen may have painted more than six thousand ship portraits between 1873 and 1916, a remarkable accomplishment and a mark of his facility and evident popularity.[1] The Mariners' Museum in Newport News, Virginia owns the largest collection of his work.

Jacobsen's masterful ability to record in meticulous detail every feature of the vessel, conveying to knowledgeable viewers a wealth of information about the ship, is strikingly evident in this picture. The presence of numerous signal flags indicates that this would have been a special portrait done to celebrate a holiday. Jacobsen cleverly places the company's name on a flag, the bow of the boat, and on a buoy in the foreground. Lively specks of paint indicate passengers crowded together on the decks. Although clients typically commissioned Jacobsen to made several replicas of a ship's portrait—he painted at least one other portrait of the Gover-

nor Dingley (ca. 1910, Maine Historical Society)—none that presents the vessel in holiday dress has yet been discovered.[2]

At the turn of the century, during the golden years of steamship passenger service, Portland was a primary destination for tourists. The maritime historian, William Frappier, has estimated that the number of visitors who arrived by ship to the Casco Bay area exceeded 450,000, not including the number of island commuters, who regularly used the ferries to travel to the mainland.[3] In Casco Bay alone, there were ninety-eight wharf landings and as many as forty-five companies operating ninety-eight coal-fired steamboats; the city of Portland operated a total of eleven wharves to handle the traffic during the peak season. Governor Dingley, the ship portrayed here, was built in 1899 by the Delaware River Ironworks and named for Nelson Dingley (1832-99), the governor of Maine from 1874 to 1882, whose primary concerns were prohibition, free public education, and reform in the taxation of railroads and corporations.[4]

Rebecca Lawton

---

[1] Harold S. Sniffen, *Antonio Jacobsen's Painted Ships on Painted Oceans* (Newport News, Virginia, 1994), 31.

[2] Letter of Louis J. Dianni to Kenneth Miron, 1 April 1994, courtesy Kenneth and Andrea Miron. See also Harold S. Sniffen, *Antonio Jacobsen—The Checklist Addenda List Number 2, Paintings and Sketches by Antonio N. G. Jacobsen (1850-1921)* (Newport News, Virginia, 1994), 29, nos. 21 and 22.

[3] William Frappier, *Steamboat Yesterdays: The Steamboat Era in Maine's Calendar Islands Region* (Toronto, 1993), 32.

[4] Robert Sobel and John Raimo, eds., *Biographical Directory of the Governors of the United States 1789-1978* (Westport, Connecticut, 1978), 2:616.

54

Douglas Harvey
British (fl. 1853-72)

Oberon and the Mermaid (1853)
Oil on canvas
53$^1/_2$" x 39"
Signature: lower left, "Douglas S. Harvey Rome 1853"
Lent by Nancy G. Harrison, class of 1974

Provenance: Sotheby's, New York, 10 November 1998, lot 135

As Jeremy Maas has written, fairy painting was very close to the center of the Victorian psyche by opposing many elements that formed part of the Victorian life, which included the escapist desires from the daily life of dreary hardship, attitudes toward sexuality restricted by religious teachings, and reactions to new technological and scientific advances. The supernatural world of fantastic creatures and settings offered an antidote to the realist dogma espoused by influential writers on art such as John Ruskin.[1]

One of the most important sources of fairy subject matter was the work of William Shakespeare, whose plays regained great popularity in 1789 with the foundation of Boydell's Shakespeare Gallery. Boydell commissioned works from leading artists, including Sir Joshua Reynolds and Henry Fuseli. These works were engraved for publication four years later. Shakespeare used Oberon as a source for *A Midsummer Night's Dream* and the subject was the inspiration for many a Victorian fairy painting, such as this one. Oberon, King of the Fairies, made his first appearance in literature in Medieval French prose romances, such as the fifteenth-century *Huon of Bordeaux*. His name ultimately derives from the French translation of Alberich, the dwarf of Teutonic legend, which is why he is often portrayed as being diminutive in stature.

Claude Piening

---

[1]   Jeremy Maas, *Victorian Fairy Painting* (London, 1997), 11.

55

Unkoku Toeki
Japanese (1591-1644)

Six-Fold Screen with Tiger
Brush and ink on paper mounted on silk
66³/₄" x 138¹/₂"
Signature: signed on bamboo, upper left edge
Lent by Joan and Robert Bernhard (Joan E. Mack, class of 1953)

Unkoku Toeki was the second son of Unkoku Togan (1547-1616), a well-known painter who served the warrior ruler of Hagi, a provincial castle town in what is presently Yamaguchi prefecture. Togan positioned himself within the artistic lineage of the eminent fifteenth-century painter, Sesshu, the artist credited with establishing a long-lasting Japanese tradition of ink painting based on Chinese models. Although most of Togan's works reveal the characteristic Sesshu stylistic tendencies of dependence on black ink, crisp description of forms, and stable compositions, the artist also strayed from the Sesshu model by painting works in color on a gold-leaf ground, as was popular in the late sixteenth century. Toeki inherited both his father's position as Hagi's official painter as well as his stylistic tendencies, and established a workshop to perpetuate the Unkoku family painting tradition. The Unkoku workshop continued as an important presence in provincial Japanese painting until the eighteenth century, when the power of its primary warrior patron declined.

This painting portrays a tiger in a bamboo grove, a subject very popular with the warrior class during Toeki's years of activity. The origins of tiger imagery are rooted in Chinese and Taoist lore, where the tiger was often paired with the dragon as beasts linked, respectively, to wind and clouds. By Toeki's time, however, the tiger was often depicted without the dragon, as a secular symbol of worldly power. The folding-screen format of this painting was very common for monumental paintings in Japan, and such screens were most often created in pairs. The missing screen in this case thus probably depicted a leopard, which was thought to be the female of the species, or a dragon.

James Mundy, class of 1974

56

Jules Lefebvre
French (1836-1911)

Rachel, or *Portrait of a Young Girl* (ca. 1900)
Red chalk with blue-pencil framing lines
19^1/$_{16}$" x 12^5/$_8$"
Signature: lower right, "Jules Lefebvre"
Inscription: upper left, "Rachel"
Private collection

Jules Lefebvre was an academic painter who exhibited no fewer than seventy-two portraits in the Parisian Salons between 1855 and 1898. He was recognized by his peers as one of the best painters of the female nude, rivaled only by Adolphe William Bouguereau (1825-1905). Indeed Lefebvre's *Odalisque* of 1874 "exemplifies the hot-house bourgeois eroticism for which France was famous throughout the nineteenth century," a quality that made him especially sought after by American collectors during the period.[1]

When Lefebvre drew this study of the biblical heroine, Rachel, he was a professor at the Académie Julian in Paris, and respected for his "sensitivity to precision in his students' life drawing despite the abstract idealism of the figures in his own [work]."[2] His handling of different textures and surfaces in this chalk drawing nonetheless attests to his careful observation of nature and his brilliance as a draughtsman. Rachel's skin is soft and youthful, light reflects off the metal earring, and the flowing wrap around her head is clearly distinguished from the long hair it covers. Lefebvre's *Rachel* also embodies the ideal, for she was the woman with whom Jacob fell in love and for whose hand in marriage he worked no less than fourteen years in the service of Laban, her father.

The quick strokes and flourishes, especially in Rachel's dress and hair, may also attest to this veteran painter's move, around 1900, toward a style more characteristic of the Belle Epoque than his earlier Salon portraits.

Francesca Consagra

---

[1] Richard R. Brettell, *French Salon Artists: 1800-1900* (New York, 1987,) 99.

[2] Julius Kaplan, "Jules(-Joseph) Lefebvre," in *Dictionary of Art*, ed. Jane Turner (New York, 1996), 19:65-66.

Rachel.

57

Charles-Emile-Auguste Carolus-Duran
French (1837-1917)

Portrait of a Studio Model (1885)
Oil on canvas
18⅛" x 15"
Signature: upper right, "C D 85"
Private collection

Charles-Emile-Auguste Carolus-Duran is best known to the American audience as the Parisian teacher of the great Anglo-American portraitist, John Singer Sargent, and the subject of one of Sargent's most impressive likenesses, now in the collection of the Sterling and Francine Clark Institute in Williamstown, Massachusetts. Carolus-Duran himself has not been the subject of much intensive scholarly study. A native of Lille, he moved to Paris in 1853, where he studied with the David pupil, François Souchon, and exhibited at the Salon for the first time in 1859. He became part of the realist circle around Courbet and Manet during this period. The artist resided in Rome between 1862 and 1866 and returned to France via Spain in 1868. He sat out the 1870 Commune in Brussels and returned to Paris to open a studio in 1872. From this period, he derived his livelihood primarily as a society and celebrity portraitist, whose sitters included Manet and Gustave Doré. In addition, he won several commissions later in his career for religious and history painting. He became the director of the Académie de France in Rome in 1904.

This study of a bearded model, dated 1885, has not yet been connected to a known composition by the artist, and its execution may have been the result of an academic exercise in the studio of the by then well-established and successful artist.

James Mundy, class of 1974

58

Edgar Degas
French (1834-1917)

Dancer Tying her Slipper (1880-85)
Pastel and black chalk on buff paper mounted at edges on board
18⅝" x 16⅞"
Signature: lower left, "Degas"
Lent by Anne Hendricks Bass, class of 1963

Provenance: Boussod, Valadon et Cie, Paris, until 1907; Mr. and Mrs. H. O. Havemeyer, New York, 1907-29; Electra Havemeyer Webb, New York, 1929-60; Electra Webb Bostwick from 1960; Hirschl and Adler, New York; Acquavella Galleries, New York, until 1981; Thomas Gibson Fine Art, London; Juan Alvarez de Toledo; Christie's, New York, 12 November 1985, lot 22

Literature: Lilian Browse, *Degas Dancers* (London, 1949), 378, no. 119; *H. O. Havemeyer Collection: Catalogue of Paintings, Prints, Sculpture and Objects of Art* (Portland, Maine, 1930), 380; P. A. Lemoisne, *Degas et son œuvre*, 4 vols. (Paris, 1946), no. 913; George T. M. Shackelford, *Degas: The Dancers* (Washington, D.C., 1984), 93-94 and 141, no. 39; *Splendid Legacy: The Havemeyer Collection* (New York, 1993), 333, no. 233, pl. 41; Frances Weitzenhoffer, *The Havemeyers: Impressionism Comes to America* (New York, 1986), 130

Exhibitions: *Prints, Drawings, and Bronzes: By Degas*, Grolier Club, New York, 26 January-28 February 1922, no. 33; *Degas: The Dancers*, National Gallery of Art, Washington, D.C., 22 November 1984-10 March 1985, no. 39; *Splendid Legacy: The Havemeyer Collection*, Metropolitan Museum of Art, New York, 27 March-20 June 1993, no. 233

Edgar Degas's life-long fascination with ballet and its dancers as subjects is well known. So thoroughly and well did he mine the subject for its beauty and complexity that it seems to have deterred later artists from approaching the subject. Of the hundreds of paintings, drawings, prints, and sculptures that focus on the world of dance, some of the most compelling are the studies of dancers at rest, usually in the context of instruction and rehearsal. While the body as performing instrument makes for a dramatic subject, the candid poses of dancers rubbing sore muscles, adjusting their costumes, yawning, or waiting, combine aspects of formal compositional beauty with that of the humanity, heroic anonymity, and universality of the gestures of everyday life. In this way, Degas's dancers form a cultured counterpoint to the same heroic anonymity of the women in Winslow Homer's art.

This exquisite pastel in blues, yellows, and whites over a matrix of black chalk portrays a young dancer caught off-guard while tying the ribbon of her slipper. Her face is averted from the viewer, as are many of Degas's dancers. The elevated point of view selected by the artist helps us concentrate on the most abstract arrangement of forms that her pose achieves. The visual flourish of the stiff tulle of the tutu reminds us of a rose, or one of the confections in the millinery shops that Degas also liked to depict.

Shackelford has skillfully demonstrated how the Bass pastel served, in a sense, as a middle point in a sequence of studies beginning with that which finds fruition in a painting in the Metropolitan Museum (also a Havemeyer picture) and a pastel in the collection of the Dixon Gallery and Gardens in Memphis. The immediate study for the Met's painting was published by Browse as figure 115a and is now in the National Gallery of Victoria, Melbourne.[1] Degas's interest in and ability to follow the full range of such a gesture has an almost cinematic quality to it, or, more likely, a sequence more scientifically demonstrated by the contemporary motion photography of Marey and Muybridge.

The illustrious pedigree for this pastel can be traced, practically without pause, to the artist. There is some disagreement among scholars as to when it emerged from Degas's studio, the authors of the 1993 Havemeyer exhibition at the Met state that it was in the Havemeyers' hands as of 1907, while Browse cites a reference to it in the public sales catalogues of the Degas studio of 1918-19.[2]

James Mundy, class of 1974

---

[1] Lilian Browse, *Degas Dancers* (London, 1949), 376.

[2] Alice Cooney Frelinghuysen et al., *Splendid Legacy: The Havemeyer Collection* (New York, 1993), 333, no. 233, pl. 41; Browse, Degas Dancers, 378, no. 119.

59

Edgar Degas
French (1834-1917)

Horse Balking (modeled 1888-90; cast 1919-21)
Bronze
Height, 11³/₈"
Inscription: "cire perdue A.A. Hébard Degas #48 D"
Promised Gift of Marian Phelps Pawlick, class of 1948

Provenance: Mark Oliver, London; Alex Reid and Lefevre, London; Sir Archibald Jamieson, London; Lady Jamieson, Washington, D.C.; Alex Reid and Lefevre, London; Private collection, Hewlitt Bay, New York

Degas's bronze sculptures, all produced posthumously without the artist's consent, introduce a number of complicated questions into the discussion of their place in the history of art and the artist's own œuvre. Following the artist's death in 1917, a large number of fragile wax and clay sculptures were found in his studio and seventy-three of them were cast in editions of twenty-two examples, each identified by a letter from A to T plus two, inscribed "HER" and "HERD," not intended for sale, that went to the foundry and the Degas heirs. Fifteen of the seventy-three sculptures portrayed horses. The present sculpture is the fourth bronze cast of the forty-eighth sculpture.[1]

Wilkin quotes from the memoir of a friend of the artist's, François Thiébault-Sisson, who recalled in 1921 that Degas said, "I modeled animals and people in wax for my own satisfaction, not to take a rest from painting or drawing, but to give more expression, more spirit, and more life to my paintings and drawings. They are exercises to get me started…and since, after all, no one will ever see these efforts, no one should think of speaking about them, not even you. After my death, all that will fall apart by itself, and that will be better for my reputation."[2] Historically, then, we view these sculptures as we would sketches, works not necessarily intended for the public's view with the artist's imprimatur, but nevertheless important for our fullest understanding of his creative breadth. It is well to keep in mind however that, unlike a sketch made by the hand of the artist, in these bronze casts we are looking at something removed at least one step farther from the artist, since they are based on figures molded in wax and clay. The introduction of a further intermediate set of hands, namely those that make the plaster mold from the wax original, of course raises questions as to whether we should be experiencing these works in the chosen bronze medium. These and further aspects of the problematic relationship between wax originals and the posthumous bronze casts are reviewed by Roger J. Crum.[3]

The "A" and "P" castings of *Horse Balking* have recently been exhibited.[4] In their publication we are reminded that Millard was the first to note that a number of Degas's drawings and sculptures of horses, including the one here, were modeled after the photographic motion studies of Eadweard Muybridge, published in 1887. Gary Tinterow has made a persuasive case for understanding this sculpture not, as previously thought, as a horse about to clear an obstacle, but rather one imbued with a balking and rearing hesitancy that combines a number of more expressive motivations than simple jumping.[5] Tinterow's deduction is important because it underscores the range of nuance with which Degas was able to engage by modeling his series of fifteen horses. The final results move from the classic in pose to the more spontaneous, and connect, finally, with his long-term interest in horses, their riders, and, logically, the racecourse.[6]

Degas's *Horse Balking* is an important work because it engages the student in questions regarding issues at the core of artistic creation and, ultimately, beauty. It helps to reveal an intimate aspect of the artist's working method and artistic sensibility, for which the beholder must ultimately acknowledge the positive effect of the bronzes' salvation from destruction in 1917.

James Mundy, class of 1974

---

[1] For full discussion of these issues, see Karen Wilkin, "Considering Edgar Degas," in idem, *Edgar Degas: The Many Dimensions of a Master French Impressionist* (Dayton, Ohio, 1994), 22-30; and Charles Millard, *The Sculpture of Edgar Degas* (Princeton, 1976).

[2] Wilkin, "Considering Edgar Degas," 23.

[3] Roger J. Crum, "Degas Bronzes?" *Art Journal* 54 (Spring 1995): 93-98.

[4] Jean Sutherland Boggs, *Degas* (Paris, Ottawa, and New York, 1988), 460-61, no. 280.

[5] Ibid.

[6] For more on this topic, see Denys Sutton, "Degas: Master of the Horse," *Apollo* 266 (April 1984): 282-93.

60

Edgar Degas
French (1834-1917)

Mary Cassatt at the Louvre, The Etruscan Gallery (ca. 1879-80)
Softground etching, aquatint, drypoint, and etching printed in black; ix/ix
10⅝" x 9¼", platemark
Promised Gift of Marian Phelps Pawlick, class of 1948

Degas intended to use this print to advertise the first issue of a projected journal, *Le Jour e la Nuit,* in conjunction with the fifth Impressionist exhibition of 1880. The print is considered the first that Degas clearly intended to publish and exhibit.[1] Understandably, he wanted to present himself as a skilled professional in his debut as a printmaker. He thus composed a number of preliminary drawings and nine different states of the print before he thought it publishable.

The print depicts two women studying a tomb sculpture in the Etruscan Gallery of the Louvre. Although Degas himself did not identify them, his first cataloguer, Loys Delteil, described the elegant standing figure as the American artist, Mary Cassatt.[2] Her seated companion has sometimes been regarded as Cassatt's older sister, Lydia, who came to live with the artist in Paris in 1877.[3] Callen notes that Degas rendered Cassatt in anonymity, as a bourgeois woman enjoying a socially acceptable pastime, with her back toward the viewer.[4] Degas, she argues, would never have depicted a male peer in such a manner; instead the artist would have presented him as an acknowledged professional in a public space.

The print itself is richly intricate. Degas demarks different textiles, reflections, and gestures by using numerous printmaking techniques. He translates the light reflections in the gallery by burnishing portions of the acquatint around the glass case, the rich fur of the hats by adding drypoint, and the parallel lines of the etching needle to characterize Lydia's light-colored coat over her skirt, which is darkly rendered in acquatint.

This impression is the final state from an edition of fifty for the proposed journal.[5]

Francesca Consagra

---

[1] Richard R. Brettell and Suzanne Folds McCullagh, *Degas in the Art Institute of Chicago* (New York, 1984), nos. 50-51.

[2] Loys Delteil, *Le Peintre-graveur illustre* (Paris, 1919), 9:no. 30.

[3] Frederick Arnold Sweet, *Miss Mary Cassatt, Impressionist from Pennsylvania* (Norman, Oklahoma, 1966), 33.

[4] Anthea Callen, *The Spectacular Body: Science, Method, and Meaning in the work of Degas* (New Haven, 1995), 172.

[5] Delteil's sixth state, and Reed and Shapiro's ninth; see Sue Welsh Reed and Barbara Stern Shapiro, *Edgar Degas: The Painter as Printmaker* (Boston, 1984), 174.

61

Camille Pissarro
French (1830-1903)

Le Clos de la Mère Lucien, Éragny (1898)
Oil on canvas
21^1/$_4$" x 25^1/$_2$"
Signature: lower left, "C. Pissarro. 1898"
Promised Gift of Marian Phelps Pawlick, class of 1948

Literature: L. R. Pissarro and L. Venturi, *Camille Pissarro: Son Art—Son Œuvre* (Paris, 1939), 1:225, no. 1033 and 2:pl. 207

About two hours' traveling distance from Paris, Pissarro's country home in Eragny provided him with a rich source of artistic inspiration and a place to retreat from the professional, social, and political pressures of Paris. The artist portrayed his house and grounds, rich in fruit trees and flowers, well over two hundred times between his acquisition of the property in March 1884 and his death in 1903. This painting of his house and orchard was executed, judging from the early growth on the trees, in May 1898, just after Pissarro returned to Eragny after spending the first part of the year in Paris, executing a series of city scenes from his room in the Grand Hôtel du Louvre. *Le Clos de la Mère Lucien, Éragny* was painted with a couple of other canvases at Eragny before Pissarro and his wife, Julie, went on a trip to Dijon, Mâcon, Lyons, and Grancy-sur-Ource in June. By far the most canvases of this year were painted in Rouen between August and October. Thus, it survives as one of only about eight Eragny landscapes from this year.

The painting of the house and garden at Eragny stresses very strong compositional elements, particularly the trees in the foreground, which knit the composition together in a latticelike overlay of branches.

In regard to subject matter, the later years of Pissarro's career were also times when he took a greater interest in portraying the labors of the peasantry within luminous natural environments. The stability of this painting, which combines landscape, architecture, and laboring figures, suggests a synthesis that the artist was working toward at century's end. This synthesis is also to be found in the incorporation of many lessons learned from the Post-Impressionists, Seurat, Signac, and Cézanne, who he included among his friends. The year 1898 also saw Pissarro in the role of mentor to the young artist, Henri Matisse, who sought his advice on many matters and received much encouragement from the elderly Impressionist.

James Mundy, class of 1974

62

Jean-François Raffaëlli
French (1850-1924)

Salvation Army, Jersey (ca. 1879-86)
Oil on canvas
$20^1/_2$" x $26^1/_2$"
Signature: lower right, "J.F. Raffaëlli"
Promised Gift of Marian Phelps Pawlick, class of 1948

Provenance: Henri Duhem; Christie's, 3 November 1981, lot 40

Literature: Arséne Alexandre, *Jean-François Raffaëlli* (Paris, 1909), 180

Born into a family of privilege, Jean-François Raffaëlli made his artistic reputation as a realist artist who explored the lives of those who dwelled in the margins of society, painting a cosmetically unaltered and unromanticized view of the *comédie humaine.* His portrayals of ragpickers, absinthe drinkers, peasants, and industrial workers were part of a philosophy that explored the sociological implications of these groups, a concept he named *caractérisme.* While well-known as a French realist, he also exhibited with the Impressionists in 1880 and 1881, thanks to the influence of his friend and champion, Edgar Degas. While some of the other Impressionists found his art contrary to their purposes and would not exhibit with him, critics lauded his efforts, particularly the deGoncourt brothers, Émile Zola, and J.-K. Huysmans. His most striking scenes of social realism were painted during the 1870s and 80s.

His painting, *Salvation Army, Jersey,* is undated, yet was exhibited in the Salon of 1886.[1] The choice of subject matter, a hymn-singing revival meeting on the streets of Jersey, is an unusual one. On the street is a folded copy of the Salvation Army's weekly publication, *War Cry,* which was first published in 1879.[2] This provides us with a *terminus post quem* with which to arrive at a date for the picture. Furthermore, given that the most fervent early activity of the Salvation Army in the 1880s coincided with Raffaëlli's most intense period of social commentary, it is reasonable to assign this painting to that decade. In the painting, many of the hymn-singing crowd members seem to be portrait likenesses of the type that Raffaëlli often studied. It is quite possible that he, like other realist painters of the period, made use of photography as a mode of study and reference for his art.[3]

James Mundy, class of 1974

---

[1]   B. S. Fields, "Jean-François Raffaëlli (1850-1924): The Naturalist Artist," Ph.D. diss. (Columbia University, 1979), 357. The work was no. 3259 in the Salon and listed as a "heightened drawing."

[2]   Herbert A. Wisbey, Jr., *Soldiers Without Swords* (New York, 1955), 42. On the further history of the Salvation Army and its publication, see Norman H. Murdoch, *Origins of the Salvation Army* (Knoxville, Tennessee, ca. 1994).

[3]   See Gabriel P. Weisberg, *Beyond Impressionism: The Naturalist Impulse* (New York, 1992), 24-47.

SALVATION
FOR ME TO
LIVE IS
CHRIST
WAR CRY
JF RAFFAELLI

63

Paul Cézanne
French (1839-1906)

Teapot and Oranges (also known as *The Tablecloth*; 1895-1900)
Pencil and watercolor
$18^{1}/_{2}$" x $24^{3}/_{8}$"
Lent by Elizabeth L. Eisenstein, class of 1945-4

Provenance: Paul Cézanne *fils*, Paris; Walther Halvorsen, Oslo; Conrad Pineus, Goteborg; Samuel A. Lewisohn, New York; Mr. and Mrs. Julian Eisenstein, Washington, D.C.

Literature: Paul Cézanne, *Paul Cézanne, letters*, ed. John Rewald, trans. Seymour Hacker (New York, 1984), 198; John Elderfield, "Drawing in Cézanne," *Artforum* 19 (June 1971): 56; S. A. Lewisohn, *Painters and Personality* (New York, 1937), pl. 14; J. Meier-Graefe, *Cézanne und seine Ahnen* (Munich, 1921), pl. xix, pl. 101; G. Nicodemi, *Cézanne disegni* (Milan, 1944), fig. 68; John Rewald, *Paul Cézanne: the watercolours: a catalogue raisonné* (London, 1983), no. 544; G. Riviere, *Le Maître Paul Cézanne* (Paris, 1923), 220; Theodore Rousseau, Jr., *The Lewisohn Collection: A Catalogue of the Paintings, Watercolors, and Drawings, Prints, and Sculpture Shown in a Special Exhibition* (New York, 1951); William Rubin, ed., *Cézanne: The Late Work* (New York and Boston, ca. 1977), pl. 171; Lionello Venturi, *Cézanne: Son art, son oeuvre*, 2 vols. (Paris, 1936), 2:no. 1150

Exhibitions: *Rétrospective de Cézanne*, Salon d'Automne, Paris, 1907, no. 37; *Paintings and Drawings by Paul Cézanne*, Leicester Galleries, London, 1925, no. 28; *Erste Sonderausstellung*, Galerie Thannhauser, Berlin, 1927, no. 31; *Fifth-Anniversary Exhibition*, Museum of Modern Art, New York, 1934-35, no. 9; *Cézanne Centennial Exhibition*, Marie Harriman Gallery, New York, 1939, no. 29; *Watercolors by Paul Cézanne*, Columbus Gallery of Fine Arts, Ohio, 1939-40, no. 13; *Cézanne*, Wildenstein Galleries, New York, 1947, no. 81; *The Lewisohn Collection*, Metropolitan Museum of Art, New York, 1951, 44, no. 103; *Cézanne, Paintings, Watercolors, and Drawings*, Art Institute of Chicago and Metropolitan Museum of Art, 1952, no. 87, ill.; *Exposition pour commémorer le cinquantaine de la mort de Cézanne*, Pavillon de Vendome, Aix-en-Provence, 1956, no. 78; *Centennial Loan Exhibition*, Vassar College, Poughkeepsie, New York, and Wildenstein Galleries, New York, 1961, no. 91; *Cézanne Watercolors*, Knoedler & Co., Inc., New York, 1963, 54-55, no. 60, pl. lxii; *Cézanne: An Exhibition in Honor of the Fiftieth Anniversary of The Phillips Collection*, Phillips Collection, Washington, D.C., 1971; Art Institute of Chicago and Museum of Fine Arts, Boston, 1971, no. 50

Cézanne, the central figure in Post-Impressionism, began painting watercolors seriously in the mid-1860s, and his exploration of the medium's intrinsic qualities (transparency and lightness) continued until his death in 1906. During this time, his approach varied from the heavy use of color applied in a bold and turbulent manner to a greater interplay of transparent washes as a means to create vibrantly fragmented surfaces.

Cézanne rarely dated his works, which makes it hard to pinpoint the chronology of his watercolors. It is generally believed that this well-published watercolor (once part of the Lewisohn collection) dates from 1895-1900, for several reasons. During this period, Cézanne increasingly left areas of the paper blank, giving the impression of fullness and space. The setting of the still life also becomes less important, while the objects, in this case the fruits, are solidly emphasized with strong contours and vivid hues.

Cézanne's own son-in-law, Paul Cézanne *fils*, titled this work *La nappe* (The tablecloth), because of the large white tablecloth on which the fruits and teapot rest.[1] The tablecloth takes on "the majesty of [a] mountain," with its high peaks and well-contoured folds.[2] These folds in deep translucent shadow especially add to the composition's complex richness of color and sense of depth to the

point that Rewald perceived that there were two pieces of cloth (a blue-green one overlapping the white) over a scallop-shaped wooden table.[3] Instead, it appears to be a single white tablecloth, heavily shadowed in overlapping transparent strokes of blue and green, hanging over a straight-edged table with a drawer, as seen in other still lifes done just before or around 1900.[4]

Apparent in this watercolor also is Cézanne's brilliant use of the medium, especially in the diverse use of contour lines and washes to distinguish different objects in the still life. The white teapot, for instance, is demarked only by its contours, which are penciled and then shadowed in blue wash. The body of the pot is left uncolored, and yet distinctly read as a rounded porcelain form. Cézanne then juxtaposes the teapot to the wall behind it and the top right fold of the tablecloth, both of which also show a good deal of the paper or support, uncolored and untouched. Yet, the viewer reads them as plaster and fabric respectively because Cézanne handles the contours of these areas completely differently, though always economically, with just a hint of wash or a couple of nervous lines of pencil.

It was such experimentation in his watercolors that led Cézanne to apply paint more thinly in his paintings, increasing the effect of

light and leaving patches and spaces of his canvas bare.[5] His handling of the planes of transparent wash, as evidenced in the blue-green shadowing of the cloth, also foretell cubism, in that the luminous planes begin to take on a life of their own to the left of the sheet, anchored only by the weight and solidity of the rounded forms of the oranges and teapot at right. The watercolor thus brilliantly reflects two poles in Cézanne's work: transparent splashes of color and calligraphic contours of form.

Francesca Consagra

[1] John Rewald, *Paul Cézanne: the watercolours: a catalogue raisonné* (London, 1983), 221.

[2] Theodore Rousseau, Jr., *The Lewisohn Collection: A Catalogue of the Paintings, Watercolors, and Drawings, Prints, and Sculpture Shown in a Special Exhibition* (New York, 1951), 75.

[3] Rewald, *Paul Cézanne: the watercolours*, 221.

[4] Lionello Venturi, *Cézanne: Son art, son oeuvre*, 2 vols. (Paris, 1936), 2:nos. 735, 740, 742, 743, 1567.

[5] Rousseau, *The Lewisohn Collection*, 76.

64

Auguste Rodin
French (1840-1917)

*Grande Main Crispée (*Large clenched hand; ca. 1885; cast 1964)
Bronze with brownish-black patina
Height, 18^1/$_4$"; width, 12^1/$_4$"; depth, 9"
Signature: on wrist, "A. Rodin"
Inscriptions: back lower edge toward right of base, "Georges Rudier./ Fondeur. PARIS"; "© by Musée Rodin. 1964."
Lent by Phyllis Lambert, class of 1948, Montréal

Literature: A. E. Elsen, *Rodin* (New York, 1963), 80-81; J. de Caso and P. B. Sanders, *Rodin's Sculpture* (San Francisco, 1977), 323-25, no. 68; John L. Tancock, *The Sculpture of Auguste Rodin* (Philadelphia, 1976), 616-17, no. 119

Exhibitions: *Rodin à Quebec*, Musée de Quebec, 1998, no. 83

Auguste Rodin left, at his death, a number of studies of hands and other fragments of figures intended as preparatory or alternative studies for larger projects. This expressive study of a contorted right hand, known alternatively in its English translation as *The Mighty Hand* and *The Large Clenched Hand*, is ultimately better referred to by its French appellation, *Grande Main Crispée*. Authors on Rodin are of several opinions regarding the ultimate use for these studies, some seeing a relationship between this work and the dramatic manual expressiveness of *The Burghers of Calais*, while others see this hand as a rejected preparatory model for one of the hands of the damned in his monumental *Gates of Hell* (Paris). All are of the opinion that it was modeled around the year 1885, the present cast completed some eighty years later. Numerous casts of this hand survive. Tancock lists a dozen, a figure which does not include the present sculpture. Rodin followed this clenched right hand with a left hand, which survives in fewer examples.

Tancock was also the first to delve into sources and influences on Rodin in such hand studies as this one. He cites the possible influence of the contemporary motion studies by the photographer, Eadweard Muybridge, as well as a pen-and-wash drawing entitled *The Dream*, by Victor Hugo, a friend of Rodin's, of a similar contorted hand executed at some point before the writer's death in 1885.[1] Other authors, such as de Caso and Sanders, have evoked the anguished hands of the crucified Christ in Matthias Grünewald's *Isenheim Altarpiece* (Musée Unterlinden, Colmar) as analogies in the history of art to Rodin's dramatic disembodied hand.[2]

James Mundy, class of 1974

---

[1] John L. Tancock, *The Sculpture of Auguste Rodin* (Philadelphia, 1976), 616-17, no. 119.

[2] J. de Caso and P. B. Sanders, *Rodin's Sculpture* (San Francisco, 1977), 323-25, no. 68.

65

Eugène Carrière
French (1849-1906)

Portrait of Arsène Carrière (1905)
Oil on canvas
$16^1/_4$" x $13^1/_2$"
Signature: lower left, "Eugene Carrière"
Promised Gift of Nancy G. Harrison, class of 1974

Provenance: Vente Atelier Carrière, Galerie Manzi, Joyant et cie, 2-3 February 1920, no. 84; Georges Viau, Paris; Herbert Harvey, Jr., New Orleans, sale 1981

Literature: Élie Faure, *Les maitres de l'art moderne: Eugène Carrière, peintre et lithographe* (Paris, 1908), cover illustration

One of the curiosities of art history concerns artists who, after occupying central positions within a cultural movement during their lives, plummet into obscurity after their deaths, only to be reconsidered at a later date with fresh eyes by scholars and critics. Such is the case with Eugène Carrière, the symbolist who was at the center of a circle of friends that included the artists, Rodin and Gauguin, as well as the poets, Mallarmé and Verlaine. Carrière's paintings are distinguished by a choice of usually simple subject matter taken from his domestic surroundings, such as mothers and children, sickness, figures studies, and a few landscapes painted with a monochrome palette based on variations of brown and olive pigments. One can find in his art an inversion of Impressionist purpose, where the inherent mysteries of the nocturnal and umbral replace the visceral pleasure of the visible. His was a deeply internalized and emotional world, with much of the weight yet less of the horror of Munch.

The portrait of his youngest child, Arsène, was painted during the artist's last year, while he was dying of throat cancer in 1905. It forms a complement to his *Portrait of Elise*, of the same year and roughly the same size.[1] A second, less haunting, portrait of Arsène was painted in October of the same year, now in the collection of the Musée des Beaux-Arts, Bordeaux.[2] Evocative and haunting, the portrait confronts the viewer with the paradox of the mysteries that reside within the beloved family member, the unknowable that lies deep within the well-known. Carrière's large family stood often for the family of mankind in his philosophy, hence the obscuring of specific details of likeness in a work such as the one under discussion. This could achieve the more lasting goal of suggesting eternal bonds among young and old, mothers and children.

Robert Rosenblum, in his introduction to Bantens's book on Carrière, points out that not all were sympathetic to the almost constant penumbra that seemed to envelope the artist's subjects. He cites Degas's quip upon seeing Carrière's art, that "someone has been smoking in the nursery."[3] However, this is only in support of another of the critic's points—that there is a more complicated fabric to the birth of modernism than that represented by the four major figures in France: Seurat, Cézanne, van Gogh, and Gauguin. Symbolism and, in the case of Carrière, its occasional connection to the traditions of realism in France, are also fruitful avenues to the understanding of such things as the development of Picasso's Rose and Blue Periods of the first decade of the twentieth century.[4]

James Mundy, class of 1974

[1] Illustrated in Robert James Bantens, *Eugène Carrière: The Symbol of Creation* (New York, 1990), fig. 74.

[2] Illustrated in Musée de Saint-Cloud, *Eugène Carrière, le peintre et son univers autour de 1900* (Saint-Cloud, 1996), 57, no. 25.

[3] Bantens, *Eugène Carrière*, 13.

[4] Bantens, *Eugène Carrière*, 8 and 15.

66

Edouard Vuillard
French (1868-1940)

Self-Portrait (1892)
Oil on board
$14^{1}/_{8}$" x $11^{1}/_{4}$"
Signature: lower right, "E. Vuillard"
Collection of Frances L. Brody, class of 1937

Literature: Andrew Carnduff Ritchie, *Edouard Vuillard* (New York, 1954), 101 and frontispiece; John Russell, *Edouard Vuillard 1868-1940* (London, 1971), no. 9; Elizabeth Wynne Easton, *The Intimate Interiors of Edouard Vuillard* (Washington, D.C., 1989), *22*, no. 6

Exhibitions: *Edouard Vuillard*, Museum of Modern Art, New York, 1954; *Edouard Vuillard 1868-1940*, Toronto Art Gallery of Ontario, Toronto, 1971, no. 9; *The Intimate Interiors of Edouard Vuillard*, Museum of Fine Arts, Houston, 1989, no. 6

Considering the length and breadth of Edouard Vuillard's career, his participation with the Nabis was, arguably, his period of greatest productivity and largest contribution. Vuillard started his art studies in Paris in 1886 and within three years had fallen in with a group of young painters who took the name, "Nabis," derived from the Hebrew word for "prophet." The other members of the group were Maurice Denis, Pierre Bonnard, Henri Ibels, Felix Vallotton, Paul Ranson, and Paul Serusier. The group was greatly influenced by the work of Gauguin that they saw in the exhibition, *Peintres symbolistes et synthetistes* in 1889. They also set themselves apart from the rest of society by adopting special costumes, language, and coded correspondence. By 1891, Vuillard had begun exhibiting with the Nabis at various locations in Paris and was promoted by the influential critics, Arsène Alexandre (author of the monograph on Raffaëlli), Roger Marx, and Albert Aurier. From this period until World War I, Vuillard was at the center of intellectual and artistic life in France.

This portrait, made at the height of the Nabis camaraderie, is one of three similar self-portraits of the same time. The other two are in private collections in this country and France[1] that show us a confident young artist with a forthright presentation, who assesses the world with a directness not found in Vuillard's earlier self-portraits. Light strikes his face strongly, like the sun illuminating the moon, creating contrasts between the bright yellow hair in full light and that in shadow, where it turns a deep, dark brown. The red beard and harsh, pink skin are equally and startlingly lit in similar fashion. One is reminded of some of Van Gogh's self-portraits of several years earlier.

James Mundy, class of 1974

---

[1] Illustrated in John Russell, *Edouard Vuillard 1868-1940* (London, 1971), no. 8; and Elizabeth Wynne Easton, *The Intimate Interiors of Edouard Vuillard* (Washington, D.C., 1989), *22*, no. 7.

67

Henri-Gabriel Ibels
French (1867-1936)

L'Acrobat (The acrobat) (ca. 1893)
Pastel and chalk on paper
$16^{1}/_{2}$" x $9^{1}/_{2}$"
Signature: lower left, "H.G. Ibels"
Lent by Bannon McHenry, class of 1952

Ibels was one of the original members of a group of artists known as the Nabis while still an art student at the Académie Julian, Paris, in 1888-89. The Nabis (Hebrew for "prophet") viewed themselves as heralds of two-dimensional design rather than pursuers of the standards of naturalism and Impressionism. "A picture," the Nabis spokesman, Maurice Denis, affirmed, "is essentially a flat surface covered with colors arranged in a certain order."[1] The group's emphatic use of shape and autonomy of surface design are best evidenced in the posters of two of its most famous members, Pierre Bonnard and Edouard Vuillard, during the 1890s.

Ibels was dubbed "*le Nabis journaliste*" because of his numerous illustrations, caricatures, and poster advertisements for journals, as well as his designs for sheet-music covers and theater programs.[2] Unlike some of the other Nabis, Ibels never succumbed to symbolism, partially because his anarchist-socialist views held that art should be relevant and useful to society rather than a chronicle of one's own dreams, anxieties, and desires.

Ibels's popularity as an artist was also due to his ability to capture on paper the various spectacles of the modern city with an economy of line and dynamic use of color—as seen in this pastel of a muscular gymnast or acrobat ready to take a flip, tumble, or to execute some other exercise across a platform. Ibels's use of repetitive strokes around the arms and legs of the performer emphasizes a sense of controlled and planned movement, and provides a heightened expectation about what acrobatic exercise he's about to do next. Indeed, this is not a sentimental picture of a circus entertainer, but rather of a heroically drawn figure that anticipates the socialist art movements of the 1930s.

Francesca Consagra

---

[1] Linda C. Hults, *The Print in the Western World* (Madison, Wisconsin, 1996), 509.

[2] Belinda Thomson, "Henri-Gabriel Ibels," in *Dictionary of Art*, ed. Jane Turner (New York, 1996), 15:58.

H. G. Ibels

68

Odilon Redon
French (1840-1916)

Flowers in a Vase (ca. 1905-13)
Pastel on paper
$27^1/_4$" x $23^1/_2$"
Signature: lower right, "Odilon Redon"
Promised Gift of Eugenie Aiguier Havemeyer, class of 1951

Provenance: Doris D. Havemeyer; Horace Havemeyer, 1934

Exhibitions: *Odilon Redon*, De Hawke & Co., Inc., New York, 1928; *Odilon Redon; Paintings, Pastels and Drawings*, Art Institute of Chicago, December 1928-January 1929

Redon is considered one of the great visionaries of French art who advocated imagination over the pursuit of realism. Until 1890 his reputation rested entirely on black-and-white works, or charcoals and lithographs, that were highly melancholic and filled with fantastic imagery, sometimes culled from the writings of Gustave Flaubert and Stéphane Mallarmé. Even late in his career (or sometime around 1903-05), when he started to draw richly colored still lives of flowers picked from his own garden, he drew them through a veil of imagination and recollection rather than present-ing them with the botanical precision of a realist:

> I have often, as an exercise and a sustenance, painted before an object down to the smallest accidents of its...appearance; but [that] left me sad and dissatisfied. The next day [when] I let the other source, that of imagination, run through the recollection of the forms, I was assured and appeased.[1]

Redon drew these flowers removed from nature, cut and arranged in a vase, and floating, with no apparent table-top or surface. The vases were often drip-glazed stoneware, simple in shape, on whose surfaces he added the most subtle hint of reflection of an external world. The intensity of his colors also played a role in his desire to enhance our perception of a natural element. Although he needed to use a glue-based fixative when he layered one color over another (as can be seen when he added blue over pink in the rose at bottom left of the arrangement in the pastel exhibited here), Redon did not fix the uppermost layers of the pastel so as not to compromise further the intensity of the color and texture provided by the medium itself.[2] The major drawback of the medium, however, is the speed in which it looses a great deal of its original color to light exposure. One can only imagine how much more vivid the colors were when Redon first applied them to this sheet and others. Surprisingly, almost ninety years later, the artist's initial desire to share his unabashed joy in color and form still remains. When discussing these flower pastels, Redon noted in 1913, "I have learned that, in the process of unfolding, life...can also reveal joy. If the art of the artist is the song of his life, a solemn or sad melody, I must have hit a happy note in color."[3]

Francesca Consagra

---

[1] Quoted in Gloria Groom, "The Late Work: The Emergence of a Decorative Aesthetic," in *Odilon Redon: Prince of Dreams, 1840-1916* (Chicago, 1994), 320.

[2] Harriet K. Stratis, "Beneath the Surface: Redon's Methods and Materials," in *Odilon Redon: Prince of Dreams, 1840-1916* (Chicago, 1994), 372.

[3] Quoted in Groom, "The Late Work," 305.

69

Edvard Munch
Norwegian (1863-1944)

The Scream (1895)
Lithograph with tusche on wove paper
13⁷/₈" x 10" image; 20¹/₈" x 14³/₄" sheet
Signature: graphite, lower right, "E Munch"; graphite, lower right, "an Frau Dr. Glaser in freundliche Errinerung" [sic]
Lent by Philip and Lynn Straus (Lynn R. Gross, class of 1946)

Provenance: Glaser Collection, Berlin (?); Spirwaroff Collection, Oslo, 23 October 1978

Literature: Elizabeth Prelinger, *Edvard Munch: Master Printmaker* (New York, 1983), 39-41, pl. 32; Gustav Schiefler, *Verzeichnis des graphischen Werkes Edvard Munchs* (reprint Oslo, 1974), no. 32; Bente Torjusen, "The Mirror," in *Edvard Munch: Symbols & Images* (Washington, D.C., 1987), 223

Exhibition: *Edvard Munch: Master Printmaker*, Neuberger Museum, State University of New York at Purchase and Harvard University Art Museums, Cambridge, Massachusetts, 1983

Munch was a Norwegian symbolist who worked frequently in Germany and was an important force behind the later expressionist movement. By 1892, he had become a hero of the German avant-garde and had finished the painting, *Despair* (Thielska Galleriet, Stockholm), in which he depicted two men wearing top hats walking away from a man looking over a rail, down into a fjord, with a harbor in the distance.

On 2 January 1892, Munch offered an interpretation of the painting:

> I walked along the road with two friends. The sun went down—the sky was blood red—and I felt a breath of sadness—I stood still tired unto death—over the blue-black fjord and city lay blood and tongues of fire. My friends continued on—I remained—trembling from fear. I felt the great infinite scream through nature.[1]

A year later, he painted on cardboard his best-known image, *The Scream* (Nasjonalgalleriet, Oslo), in which he took the basic composition of *Despair* and replaced the man looking over the rail with a figure turned towards the viewer. Its serpentine hands frame its skull-shaped head as it emits a scream; its curved body, dark as the fjord behind it, is part of this undulating cry of nature that the artist wished to capture.

Munch painted the picture in several versions. After taking up printmaking in Berlin in 1894, he also translated this strongly-hued image into a lithograph with stark, sinuous lines. He accentuated the painting's rhythmic delineations of harbor and clouds as a means to seize nature's scream and project it into the winding figure below. Without the aid of color to express this intense aural moment, he drew these lines as if they were carved out of wood rather than created with a smooth crayon; the impression of gouged lines only augmented the emotional rawness of the moment. Munch also heightened the diagonal lines of the road's railing and created sharper silhouettes of the companions beyond than those in the paintings, *The Scream* and *Despair*. The solidity of the man-made rail and the ignorance of the distant figures to the highly dissonant experience around them only serve to raise the level of despair and loneliness of the protagonist, an experience which Munch wanted to share with his viewers.

To some impressions, such as the Straus's, Munch added the lines, "*Ich fühlte das grosse Geschrei/durch die Natur*" ("I felt the great scream passing through nature"), only to explicate his point further. The Straus's copy also carries an inscription to Frau Dr. Glaser, probably the wife of the art historian, Curt Glaser, who wrote an important monograph on the artist, published in Berlin in 1917.[2]

Francesca Consagra

---

[1] Jurgen Schultze, "Verzweiflung, 1892," in *Edvard Munch* (Essen, 1987), no. 29.

[2] Curt Glaser, *Edvard Munch* (Berlin, 1917).

Geschrei

70

Edvard Munch
Norwegian (1863-1944)

Madonna, Liebendes Weib (Beloved woman)(1895)
Color lithograph with tusche and crayon, with three stones printed in greenish beige, brick-red, and black, and one woodblock printed in blue; S.33A/b/I or II (probably II; Prelinger identified the woodblock)
$23^3/_4$" x $17^3/_8$"
Signature: graphite, lower right, "Edv Munch"
Lent by Philip and Lynn Straus (Lynn R. Gross, class of 1946)

Literature: Elizabeth Prelinger, *Edvard Munch: Master Printmaker* (New York, 1983), 110; Gustav Schiefler, *Verzeichnis des graphischen Werkes Edvard Munchs* (reprint Oslo, 1974), no. 33

Exhibitions: *Edvard Munch: Master Printmaker*, Neuberger Museum, State University of New York at Purchase and Harvard University Art Museums, Cambridge, Massachusetts, 1983

As already noted in the discussion of *The Scream* (see cat. no. 69), Munch altered and experimented with the motifs of some of his earliest paintings as a means to create new works and to understand better his own emotions and desires. It was also a process that furthered his goals as a symbolist painter to reform art from the limitations of naturalism during the 1890s.

The original motif for *Madonna* appears to have been drawn by Munch as early as 1886, when he painted *Hulda*, a work now lost, in which a woman is seen from the viewpoint of her lover while making love. Munch's friend, Hans Jaeger, described her as "thrown back onto her bed, life-sized, naked down to her hips, both her hands raised up under her head, her elbows stretched out, and her dark hair falling in disarray over one of her naked shoulders."[1] During the next two decades, Munch depicted this image in various media and versions, including pastels, paintings, etchings, and lithographs, and in doing so he altered the mood or emphasis of the motif. In 1893, the original image of Hulda is transformed, in one instance, into an angel (see *The Hands*, Munch-Museet, Oslo), and in another, into a corpselike figure with a scarlet halo, or the famous painting, *Madonna*, now in the National Gallery of Oslo.

Munch originally exhibited *Madonna* in Berlin as part of a series of six paintings depicting "love," or "love seen in the constant, overpowering presence of death."[2] Scholars believe that the artist furnished the painting with a frame on which were drawn or carved spermatozoa and an embryo, as can be seen on this lithograph of the same title.[3]

Munch wrote about the Madonna as a motif of the chain of life, or the cycle of conception, birth, and death in his album, *The Tree of Knowledge of Good and Evil*:

The pause as all the world stops in its path. Moonlight glides over your face filled with all the earth's beauty and pain. Your lips are like two ruby-red serpents and filled with blood, like your crimson red fruit. They glide from one another as if in pain. The smile of a corpse. Thus now life reaches out its hand to death. The chain is forged that binds the thousands of generations that have died to the thousands of generations yet to come.[4]

This color impression of the lithograph is noteworthy for being one of the earliest examples of Munch's experiments in combination prints, which incorporate woodcuts into the lithographic process. Munch used three stones for the colors of beige, brick-red, and black. For the blue in the center, however, he used a woodblock that is discernible in the horizontal grain among the waves of hair.[5] Munch neither added the woodblock, nor the extended areas of blue, to all his color impressions of the Madonna. He thus appears to have wanted to emphasize the idea of water, or the fluid state of life from conception to death, in those impressions heavily colored in blue.

Francesca Consagra

---

[1] Reinhold Heller, "Love as a Series of Paintings," in *Edvard Munch: Symbols & Images* (Washington, D.C., 1987), 103-04.

[2] Ibid., 97.

[3] Arne Eggum, "Madonna," in *The Masterworks of Edvard Munch* (New York, 1979), no. 40.

[4] Edvard Munch, from Munch-museet ms. T2547; quoted in Heller, "Love as a Series of Paintings," 105.

[5] Elizabeth Prelinger, *Edvard Munch: Master Printmaker* (New York, 1983), 110.

71

Edvard Munch
Norwegian (1863-1944)

The Lonely Ones, or *Two People* (1908)
Oil on canvas
37 $^1/_2$" x 43$^1/_4$"
Signature: upper right, "E. Munch 1908"
Lent by Philip and Lynn Straus (Lynn R. Gross, class of 1946)

Provenance: Städtische Kunstsammlung, Chemnitz; H. Nobel Roede, Oslo

Literature: Elizabeth Prelinger, *Edvard Munch: Master Printmaker* (New York, 1983)

Exhibitions: *Edvard Munch*, Ateneumin Taidemuseo, Helsinki, January 1909, no. 9; *Edvard Munch*, National Galerie, Berlin, March-May 1927, no. 127; *Edvard Munch*, National Galeriet, Oslo, 1927, no. 182; *Edvard Munch*, Kunstutte, Chemnitz, 1929, no. 34; *Edvard Munch*, London Gallery, London, October-November 1936; *Edvard Munch, Utstelling Malerier, Akvareller, Tegninger, Grafik*, Kunstnernes Hus, Oslo, November-December 1951, no. 77; *Munch: Bilder i Privat eie*, Kunstnerforbundert, Oslo, January-February 1958, no. 22; *Edvard Munch*, Steinerneshaus, Frankfurt-am-Main, November 1962-January 1963, no. 42; *Edvard Munch*, Solomon R. Guggenheim Museum, New York, 1965, no. 48

One of Munch's most important and experimental subjects, *The Lonely Ones* is richly represented in the Straus collection by numerous drypoints and woodcuts dating from the 1890s and by this painted version of 1908.

The first ideas for this motif are found in Munch's sketchpad of 1891.[1] The image is a woman clothed in white with her back turned to the viewer to reveal blonde hair reaching just below the belt. In some of the drawings, the woman gazes across the fjord at the moon and at a boat, as if she is alone but waiting for someone to fill the space beside her. In 1891 or 1892, Munch repeated the figure in a painting (originally exhibited as *A Man and a Woman during a Summer Night*) that was lost in a shipwreck in December 1901. However, a black-and-white photograph of it survives and depicts not only the woman by the shore but also a man attempting to walk towards her.[2] Other than the two isolated figures, only rocks fill the foreground area along the shoreline. The image projects a weighty silence and unease between the two figures. Both appear separate and deep in their own thoughts. She looks out at the water and he looks at her. The man, darkly dressed, seems hesitant. He wants to move forward, but his feet are firmly embedded in the sand.

A color reproduction of this first painted version of *The Lonely Ones* does not exist, but Munch himself (emulating Whistler's practice of describing paintings as music) gave it yet another title, *Harmony in White and Blue*, alluding perhaps to the unity between the white woman and the blue sea, as seen in subsequent renderings of the image.[3] Heller noted that water is a frequent metaphor for life in Munch's journals and that Munch's perceptions of it were influ-enced by such writings of the philosopher, Arthur Schopenhauer (1788-1860), as: "Since all living things of this earth emerge from [water] and the infinity of the heavens is mirrored in it, its bright or dark mirror awakes in us the sensation of unending longing."[4] If the woman in *The Lonely Ones* is associated with the water, then, Heller believes, her male companion becomes allied with the dark and lifeless shoreline.

About sixteen years later, Munch painted the Straus's version of *The Lonely Ones*. At this time, Munch suffered severely from mental illness and alcoholism, and committed himself to Dr. Jacobson's clinic for nervous disorders in Copenhagen.[5] The painting differs from the first version in several ways. Firstly, the figures are reversed and the woman is now to the left of her companion. Her hair is shorter, and Munch heightens a long fold in the back of her dress with quick horizontal brushstrokes in blue. Instead of a nightscape, it is daylight, perhaps even sunset, because of the reddish hue on the sand and rocks of the beach and in the woman's hair. Red also reflects off the man's trousers. In the first version, both figures stood well below the horizon line. In this version, the woman's head just barely reaches it, while her companion's breaks the horizon line and turns more toward the water than to her. He now shares the view with her, while hesitantly moving toward her, creating a mood altogether different from the early painting.

Munch's new approach may have been influenced by the death of Aaase Nørregaard in May 1908. She was an artist who had once been his "blonde bohemian love," and about whom in a condolence letter he wrote: "I have lost much, my best woman friend...."[6] It is not difficult to imagine that Munch sought to create both a

mood of nostalgia as well as a deep unending loneliness by depicting two figures looking at the horizon, across the fjord's icy water, as
they themselves are infused with the red glow of the sun setting.

Francesca Consagra

1   Gerd Woll, "The Frieze of Life: Graphic Works," in *Edvard Munch: The Frieze of Life*, ed. Mara-Helen Wood (London, 1992), 88.

2   Woll, "The Frieze of Life," 88; and Reinhold Heller, *Munch: His Life and Work* (Chicago, 1984), 95.

3   Heller, *Munch: His Life and Work*, 95.

4   Ibid., 88.

5   Arne Eggum, "Edvard Munch: A Biographical Background," in *Edvard Munch: The Frieze of Life*, ed. Mara-Helen Wood (London, 1992), 23.

6   Heller, *Munch: His Life and Work*, 194.

72

Egon Schiele
Austrian (1890-1918)

Standing Nude with Raised Arms (1911)
Tempera and pencil
18¹/₂" x 11¹/₂"
Lent by Mary Sharp Cronson, class of 1947

Although the Austrian expressionist artist, Egon Schiele, is best known for the eroticism of his figurative works, many of his images of nudes belie any fulfillment of passion or sensuality. They appear instead as tormented figures living in perpetual tension and discomfort. The grotesquely thin nude exhibited here is covered with patches of green, red, and brown, which suggest illness and starvation. The drawing belongs to a group of works referred to by contemporary critics as the "rabbit pictures" because the nudes looked like skinned rabbits in a butcher's display.[1]

Although the drawing is signed as a vertical, and properly displayed as such, it should be noted that the awkwardness of the pose stems from Schiele's customary manner of placing his models on low sofas or mattresses and drawing them from above while he perched on a stool or ladder. He omitted adding props to the composition and, as in this case, would employ a white outline around the contours of the figure in order to set the figure off from the buff-colored tint of the packing paper.[2]

The identity of the sitter is unknown. She may be one of the adolescent prostitutes that Schiele began drawing towards the end of 1910, or even the dancer Moa, who had an extremely slender body with very muscular arms.[3] In a drawing of her, *Standing Female Nude with Arms Crossed over her Breast (Moa)*, also dated 1911, Schiele elongates her torso and hides her eyes. Since Schiele normally drew eyes as the focal point of the top half of his vertical images of nudes, their exclusion is a particularly unusual feature of both drawings (although this alone may not properly identify the sitter as Moa).

Francesca Consagra

---

[1] Magdalena Dabrowski and Rudolf Leopold, *Egon Schiele: The Leopold Collection, Vienna* (New York, 1997), 112.

[2] Ibid.

[3] J. Kallir, *Egon Schiele* (New York, 1994), 60.

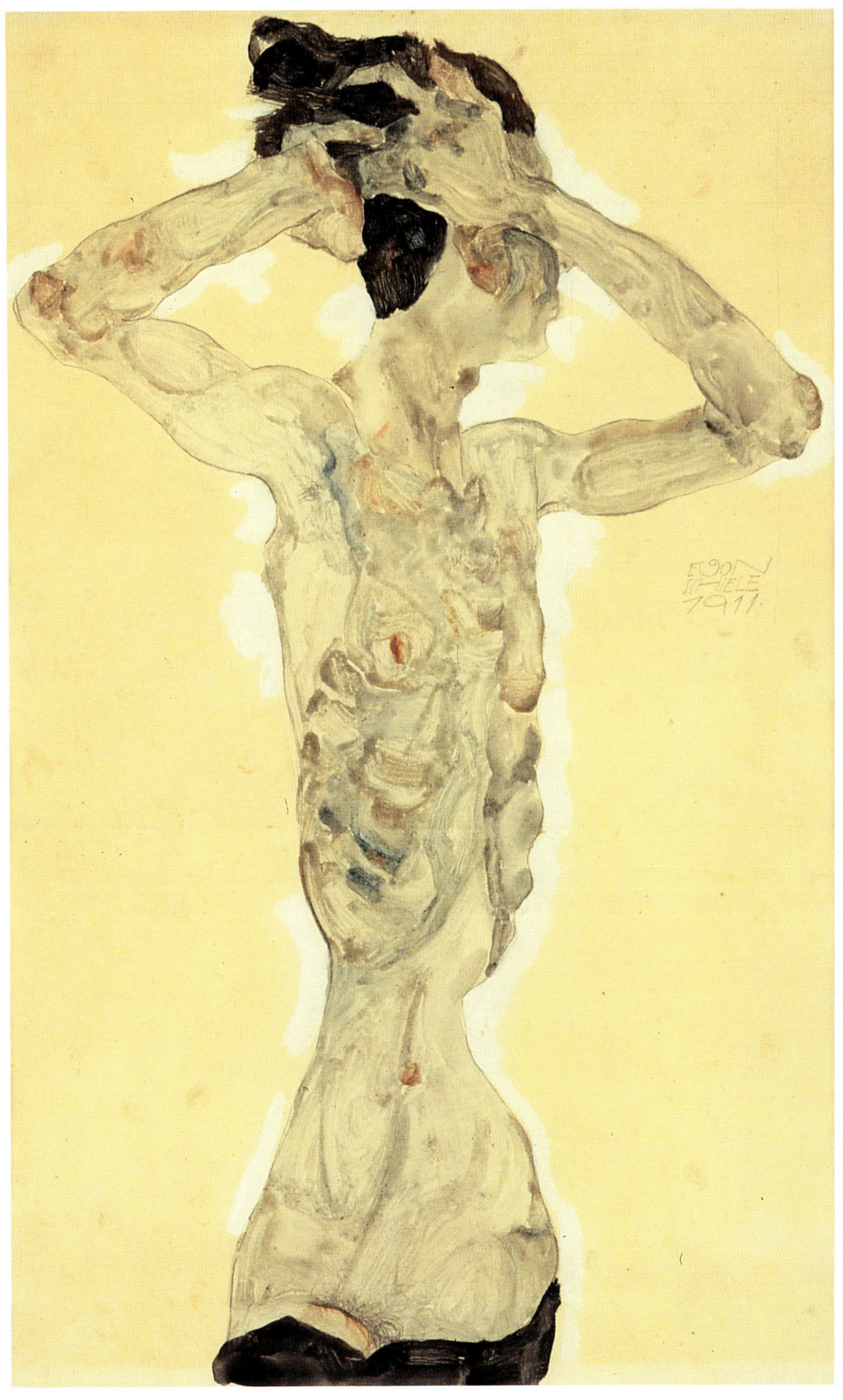

73

Egon Schiele
Austrian (1890-1918)

Self-portrait as Monk (1913)
Pencil
11" x 5^1/$_2$"
Lent by Mary Sharp Cronson, class of 1947

The Austrian expressionist painter, Egon Schiele, died when he was only twenty-eight and had been at odds with art critics and society for most of his brief life. The subjects of his work do not change drastically during the 1910s: they remain primarily self-portraits, nudes, and landscapes. The nudes, often young adolescents, had their shock value in their onanistic poses. In his self-portraits, he either presented himself naked in positions similar to the nudes, or, as in the drawing exhibited here, robed in monastic garb—which went some way to insult further both his secular and nonsecular audiences.

Originally these ecclesiastical portraits may have alluded to a "brotherhood" of artists, which included his one-time mentor, Gustav Klimt, and the *Neukunstgruppe* (New art group) in Vienna, that he helped found in 1909.[1] By 1912, they had a significantly different spirit, and Kallir suggests they were painted in reaction to his imprisonment for twenty-four days on charges of immorality.[2] He had been accused of kidnapping and seducing a minor, and found guilty only of the third charge, "distributing obscene drawings," by allowing minors to see the studies of nudes in his studio.[3] Correspondence and drawings around the time of the imprisonment reveal that the experience had shattered Schiele. After his release, he wrote, "I am still completely shaken. During the trial a drawing of mine, the one I had hanging on the wall here, was burned. Klimt is hoping to do something. He assured me that the same thing could happen to one of us one day, another the next, that we're none of us free to do as we will."[4]

The paintings of this year include *Cardinal and Nun (Embrace)* (collection of Rudolf Leopold, Vienna), in which the protagonists (personified by Schiele and his lover, Valerie "Wally" Neuzil)

appear to be having sexual intercourse wrapped in their ecclesiastical robes. These works were meant to shock and anger a society that did not understand him or his art. Up until his death, Schiele continued to present himself as a monk or hermit, and (in the next step in his exhibitionism and self-confession) as the martyred saint, as in his famous drawing, *Self-portrait as St. Sebastian* (1913; private collection, New York). Edwin Lachnit sees these self-portraits as an indication of Schiele's "conviction that in self-sacrifice he would find the source of artistic creativity not available to him in institutionalized groups such as religious communities or artists' associations."[5]

The drawing exhibited here thus presents a common theme in Schiele's art, of a self-portrait of him with a monk's cap. It also exemplifies a new drawing style that became more apparent around 1913-14, in which he depicts a face in profile in a highly geometric manner embellished with hatching and spiral lines, sometimes free, sometimes tight, to describe the hair and eyebrows, as seen in *Preacher (Nude Self-portrait with Blue-Green Shirt)* and *Crouching Woman (Study for Blind Mother)* (both in the collection of Rudolf Leopold, Vienna).

Francesca Consagra

---

[1]   J. Kallir, *Egon Schiele* (New York, 1994), 126.

[2]   J. Kallir, *Egon Schiele: The Complete Works* (New York, 1990), 308.

[3]   Kallir, *Egon Schiele* (1994), 43; and Magdalena Dabrowski and Rudolf Leopold, *Egon Schiele: The Leopold Collection, Vienna* (New York, 1997), 348.

[4]   Dabrowski and Leopold, *Egon Schiele: The Leopold Collection*, 348.

[5]   Edwin Lachnit, "Egon Schiele," in *Dictionary of Art*, ed. Jane Turner (New York, 1996), 28:88-91.

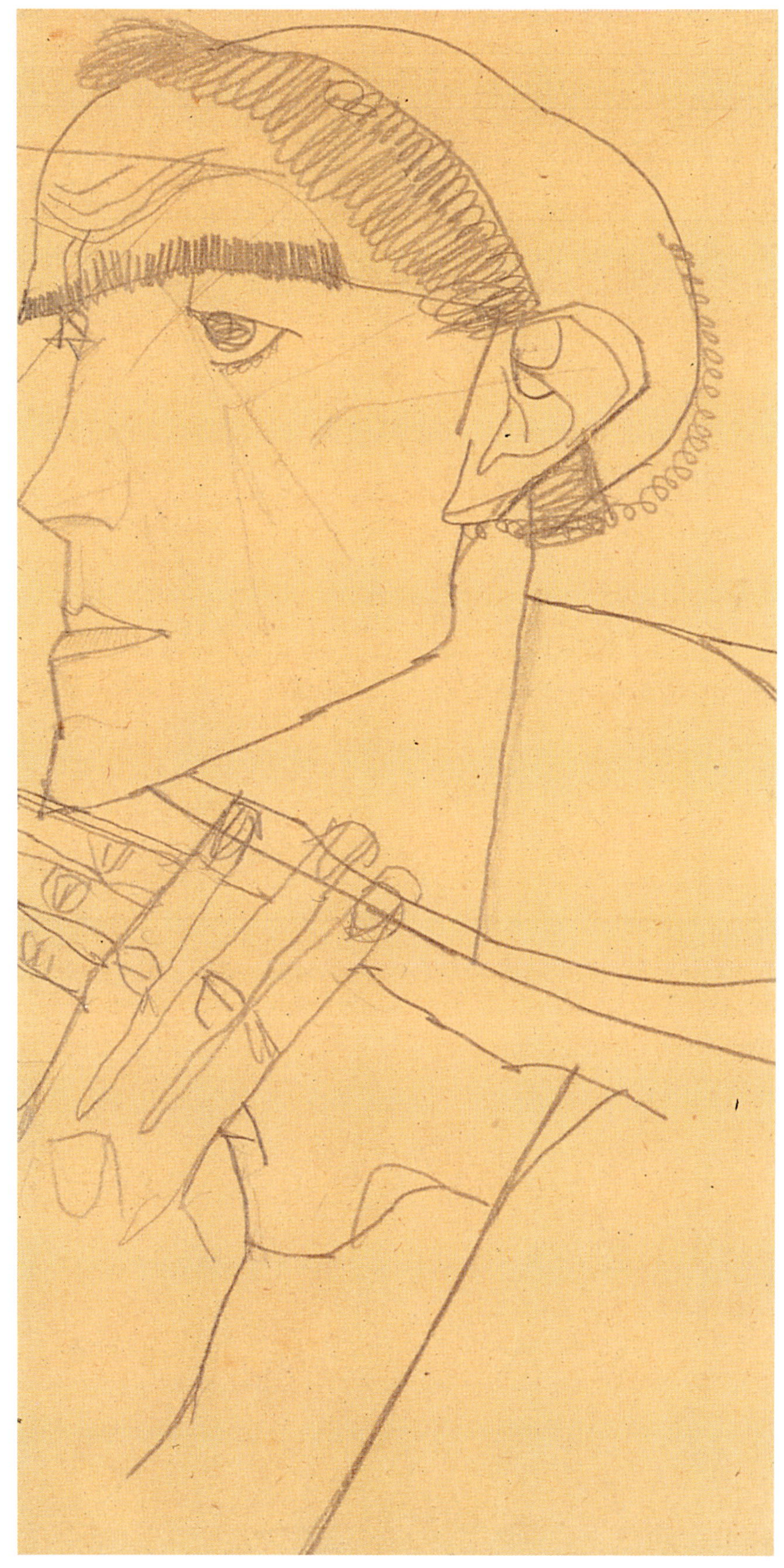

74

Emil Nolde
German (1867-1956)

Tänzerin (Dancer)(1913)
Lithograph printed in carmine, violet, ochre, and black on very thin Japan paper in Flensburg, Germany
20³/₄" x 22"
Signature: in pencil, lower right, "Emil Nolde"
Inscription: "Anfl. Nr. 29" (probably from an edition of 35)
Lent by Philip and Lynn Straus (Lynn R. Gross, class of 1946)

In 1907, while Emil Nolde was briefly a member of *Die Brücke* (a group of German expressionists who admired his "storm of color"), he produced his first significant group of lithographs. Between 1909 and 1911 his interest in Old Testament themes and ethnographic art flourished, and with them his fascination for the erotic frenzy of ritualistic dances of non-Christian peoples. Nolde's interest in color, dance, lithography, and ethnography culminated in 1913, in what many consider the most important print of Nolde's career[1], and one of the "greatest examples of color printing in this century."[2]

Tänzerin (The dancer), exhibited here in an excellent impression, is printed in carmine, violet, ochre, and black on very thin Japan paper. Nolde made it at the end of an intense eight-week period in 1913, at the Westphalen lithography workshop in Flensburg, Germany, where, he writes:

> To my heart's content I could do as I liked. Colors were used up, were ground, and I stood continually drawing, etching, grinding, mixing, pondering, switching from color to color, and the large works were pulled from the press, almost all in the most diverse nuances and states. It was a delight and gave me great pleasure when I could carry off all the rolled up sheets.[3]

Nolde himself regarded *Tänzerin* as a symbol of "all the passion and joy" that he had felt working at this shop.[4] This color lithograph depicts a woman dancing topless on a dais, which is lit by a large torch, with two male spectators seated at the far left. She dances in total abandonment, with her dark mass of hair thrown to one side, her mouth wide open, and her eyes closed as if in a trance. Her grass skirt sways right, her arms sway left, and her legs are wide apart as she balances herself on the toes of one foot. The black triangular pubic area counters the triangular shape of the legs; the nipples are prominent, round, and colored in carmine, the same color as her cheeks and skirt. The effect is rhythmic, erotic, and joyous, with a feeling of spontaneity, not only in the woman's movements, but also in the very printing of the stones, where the registration of the various colors is not exact, especially around the nipples and arms, and one layer of translucent color is printed over another to great effect. This impression of *Tänzerin* is also printed on a thin Asian paper that is wonderfully receptive to the inks, which shimmer on the lustrous surface.

How appropriate that *Tänzerin* was the last lithograph Nolde made before joining the ophthalmologist, Alfred Leber, on an expedition for the Department of Colonial Affairs to German New Guinea.[5] The trip took Nolde and his wife, Ada, through Korea, Japan, China, and the South Seas, where natives may well have enraptured them in jubilant torchlight dances similar to the one depicted in this print.

Francesca Consagra

[1] Andrew Robison, "Prints of the Brücke Artists" in *German Expressionist Prints from the Collection of Ruth and Jacob Kainen* (Washington, D.C., 1985), 56.

[2] Victor Carlson, "The Lithographs," in *Nolde: The Painter's Prints* (Boston, 1995), 50.

[3] See Emil Nolde, *Jahre der Kämpfe* (Berlin, 1931), 228-29, for original German; English translation is in Victor Carlson, "The Lithographs," 47.

[4] Ibid.

[5] Susan V. Cloeren, Chronology, in *Nolde: The Painter's Prints* (Boston, 1995), 299.

75

Gabriele Münter
German (1877-1962)

Clouds Over Murnau (1908-10)
Oil on cardboard
14" x 16"
Promised Gift of Joan Quigley, class of 1946, in memory of Mr. and Mrs. John Baird Quigley

Provenance: Dazell Hatfield Gallery, Los Angeles, 1958; Mr. and Mrs. John Baird Quigley; by descent to the owner

Gabriele Münter was born in Berlin and received her first formal art training in Düsseldorf. After a trip to visit relatives in Missouri, Arkansas, and Texas, in 1898-1900, she enrolled in the painting classes of Wassily Kandinsky in Munich in 1902. After traveling together with Kandinsky in North Africa, Italy, and Paris, they returned to Munich in 1908 and both exhibited with the *Neue Künstler Vereinigung*, a secessionist modern movement.

By 1911, they had split from the *Vereinigung*, together with Franz Marc, and organized a competing group known as *Der Blaue Reiter*, whose first exhibition took place in December of that year. Münter continued to exhibit in avant-garde exhibitions until the outbreak of World War I, at which time she left for Stockholm, not returning to Germany until 1920, by which time her relationship with Kandinsky had ended. While she continued working professionally as an artist through World War II, her works were censored by the Nazis. Münter was most influenced by traditional Bavarian glass painting and the Fauve manner of working imported through her and Kandinsky's sojourn in Paris and through their friend, Alexi Jawlensky, who had worked in Matisse's studio in 1907.

This hitherto unpublished and unexhibited landscape by the German expressionist and founding member of *Der Blaue Reiter* was painted during 1904-16, the first two years that she and Kandinsky lived in the rural village of Murnau, about an hour south of Munich in the Bavarian Alps. In 1908, they purchased not only a property in Munich but also a new structure without plumbing in Murnau, known to the villagers as the *Russenhaus* (house of the Russians),

owing not only to Kandinsky's background, but that of their early frequent visitors, the painters Alexi Jawlensky and Marienne von Werefkin. The landscape around the Murnau countryside was a constant source of inspiration to both Münter and Kandinsky, and their productivity during these early years was intense during all seasons.

The Quigley picture depicts the small onion-domed spire of the village church at Murnau, a view based on that from the window of their house as demonstrated through a comparison of paintings and photographs taken from the house.[1] The same basic view was used by Münter in *Landscape with Church* (1909; Saarbrücken, Saarland Museum[2]); *Sunflowers with Church* (1910; private collection; illustrated in Cole, pl. 33); and *Countryside in Bloom* (1910; private collection, illustrated in Cole, pl. 35); and also by Kandinsky in several of his paintings from the same years. Each of the paintings by Münter are executed on artist's cardboard of the same size as the Quigley painting. It is assumed by certain authors that the more expensive canvas support was reserved for special composi-tions by both artists at this stage of their careers.

James Mundy, class of 1974

---

[1] By Brigitte M. Cole, "Gabriele Münter and the Development of her Early Murnau Style," M.A. thesis (Southern Methodist University, 1980), 64-71 and pls. 32-36.

[2] Illustrated in Reinhold Heller, *Gabriele Münter: The Years of Expressionism 1903-1920* (Munich, 1997), 137.

76

Paul Klee
Swiss (1879-1940)

The Second Wave Attacks (1933)
Watercolor
18$\frac{1}{2}$" x 24$\frac{1}{2}$"
Signature: lower left, "Klee"
Inscriptions: upper right, "Angriff der Nacht folgenden"; upper left, "1933 v 19"
Collection Anne Keating Jones, class of 1943

Provenance: Eugene Thaw, New Gallery, New York, 1956

Paul Klee was a major contributor to the history of twentieth-century art as both an artist and a theoretician. "In much of his work," Temkin notes, "he aspired to achieve a naive and untutored quality, but his art is also among the most cerebral of any of the twentieth century."[1] He is associated most commonly with the Bauhaus school in Wiemar and Dessau, Germany, where he taught and wrote handbooks under the guidance of Walter Gropius from 1920 to 1931, when Klee terminated his contract and began to teach at the Düsseldorf Art Academy. On 30 January 1933, Hitler became chancellor of the German Reich and soon proposed an enabling act empowering him to institute laws on his own authority for the next few years. Art academies all over Germany then effected a new policy of "restoring the indigenous character of German art instruction," in which Klee's abstractions, his concentrated pictorial sign system, and experiments with creative spontaneity played no part.[2] A Nazi appointee to the academy in Düsseldorf dismissed him in April, and Klee and his wife left Germany and returned to his father's house in Berne, Switzerland in December of that year.

In 1933, perhaps due to the rising insecurity in his life, Klee's drawing style changed. It became more calligraphic, using fewer lines than his earlier work, and the drawings seem to have been done in no time at all. Klee wrote in a letter, "The year 1933 has begun with some new drawings made with impertinent lines which are supposed to be straight....How much happiness can lie in a few lines."[3] It is in the titles of the year's drawings that he refers to the social and political disturbances of the time, for example, *Manhunt, Emigration, Deadly Enemy*, and *The Battle Remains*.

The Second Wave Attacks not only has a similar dark and foreboding title but it may also carry a subliminal message in the form of the letters, however loosely drawn, of N, A, Z, and I.[4] The thickly drawn arrow at the top and the stick-figure legs marching towards the right, off the sheet, also may refer to a second wave of Nazi force within Germany's political system, or even a self-referential statement about Klee's dismissal from the art academy in Düsseldorf and ultimate exile from Germany.

Francesca Consagra

---

[1] Ann Temkin, "Paul Klee," in *Dictionary of Art*, ed. Jane Turner (New York), 18:108.

[2] See Lisa Dennison and Andrew Kagan, *Paul Klee at the Guggenheim Museum* (New York, 1993), Introduction and 44-45, respectively.

[3] Marcel Franciscono, *Paul Klee: his work and thought* (Chicago, 1991), 270.

[4] As noted in conversation by the present owner of the drawing, Anne Keating Jones.

77

Henri Matisse
French (1869-1954)

Lorette in a White Blouse (1916-17)
Oil on cradled panel
21⅝" x 17⅝"
Lent by Elizabeth L. Eisenstein, class of 1945-4

Provenance: Sam A. Lewisohn, New York; by descent to owner

Exhibitions: *Matisse: His Art and his Public*, Museum of Modern Art, New York, 1951, 226-27; *The Lewisohn Collection*, Metropolitan Museum of Art, New York, 1951, 14, no. 50, illus. p. 48

Perhaps Matisse's favorite Parisian model during the period 1915-17, the attractive, broad-faced Italian woman with high cheek bones, known only as Lorette, was portrayed at least fifty times by the artist during these years. These works reside presently in public and private collections in New York, Paris, Richmond, Houston, West Palm Beach, Berne, Stockholm, and Washington, D.C., among other locations. While the artist left Paris and traveled south to Nice beginning in 1916 for half the year, he returned to his studio on the quai St. Michel and to the many pensive portrayals in both half- and full length of the raven-haired, almond-eyed Italian. The majority of the portraits were composed of shades of black, white, and flesh tones, but occasionally Matisse included the bold colors of an enveloping armchair or chaise.

Alfred Barr referred to the present portrait as "one of the most distinguished portrait studies of this model" and cites an experimental return by the artist to the "firm, sensual paint surface" he had abandoned since 1903.[1] Indeed, the close proximity of the sitter to the picture plane in this and other studies of Lorette from these years bring to mind the half-Fauve, half-expressionist portraits by

Alexi Jawlensky from the same years. This is particularly true of the close head study, *Lorette with the Long Curls* (1916-17; Norton Gallery, West Palm Beach)[2], most likely painted on the same day as the Eisenstein picture. This and other paintings executed during World War I have been seen by critics as possessing a severe aspect devoid of the "hedonistic exuberance" of Matisse's art.[3] This might be seen as a reflection of the anxieties associated with the war. While it is difficult to generalize successfully on this question, the many portrayals of Lorette move between the somber and the more decorative, a result, perhaps, of the first trip to Morocco by the artist.

James Mundy, class of 1974

---

[1]   Alfred Barr, *Matisse: His Art and his Public* (New York, 1951), 192.

[2]   Illustrated in Jack Cowart and Dominique Fourcade, *Henri Matisse: The Early Years in Nice: 1916-1930* (New York, 1986), pl. 8.

[3]   See John Elderfield, *Henri Matisse: A Retrospective* (New York, 1992), 237.

78

Henri Matisse
French (1869-1954)

Vase with Flowers and a Plate of Oysters (1940)
Oil on canvas
20" x 24"
Signature: upper left corner, "Henri Matisse 12/40"
Promised Gift of Anonymous, class of 1953

Provenance: Galerie Bernheim-Jeune, Paris; Paul Petrides, Paris; Acquavella Galleries, Inc., New York; Frances W. Pick (class of 1927) ca. 1975; to the owner by descent

Matisse lived out both World Wars in France, seeking creative calm in the south of France. The year 1940 was divided between stays in Nice at the Hôtel Regina (January-April; September-December), Saint-Gaudens at the Hôtel Ferrière (July-August), and Paris (late April-May), where he was making final his separation from Madame Matisse and preparing to make a trip to Brazil. The German invasion of France scuttled his travel plans to South America and forced his return to Nice. The attempts in December of that year by Varian Fry, the chief American agent for the Emergency Rescue Committee, to get Matisse a visa to the United States were rebuffed. This period was one of multiple anxieties for the artist resulting from the legal problems of the separation, the escalating war in Europe, and the worsening of his health, resulting in surgery for duodenal cancer in January of the next year.

In spite of these travails, Matisse was determined to paint still lifes. He wrote to his son Pierre on 1 September 1940 that he had "set up several arrangements in my studio—but this kind of uncertainty in which we are living here makes it impossible; consequently I am afraid to start working face-to-face with objects which I have to animate myself with my own feelings."[1] At around this moment, Matisse was photographed in his studio at the Hôtel Regina surrounded by numerous still-life elements.[2] Among the objects spread upon several tables were the vase and pitcher that appear in the present still life of flowers, possibly camellias, and oysters, painted in December when Matisse was in very poor health and working little. The compositional organization relies on the loosely painted and similar shapes and colors of the oyster shells and the flowers, each of which moves aggressively out from the strong red background of tablecloth and wall. Indeed, it is easy to read the empty shells as flowers that have fallen from the stalks. A second variation of this still life exists in a slightly larger format (25" x 32") in the Kunstmuseum, Basel and is also signed and dated by Matisse "12/40".[3] The major difference between them is the introduction of a rich blue placemat under the plate of oysters in the Basel version and the removal of the vase of camellias.

James Mundy, class of 1974

---

[1] Alfred Barr, *Matisse: His Art and his Public* (New York, 1951), 256.

[2] Illustrated in John Elderfield, *Henri Matisse: A Retrospective* (New York, 1992), 364.

[3] Illustrated in Elderfield, *Henri Matisse*, fig. 348.

79

Marc Chagall
French, Russian-born (1887-1985)

Flowers and Profiles (1930)
Oil on canvas
30" x 24"
Signature: lower left, "Marc Chagall"
Promised Gift of Mary Pick Hines, class of 1953

Provenance: Dr. Yngar Nielsen; Acquavella Galleries, Inc., New York; Frances W. Pick (class of 1927); by descent to owner

Exhibitions: Liljevalchs Konsthall, Stockholm, 1954; *19th and 20th Century Master Paintings*; Acquavella Galleries, Inc., New York, May-June 1981

Marc Chagall was born in Vitebsk, Russia, in 1887. His parents were Hasidic Jews, and the spirit of Jewish mysticism is one of the fundamental themes in Chagall's work. Chagall's memories of his childhood in Vitebsk surface repeatedly in his imagery. Chagall was in Paris between 1910-14 and was impressed by the Old Masters and contemporary art he saw there, forcing a change of style and palette in response to Van Gogh, Gauguin, and Matisse. He returned to Paris in 1923, where he remained until his death, with the exception of the period when he sat out World War II in the United States.

The art of Chagall is at times difficult to interpret because it combines images of memory, those of the present reality, those of fantasy, and those of the subconscious dream world. This outwardly simple still-life painting is just such an example. Painted in 1930, after Chagall and his family were well-established in Paris in the house they bought in 1929, called Villa Montmorency on the Avenue des Sycomores near the Porte d'Auteuil, this image is one of many painted during these years that focuses on a floral still life, in this case a huge bouquet of yellow and delphinium-blue wildflowers, combined with figural elements in a virtually unspecified setting, yet presumably one with a blue sky interwoven with light cirrus clouds.

Near the upper left-hand corner, where a fragment of a red sun is placed, hovers a figure often found in Chagall's paintings, one suggestive of Jewish mystical traditions and, possibly, Greco-Roman mythology (Helios?). In the foreground, next to the vase of flowers, are two figures in profile. While the viewer's first inclination is to interpret them as contemporary references to Chagall's

family or friends, they seem to be a direct reference back to a series of half-length paintings of lovers the artist made in the years 1915-17, at the time of his marriage to Bella, while still in Russia[1], most specifically the painting entitled *Lovers in Gray*, of 1916, where the female lover (the archetypal Bella) is posed in profile in the same red dress with a white lace collar, left arm raised and bent toward her face, in this case cradling the head of the male lover, also seen in profile and in the same position as that in the painting of 1930. Chagall referred back to the period 1915-17 as a happy one thanks to Bella, when "blue air, love, and flowers filled the house."[2] Thus, it seems that while the flowers might have been fresh in Paris in 1930, when the Hines painting was executed, the moment of greatest import to the understanding took place fourteen years before, in another culture.

Works similar to this one from the period around 1930 can be found in the Sara Lee Corporation Collection, and two private collections[3] and also one entitled, *The Lovers in the Flowers (Lilacs)*, 1931, formerly in the collection of Josef von Sternberg, Hollywood.[4]

James Mundy, class of 1974

[1] Formerly in the collection of Ida Chagall; illustrated in Aleksandr Kamensky, *Chagall the Russian Years 1907-1922* (New York, 1989), 252-53.

[2] Kamensky, *Chagall the Russian Years*, 234.

[3] Illustrated in Jacob Baal-Teshuva, *Marc Chagall 1887-1985* (Cologne, 1998), 130-31.

[4] Illustrated in James J. Sweeney, *Marc Chagall* (New York, 1946), 59.

80

Pablo Picasso
Spanish (1881-1973)

The Frugal Repast, from *The Acrobat's Suite* (1904; possibly 1913 edition)
Etching
6⅞" x 5¾"
Promised Gift of Marian Phelps Pawlick, class of 1948

In the spring of 1904, Picasso finally settled in Paris, moving into a rundown studio complex in Montmartre known as the *Bateau Lavoir*, named for its resemblance to a laundry barge.[1] The artist was, at the time, painting in what is known as his late Blue Period style, in which emaciated figures with long, Mannerist limbs peopled his predominantly blue-hued canvases.

Fernande Olivier recalls that when she met the artist in August 1904 he "was working on an etching, now famous: a man and a woman sitting at a table in a tavern; this hungry couple emits an intense expression of misery and alcoholism of an astounding realism."[2] The emphasis on the hands, creating a circular movement around the frontal figure of the woman, may refer to the art of the *Saltimbanques*, or low-class acrobats and jugglers that performed in the streets of Paris. The print was the first of a series of fifteen plates devoted to this group of marginal artists.[3] Scholars have attempted to understand Picasso's fascination with them during the Blue Period, and some see it evolving out of his desire to identify with social misfits and his need to romanticize them as starving artists or martyrs of their art and desires, with the traditional symbols of self-sacrifice, the bread and the wine, in the forefront of the image.[4]

Five years earlier, Picasso had attempted to make his first etching in Barcelona. He then abandoned the art until he came to Paris and started working on *The Frugal Repast*.[5] His renewed interest was likely inspired by his need for money in a city with a strong tradition of print publishing and an active print market. In order to economize, he worked on an already-used zinc plate that bore a landscape by another artist, which is still visible at the top right of the image. It was most likely Eugène Delâtre who issued small editions of Picasso's plates in 1904-05. The famous publisher, Ambroise Vollard, then acquired and steel-faced them in 1913, and issued them as a series under the title, *Les Saltimbanques*.[6]

Francesca Consagra

---

[1]   John Richardson, *A Life of Picasso* (New York, 1991), 1:296-98.

[2]   Quoted in Nuria Rivero, *Picasso, 1905-1906: From the Rose Period to the Ochres of Gósol* (Barcelona, ca. 1992), 124.

[3]   Riva Castleman, "The Frugal Repast," in William Rubin, *Picasso in the Collection of the Museum of Modern Art* (New York, 1972), 30.

[4]   See Linda Hults, *The Print in the Western World* (Madison, Wisconsin, 1996), 650-52.

[5]   Castleman, "The Frugal Repast," 28.

[6]   Ibid., 30.

81

Pablo Picasso
Spanish (1881-1973)

Blind Minotaur Led through the Night by Girl with Fluttering Dress (1934)
Aquatint, drypoint, burin; iii/iii, Bloch #225
9³/₄" x 13⁵/₈"
Signature: lower right margin, "Picasso"
Collection of Dorothy Seiberling, class of 1943

"If all the paths I've taken were marked on a map and joined up with a line, it might represent a Minotaur." Pablo Picasso[1]

In the fall of 1934, Picasso made four intaglio plates and several drawings devoted to the Blind Minotaur (*Le minator aveugle*). Although they are part of the set of a hundred prints, referred to today as the *Vollard Suite*, they were never commissioned by publisher, Ambroise Vollard. Instead he issued them after World War II, along with five other sets of Picasso's prints, *The Sculptor's Studio*, *The Rape*, *The Minotaur*, *Rembrandt*, and three portraits of Vollard.

Picasso began the *Blind Minotaur* series on 22 September with *Blind Minotaur Led by Girl with Fluttering Dress: I* (Bloch #222), in which fishermen bring their boat to shore and a small girl holding a bouquet of flowers guides the Blind Minotaur by the hand along the beach past another fisherman standing at the far left of the image. In the second print of the series, the fishermen have left shore in their boat, and the girl now holds a dove and walks before the Minotaur towards a doorway with steps. They no longer walk toward the isolated fisherman, but rather away from him. The last print of the series, seen here, is richly incised with drypoint to set the scene at night, and Picasso reverts more or less to the original composition, but adds stars and a fire on the beach, while the girl holds the dove in one hand and guides the Minotaur with the other.

We are as in the dark as the Minotaur. The effect is stunning and by far the best of this set, if not the entire *Vollard Suite*.

The mood is much more melancholic here than the prints of the Minotaur done only a year earlier, in which the mythological creature is depicted as a *bon vivant*, drinking wine, caressing women, and enjoying banquets. He is now no longer the triumphant figure representing sexual urges, but is rather tragic and defeated, led by a small girl along a beach, and he may no longer symbolize the artist. Instead, he may stand for a country in strife: the blind creature, half-man and half-bull (the symbol of Spain), is being led by the girl holding the dove (the symbol of peace). Although Picasso preferred to remain apolitical in the early stages of the Spanish Civil War (1936-39), it is nonetheless interesting to note that at the time he was working on the *Blind Minotaur* series, there were general strikes in Valencia and Zaragoza, fighting in Madrid and Barcelona, and a bloody uprising by miners in Asturias that was suppressed by troops led by Generalissimo Francisco Franco. This print may thus stand as one of Picasso's first political prints concerning the plight of Spain during the 1930s.

Francesca Consagra

---

[1] Quoted in Janie Cohen, ed., *Picasso, inside the image: prints from the Ludwig Museum, Cologne* (Burlington, Vermont, ca. 1995), 78.

82

Jacques Lipchitz
French (1891-1973)

Musician with Sheet Music and Clarinet (1917-18)
Terracotta
Height, 18"; width, 6"
Lent by Virginia Herrick Deknatel, class of 1929

Pablo Picasso significantly changed the direction of Lipchitz's work after the two met in Paris while Lipchitz was an art student in 1915. At this time, Lipchitz moved away from the classicism of Aristide Maillol (1861-1944) toward the reduced geometric style of cubism. The sculptures of 1915-16 were so abstract that the subjects, primarily standing "personages," were almost illegible.

Musician with Sheet Music and Clarinet belongs to a body of work Lipchitz made in reaction to the austerity of his previous work. In 1917-18, he turned to common cubist subjects like musicians, dancers, and harlequins, the majority of which carried some kind of prop. Lipchitz himself noted that he began to use in his sculptures a musical instrument like a guitar or a clarinet, because it could act as a "point of reference, a stabilizing influence around which the figure is organized, while the figure may be largely disintegrated. The existence of the [instrument] assists in the visual recomposition of the figure into a new and different kind of reality."[1] In the 1920s, Lipchitz continued to experiment with the organization of space and form that he had begun to understand while making such works as *Musician with Sheet Music and Clarinet*, and it led him to produce bronzes casts from constructions in wax and cardboard, which ultimately influenced the metal constructions of Picasso and Julio González of 1928, and helped change the course the twentieth-century sculpture.

Francesca Consagra

---

[1]   Jacques Lipchitz with H. H. Arnason, *My Life in Sculpture* (New York, 1972), 50.

83

Hans Arp
French (1886-1966)

Leaf on a Crystal (1954)
Bronze
Height, 24"; width, 10"; depth, 10"
Lent by Mary Sharp Cronson, class of 1947

Hans Arp was a pioneer of abstract art and one of the founders of Dada in Zurich in 1916. The concept of chance and a dependency on natural forms were the two forces that freed him from academic conventions and allowed him to work from his subconscious and be spontaneously inventive. As early as 1916-17, the debris thrown up on a beach inspired his investigation into biomorphism in his paintings, and from that time on, he investigated and reveled in the creation of simple terrestrial forms arranged by chance.

Sometime around 1930, he created his first sculptures in the round, known as Concretions, which were based on natural forms modeled in plaster and carved in wood or stone. They had rounded contours, smooth surfaces, and appeared weightless. Arp preferred sculptures that didn't stand on bases in order to enhance their aerial, transcendental qualities so that they might take their place in their natural surroundings instead of being separated from them.[1]

Arp did use modeled bases, however, when he wanted to link together a fluid natural form and a crystallized formal one, a combination that occurs in a group of sculptures done over a period of decades, known as his *Geometric-Ageometric* series, to which *Leaf on a Crystal* belongs. Georg Schmidt, an art critic and contemporary of Arp, described this "organic-geometrical antithesis" in terms of the two modes or schools of abstract expressionism:

While the geometrical abstractionists like to bring a single formal law to light, the organic abstractionists show creations that have been worked on by many shaping forces. The crystal is the symbol of geometrical abstract art, the pebble the symbol of organic abstract art.[2]

Part of Arp's desire to link the two symbols stemmed from his collaboration with his wife, Sophie Taeuber-Arp, an accomplished artist who worked within the parameters of geometrically formal language, rather than Arp's spontaneously natural one. After her death in 1943, he continued to pay tribute to her by combining the crystal with his biomorphic forms. An example of his continued devotion to her and his interest in the geometric-ageometric sculpture is *Leaf on a Crystal*, created in 1954, the same year that Arp was awarded the International Sculpture Prize at the Venice Biennale at the age of 68.[3]

Francesca Consagra

---

[1]   Greta Stroeh, "Hans Arp," in *Dictionary of Art*, ed. Jane Turner (New York, 1986), 2:488-91, esp. 490.

[2]   Schmidt's statement was first published in *Plastique*, the journal that Taeuber-Arp herself published; see "Informations," *Plastique* 3 (Spring 1937): 14. The passage here is quoted in Stephanie Poley, "Geometric-Ageometric," in *Arp, 1886-1966* (Minneapolis, 1987), 210.

[3]   Arp made another version of the sculpture in white marble; see Carola Giedion-Welcker, *Jean Arp* (New York, 1957), cat. no. 76.

84

Edward Hopper
American (1882-1967)

Standing Woman (1899)
Black ink on paper
15" x 10"
Signature: ink, lower right, "EHopper/99"
Gift of Ellen G. Milberg, class of 1960, in honor of the twenty-fifth anniversary of the Friends of the Frances Lehman Loeb Art Center

Exhibitions: *Edward Hopper Drawings: The Poetry of Solitude*, Hunter Museum of Art, Chattanooga, Tennessee, 9 September-15 October 1995; *The Early Drawings of Edward Hopper (1882-1967)*, Kennedy Galleries, New York, 4-25 November 1995, no. 7

Hopper, the great exponent of American scene painting of the twentieth century, began his career as a commercial artist. His early preference for ink drawings lent itself well to a career in illustration. It was, after all, the most common method of drawing for the new photographic engraving processes available to publishers of magazines and books at the turn of the century.[1]

In 1899, Hopper graduated from Nyack High School in Nyack, New York and began "to travel daily,"[2] at his parents' urging, to the Correspondence School of Illustration in New York City. Little is known about his year at the school, but it is likely that he made this pen drawing of a woman while a student there in the fall of 1899.

Standing Woman thus was done when Hopper was only seventeen years old and attests to his early facility with pen and ink, and it marks the beginning of his training as a commercial artist. For the next two decades, he would make a living drawing illustrations for books and magazines, while longing to spend his time painting. He would have to wait until he was forty-two for his career as an artist to be launched, finally, at the Frank K. M. Rehn Gallery in New York, in 1924 (see cat. nos. 85-86).

Francesca Consagra

[1] See Gail Levin, "The Early Years of Edward Hopper" in *The Early Drawings of Edward Hopper* (New York, 1995), 2.

[2] Gail Levin, *Edward Hopper: Perspectives on His Life and Work Edward Hopper: A Catalogue Raisonné*, 3 vols. (New York, 1995), 1:27.

85

Edward Hopper
American (1882-1967)

Rockland, Beam Trawler Widgeon (1926)
Watercolor on paper
13⅝" x 19½"
Signature: "Edward Hopper/Rockland, Me."
Gift of Virginia Lewisohn Kahn, class of 1949

Literature: Gail Levin *Edward Hopper: A Catalogue Raisonné*, 3 vols. (New York, 1995), 2:120, cat. no. W-151

During the summer and early fall of 1926, Hopper and his wife, Jo, visited Rockland, Maine, where he spent a great deal of his time painting watercolors that may be grouped into informal series, each with a particular theme: houses in town, rocks at the local quarry, and a group of beam trawlers in the harbor. Sometime later, an interviewer for *Scribner's Magazine* described how Hopper began drawing this group of trawlers:

> Mr. Hopper had accidentally come upon a fleet of lumpy fishing boats equipped with gigantic nets for ground fishing. These had originally been built for the French government during the [First World] War, but with the Armistice they were sold to a large fishing company.[1]

Hopper had already painted at least five watercolors of trawlers in Gloucester, Massachusetts during the summer and fall of 1923 or 1924, when he was preparing for his first one-man show to be held at the Frank K. M. Rehn Gallery in New York. Sixteen watercolors were sold at $100 each.[2] Although none sold were recorded as being trawlers, Hopper had delivered three watercolors of these fishing boats to the gallery in October 1924, the same month as the opening of the exhibition.[3]

Watercolors of trawlers must have been popular (or interesting) enough to encourage Hopper to return to them when preparing for his next exhibition at the Rehn Gallery in February 1927, which was tremendously successful and established his reputation as a painter of the "American Scene."[4] Levin records seven watercolors from this trawler series, which Hopper delivered to the Rehn Gallery in two shipments on 15 August and 30 September 1926. *Beam Trawler Widgeon* belonged to the latter shipment, and Hopper recorded the composition in his record book as "*Rockland. Beam Trawler Widgeon*. Chocolate profile & rigging, far shore sharp."[5]

After 1926, Hopper preferred to concentrate on watercolors of buildings and landscapes. He rarely painted boats in this medium, and when he did, his interest turned to dories and coast guard boats (1929), freighters and tugboats (ca. 1934-38), or the splendid *Yawl Riding a Swell* (1935, Worcester Art Museum). *Beam Trawler Widgeon* was thus one of Hopper's last watercolors of trawlers, and created at an important time in his early career, between his first and second one-man exhibitions in New York.

Francesca Consagra

---

[1] Bernard Myers, ed. "Scribner's American Painter's Series, No. 7," *Scribner's Magazine* 102 (September 1937): 32.

[2] Gail Levin, *Edward Hopper: A Catalogue Raisonné*, 3 vols. (New York, 1995), 1:6.

[3] See Ibid., 2:cat. nos. W-92, W-98, W-99.

[4] Ibid., 1:8.

[5] Ibid., 2:cat. no. W-151.

86

Edward Hopper
American (1882-1967)

Factory (1928)
Charcoal on paper
12" x 18"
Lent by Christopher Tunnard

Edward Hopper painted American cityscapes with a disturbing realism that expressed the world as a strange and vacuous space, with few, if any, inhabitants. He had developed his own personal style of realism (from such important influences as Thomas Eakins, Winslow Homer, Edgar Degas, and John Sloan) as early as 1925. From that time forward, few significant changes occurred in his art or in his life. The charcoal drawing exhibited here, of a factory, most likely dates from his visit to Gloucester, Massachusetts in 1928, the same year that he painted *Freight Cars, Gloucester* (Addison Gallery of American Art, Phillips Academy, Andover, Massachusetts), and *Blackwell's Island* (on extended loan to the Frances Lehman Loeb Art Center).[1]

Hopper had begun to draw factories in Gloucester before 1925,[2] but he had dramatically changed the viewpoint and composition of them by 1928. He himself noted experimenting that year with a "very long horizontal shape...to give a sensation of great lateral extent," and that by "carrying the main horizontal lines of the design with little interruption to the edges of the picture...[it made] one conscious of the spaces and elements beyond the limits of the scene itself."[3]

Hopper explored the use of strong horizontal sweeps in other works of factories dated 1928, including *Box Factory, Gloucester* (Museum of Modern Art, New York), and *Factory and Shed* (Whitney Museum of American Art, New York). The drawing exhibited here, however, is compositionally most like the oil painting, *Freight Cars, Gloucester*, with its sweeping, dark, horizontal form moving from right to left, a strong vertical telegraph pole, and a break in the horizontal by a gabled roof at far left.

Regardless of the medium or size of the work, Hopper's compositions express the same monumental character that are "short, isolated moments of figuration....The shadow of dark hangs over them, making whatever narratives we construct around them seem sentimental and beside the point."[4]

Francesca Consagra

---

1   The rich use of the charcoal used on this sheet is also similar to the small study for the oil painting, *Manhattan Bridge Loop*, done the same year. (Both are owned by the Addison Gallery of American Art).

2   See his watercolor, *Gloucester Factory and House* (Collection of Mr. and Mrs. S. Roger Horchow), signed and dated 1924 and reproduced in Gail Levin, *Edward Hopper: A Catalogue Raisonné*, 3 vols. (New York, 1995), 2:cat. W-102.

3   Hopper to Charles H. Sawyer, writing about *Manhattan Bridge Loop*, letter of 19 October 1939, Addison Gallery of American Art, Phillips Academy, Andover, Massachusetts. Quoted in Lloyd Goodrich, *Edward Hopper* (New York, 1971), 163.

4   Mark Strand, *Hopper* (Hopewell, New Jersey, 1994), 23.

87

Alice Neel
American (1900-1984)

Snow on Cornelia Street (1933)
Oil on canvas
30" x 24"
Collection of Peggy Brooks, class of 1940

Literature: Pamela Allara, *Pictures of People: Alice Neel's American Portrait Gallery* (Hanover and London, 1998), 69, fig. 35; Ann Sutherland Harris, *Alice Neel* (Los Angeles, 1983), 8, no. 1

Alice Neel arrived in Greenwich Village, then the epicenter of American bohemian life in 1931, to fulfill her childhood ambition to be a painter. Before her death in 1984, she told an interviewer, "I had a very hard life, and I paid the price for it, but I did as I wanted."[1] Raised in the small town of Colwyn, Pennsylvania and trained at the Philadelphia School of Art (now Moore College of Art), Neel only attained mainstream recognition as an artist in the 1960s. In the 70s, she won numerous prestigious awards and lectured frequently on her art. The Public Broadcasting System made a film on her life, and the Whitney Museum of American Art mounted a retrospective of her work. She entered the pantheon of great twentieth-century women artists when President Jimmy Carter honored her, and four other artists, at the end of the decade as the first recipients of the Women's Caucus for Art awards. Neel's celebrity status was such that in the years before her death, she appeared twice as a guest on Johnny Carson's television program, *The Tonight Show*.

Neel achieved fame for portrait painting. Her portraits were not flattering to her sitters, many of whom sat for her in the nude and rarely purchased their likeness. Her unique style combined realism with expressionistic distortion by exaggerating certain of her subject's distinctive physical characteristics. Neel used glaringly bold colors and painted her sitters with harsh outlines that emphasized the linear rather than sculptural quality of the human form.

Neel painted *Snow on Cornelia Street* in 1933, the day the federal government's Public Works of Art Project hired her as an easel painter. Since her arrival in New York two years earlier, Neel had been struggling to survive, living in poverty and suffering from depression, a result of the dissolution of her marriage and concomitant break-up of her family. Despite living in such anguish, *Snow on Cornelia Street* is unequivocally the work of an assured artist. Here, she has painted a view from her rear window, striking in its simplic-

ity and sense of place. As a formal composition, it is structurally well defined, with contours softened by snow, although the perspective is in no way pictorially correct. Anne Sutherland Harris has remarked that the painting "is a work of strength and sobriety, which holds its own beside earlier New York snow scenes by John Sloan and Edward Hopper."[2]

Snow on Cornelia Street belongs to the body of work Neel accomplished in the 1930s, some of which overtly reflected her political sympathies for the left, and all of which showed her remarkable talent as a social realist. She acknowledged the historical importance of art and art training, and believed that "more is communicated about [an] era and its effect on people by a revealing portrait than in any other way."[3]

Neel's art, including her portraiture, has always referred to the artist herself; her paintings are as much about her emotional response and sentiments as they are about her subjects. Such is the case with *Snow on Cornelia Street*, though neither she nor any other human element is physically present in the picture. Rather, the painting can be considered a reflection of her inner world, the isolation she felt as an artist, but also like the freshly laid blanket of show, representing a cleansing and rejuvenation of her spirit on the day the federal government employed her as an artist.

Rebecca Lawton

[1]   "Alice Neel Dead; Portrait Artist," *New York Times* (14 October 1984), 44.

[2]   Ann Sutherland Harris, *Alice Neel Paintings 1933-1982* (Los Angeles, 1983), 8, no. 1.

[3]   *Memorial Exhibition* (American Academy and Institute of Arts and Letters, 1985), unpaginated; in Curatorial Files, Frances Lehman Loeb Art Center.

88

Andrée Ruellen
American (born 1905)

Mural Study for Delhi, N.Y., Post Office (presentation drawing for the 48 States Competition; 1939)
Oil on board
15$^1/_2$" x 39$^1/_2$"
Inscription: pencil, on verso, "Delhi, N.Y."
Promised Gift of Steven R. and Susan Hirsch (Steven R. Hirsch, class of 1971)

Exhibitions: Donald D. Keyes, *Andreé Ruellen*, Georgia Museum of Art, University of Georgia, Athens, 30 January-21 March 1993; *The Hyde Collection*, Gibbs Museum of Art, Charleston, South Carolina, 27 June-22 August 1993, 15 September-31 October 1993, 23, no. 16

As a child, Andreé Ruellen's liberal-minded parents, both French-born immigrants, exposed her to a wide range of cultural activity in New York City. Born there in 1905, Ruellen displayed a precocious talent for art and a particularly dexterous hand at drawing. She studied at the Art Students League on scholarship in the early 1920s, at a time when male instructors could still deny female students access to drawing from life; one of Ruellen's League instructors had prevented her from taking his life-drawing class. A self-taught painter, Ruellen befriended dozens of artists in New York, Rome, and Paris, who in turn exposed her to modernism and encouraged her career. The artist, Adolf Dehn, for example, introduced Ruellen to Carl Zigrosser, then director of New York's prestigious E. Weyhe Gallery, who mounted her first solo exhibition in April 1928 and thus established her reputation within the city's art circles. In 1929, Ruellen married a fellow artist, John "Jack" Taylor, and moved into his house in Shady, New York, near the legendary Woodstock Art Colony. There, she joined a group of European-trained artists, such as Konrad Cramer (see cat. no. 90), and Andrew Dasburg, and became active in the Woodstock Artists Association.

By living modestly and by having steady sales of her work, Ruellen did not require relief employment within the various WPA agencies, which operated from late 1933 to 1943, to support American artists during the Depression. However, she submitted drawings to a nonrelief-based program, the Treasury Department's Section of Painting and Sculpture, which sponsored a nationwide contest to place murals in federal buildings.[1] Since the competition required winners to pay all expenses associated with the execution and installation of their work, Ruellen, no doubt, chose Delhi because the village was located not far from Woodstock. She approached mural painting as she approached art in general, basing her designs upon the direct observation of modern life. Her proposal, a scene of farming, is in keeping with the Section's recommendation for artists to choose subject matter of local interest, whether it be from history or contemporary life.

Section officials "offered" artists various themes, agriculture among them, to help them create a "distinguished and vital design."[2] During the Depression, images of agriculture, especially those of the rural past, posited the family farm as essential to the nation's well-being. Further, the blame placed upon industrial America for the country's economic problems inspired the public to view rural farm life as a model for rediscovering humane values. The centuries-old tradition of the yeoman farmer as the embodiment of the American character was a popular theme for artists working on government-sponsored projects. The prototypical American hero, Thomas Jefferson, had recognized the farmer's importance to the republic in 1785, during a trip to Paris: "Cultivators of the earth are the most valuable citizens. The are the most vigorous, the most independent, the most virtuous, and they are tied to their country and wedded to its liberty and interests by the most lasting bonds."[3] Ruellen's choice to present a scene of non-rather than preindustrial farming presents Delhi as an exceedingly pleasant community. Her proposed mural shows a farmer at left, standing in a wheat field, while two young children observe him in the process of sharpening his scythe. At right, a second farmer works the field with a horse-drawn cutting rig. Also at right, Ruellen situated a red barn in the background and a boy petting his dog, foreground. In the distance at left, is a small bridge over the West Branch of the Schoharie River, which runs through Delhi.

Here, children are presented as spectators, passively observing men at labor. With children no longer required to work as field hands, nature takes on the role of a playground, a place for them to engage in activities of idle interest. Ruellen has balanced her composition by creating pairs—a girl and a boy, and a brown and a white work horse pulling the rig. Not the least obvious is Ruellen's placement of a pair of trees at center—one in full bloom, the other exposing dead branches.

Given Ruellen's leftist politics, her support of the Popular Front, Spain's anti-Fascists, and the American Artists' Congress—she may have used the scythe to symbolize more than just a harvesting

210

tool. Long used in Europe as a symbol of the peasantry, the scythe points to a celebration of the relationship between man and nature, just as it also signals oppression and further suggests anti-industrial sentiments.

Ruellen's great admiration for the graphic art of the German artist, Käthe Kollwitz, who used her own art as a form of social protest, particularly against the spread of capitalism, exerted a strong influence upon her.[4] Kollwitz's graphic art in fact engendered strong interest among American print connoisseurs during the mid- to late thirties. Zigrosser promoted Kollwitz's work at the Weyhe Gallery as early as 1936, providing Ruellen with the opportunity to study her work in detail. In June 1938, both Ruellen and Kollwitz had exhibitions in New York galleries, which were reviewed in the same issue of *The Magazine of Art*. The meaning of the scythe as employed by Kollowitz in such haunting prints as *Whetting the Scythe, 1905* from the *Peasants' War* cycle, could not have escaped Ruellen, who nonetheless chose not to make politics her subject matter.

The size and layout of the post office dictated that designs be formatted as a classical frieze and, in certain cases, artists submitted sketches to accommodate the location of the postmaster's door at center. Ruellen's study, done in oil with brisk brushwork, uses the horizontal format in full measure by creating a uniform play of bright sunlight throughout the composition. The clarity of her design and her use of bright, contrasting colors successfully achieve the vitality Section officials sought in the winning designs. Despite this, Ruellen lost the contest to Mary Early, who received the commission for the Delhi Post Office with a historical subject, *The Down-Rent War of 1845* (1939). Ruellen's preliminary study did not go unnoticed, as Section officials later awarded her two post-office commissions, *Country Saw Mill* (1941) for Emporia, Virginia and *Spring in Georgia* (1942) for the Lawrenceville Post Office and Agriculture Building (presently located in the Office of Fine Arts and Historic Preservation, Government Services Agency, Washington, D.C.).

Rebecca Lawton

[1] See *Section of Painting and Sculpture Bulletin* 19 (June 1939): 4-30; and Karal Ann Marling, *Wall to Wall: A Cultural History of Post Office Murals in the Great Depression* (Minneapolis, 1982), 81.

[2] *Section of Painting and Sculpture Bulletin*, 5.

[3] Joseph B. Ross, "The Agrarian Revolution in the Middle West," *North American Review* 189 (September 1909): 376; as quoted in Charles C. Eldredge, *Georgia O'Keeffe: American and Modern* (New Haven and London, 1993), 191.

[4] Marlene Park, "Andrée Ruellen: Her Life in Art," in *Andrée Ruellen* (Athens, Georgia, 1993), 56.

89

Reginald Marsh
American (1898-1954)

Bowery Scene (White Tower Hamburger) (1945)
Brush and Chinese ink over charcoal
22¹/₂" x 30"
Signature: ink, lower right, "Reginald Marsh-1945"
Lent by Ellen G. and Leonard Milberg (Ellen D. Gordon, class of 1960)

Provenance: Kraushaar Galleries

From the mid-1920s, when Reginald Marsh began his artistic career, until his death, his art was synonymous with the social realism that was spawned in the circle of artists around Robert Henri and grew to maturity during the Depression. Marsh was the son of the painters, Fred Dana and Alice Randall Marsh. He grew up in Nutley, New Jersey and New Rochelle, New York, suburbs of New York City, but his art would always be about the city and its people. He attended Yale and graduated in 1920, afterwards receiving work as a freelance illustrator for magazines such as *Harper's Bazaar*, *Vanity Fair*, and *The New Yorker*. In the same year he went to Europe, where he resided for six months, returning and falling under the influence of the painter of urban themes, Kenneth Hayes Miller. This would set the stage for the next thirty years of Marsh's career, during which city scenes from bawdy entertainments to public transportation became grist for his mill.

This previously unpublished drawing is an important one in many ways within the context of Marsh's work. It is a large, heroic, and beautifully articulated wash drawing of the area under the old Third Avenue elevated railway at Chatham Square, at the lower end of the Bowery. Stebbins has remarked on the exceptional quality of a similar drawing of the same location, same size, and done at the same time, apparently part of a series that includes the Milberg drawing.[1] Here, in our drawing, among the signs of the urban environment—the White Tower Hamburger restaurant with its sign reading, "buy a bagful"; the fire alarm box; and the erect, staggering, and unconscious denizens of the Bowery—we are greeted by a composition replete with unexpected elements of "high" art and classical allusion.

The setting under the steel supporting columns, spandrels, and girders of the El is presented obliquely, with an emphasis on the lofty space it encloses, calling to mind one of Piranesi's fantastic *Carceri* series, and suggestive, therefore, of another form of urban imprisonment. The emphasis on classicism is further enhanced by the carefully placed reclining derelict in the lower-left corner, his drunken head bowed and his near arm wrapped around a standpipe. This classic *repoussoir* element anchors the composition and refers in pose to a classic river god, as in Renaissance paintings and prints. It also quotes verbatim from the art of Michelangelo and presents an updated version of the Renaissance master's "proto-inebriate" Moses, the father of all drunks, from the relevant scene on the ceiling of the Sistine Chapel.[2]

While at first seemingly incongruous, Marsh's quotation of the great masters of art should come as no surprise. Goodrich tells us that his parents' home was covered with reproductions of the great works by Titian, Tintoretto, Rubens, and Rembrandt, as well as scores of art books.[3] Goodrich also published a number of sheets of sketches made by Marsh after Raphael, Leonardo, Rubens, and Michelangelo. The drawings after Michelangelo include studies of the large marble *David*, and that of *Adam* and the *Libyan Sibyl* from the Sistine Ceiling. The latter two drawings were likely made after the drawings by Michelangelo, owned by the Metropolitan Museum.[4]

James Mundy, class of 1974

---

[1]   Theodore E. Stebbins, Jr., *American Master Drawings and Watercolors* (New York, 1976), 295, fig. 255. This drawing is in the collection of the Whitney Museum of American Art.

[2]   For this image see, *inter alia*, Charles de Tolnay, *Michelangelo* (Princeton, 1975), fig. 55.

[3]   Lloyd Goodrich, *Reginald Marsh* (New York, 1972), 17.

[4]   Ibid., 210-15. In 1972, these drawings were in the collection of the artist's widow.

7UP
SOLD HERE
WHITE TOWER
HAMBURGER
Buy
a bagful
Towers
Mean
WILLIAMS
FOOD
CHATHAM SQ
DOYERS
Reginald Marsh - 1945

90

Konrad Cramer
American, German-born (1888-1963)

Abstraction (ca. 1913)
Oil on canvas
19" x 16"
Lent by Mr. Steven R. and Susan Hirsch (Steven R. Hirsch, class of 1971)

Provenance: Estate of the artist

Exhibition: *Concerning Expressionism, American Modernism, and the German Avant-Garde*, Hollis Taggert Galleries, New York, 20 May-31 July 1998, 60, no. 31

Born in 1888 in Würzburg, Germany, Konrad Cramer arrived in America in 1911 with his American wife, Florence Ballen, also an artist. From 1906 until 1908, he studied at the Karlsruhe Academy of Fine Arts. Cramer met *Der Blaue Reiter's* theoretician-artists, Wassily Kandinsky and Franz Marc, in Munich in 1910. His subsequent move toward pure abstraction was a direct result of his association with Kandinsky and Marc, whose aesthetic theories postulated art as the embodiment of the spirit. Form, as defined in the nineteenth century by realism, was rendered meaningless unless it expressed the artist's inner feelings.

Cramer was one of the first artists in America to experiment with pure abstraction as articulated chiefly through Kandinsky's critical writings. Though he produced nonrepresentational works for a relatively short period, paintings such as the canvas under discussion here reflect Cramer's distinctive contribution to nonobjective art. Far less derivative than many of his other paintings produced around the same time, which are strikingly akin to Kandinsky's work, *Abstraction* employs vivid unmodulated colors and brisk, highly visible, and seemingly erratic brushwork. In certain areas, Cramer has worked the edge of the paint, refraining from placing colors directly adjacent to one another, allowing slivers and spots of primed canvas to appear as part of the painting. The structural underpinnings of the painting are solely dependent upon color forms, both organic and geometric shapes, which in turn embody its emotive content. In this respect, *Abstraction* stands as a precursor to the abstract expressionism developed by American artists in the 1950s.

Rebecca Lawton

91

Patrick Henry Bruce
American (1881-1937)

Peinture/Nature morte (Painting, Still life)(ca. 1923-24)
Oil on pencil on canvas
31¼" x 38½"
Collection of Dorothy Seiberling, class of 1943

Provenance: Patrick Henry Bruce; Henri-Pierre Roché; Mme Henri-Pierre Roché; Knoedler & Co., Inc., New York, 1965-67; Noah Goldowsky Gallery, New York, 1967

Literature: William Agee and Barbara Rose, *Patrick Henry Bruce: American Modernist, A Catalogue Raisonné* (New York, 1979), 203, no. D15

Exhibition: Noah Goldowsky Gallery, New York, 1967

Patrick Henry Bruce was a little-known, somewhat enigmatic painter until William Agee and Barbara Rose published their monograph and catalogue raisonné in 1979.[1] Born into a Southern family of great ancestral wealth in 1881, Bruce died in poverty in New York in 1936. He ended his own life at the age of fifty-five, leaving behind a small, but remarkable body of work and an important legacy as an early American modernist. It is odd that Bruce, who had close contact with nearly all of the major American and European artists and patrons of his generation, nearly escaped recognition as one of the most original painters of the twentieth century.

Bruce's training was conventional. He studied art with William Merritt Chase and Robert Henri at the New York School of Art in 1902-03. By 1904, he was in living in Paris, where, four years later, he became an original member of the Matisse School. Through Matisse, Bruce developed a strong affinity for Cézanne's work and an encyclopedic knowledge of European modern art that is evident in a series of still lifes Bruce painted during the years 1908-12. After meeting Robert and Sonia Delaunay, pioneers of the cubist-based abstract style of painting called orphism, in late 1912, Bruce experimented with their theory of achieving a sense of movement by contrasting high-keyed colors of varying hues and values. His art developed along the lines of the synchromists, who employed a systematic technique to produce harmonious combinations through the separation, rather than gradation, of colors, and the futurists, who were preoccupied with using color and composition to achieve a sense of motion in their work.

Bruce was among a handful of artists, and the only American artist, to remain in Paris during and after World War I. Within that period, roughly 1916-17, his painting shifted, progressing from the synchromist and futurist interest in movement to a classicizing cubism that advocated reducing forms to simple geometric struc-

tures. Bruce's work became composed of stable forms rendered with machinelike precision and painted in pure, unmodulated colors.

The work discussed here belongs to a group of twenty-five known geometric still lifes that Bruce produced late in his career between circa 1917 and 1930. Originally owned and catalogued by Bruce's friend, the novelist Henri-Pierre Roché, according to William Agee this painting is one of twelve works to receive alterations from an unknown source sometime between January 1964 and September 1965, when Roché's widow had them in her possession. In the late geometric abstractions, all of which are based upon the tradition of the still life, Bruce gradually distilled his subject matter into three-dimensional elements such as triangles, wedges, and cylinders. Many of these elements appear to be the remnants of wood from which craftsmen had cut pieces to fashion into furniture and architectural fittings. The objects Bruce chose for his paintings have been identified from photographs of his Paris home and studio as his personal affects, his straw boater, his furniture, and dinner-ware, as well as the wood cutouts the artist discovered while buying antiques.[2]

In a number of the late geometric paintings, Bruce returned to his earlier interest in Cézanne's work. Thus, his still lifes can be considered as both paeans to, and a radical departure from, Cézanne's late still-life paintings of fruit. In these works, Bruce deliberately left areas of the canvas unpainted, just as Cézanne had in his own works. The painting under consideration here can also be categorized as belonging to a fifth group of works within the larger group of geometric still lifes. There are thinly painted canvases with visible traces of pencil and extensive erasures. Agee has dubbed these works "triangular arch" or "collapsed beam"

paintings, because in all these works, Bruce has introduced an inverted V shape into the background[3], an attempt to make his compositions more complex. In this work, Bruce has increased the number of elements and tried to make it appear as if the table and its contents were merged into the spatial setting, thereby taking his subject to the point at which it is about to lose its structure and dissolve into complete nonobjective abstraction.

Critics, who misunderstood Bruce's intentions, responded negatively to the geometric paintings, causing the artist to stop exhibiting his work. Bruce's health declined rapidly after 1930. In July 1936, he returned to America to live with his sister in New York and died there less than four months later.

Rebecca Lawton

[1]   William Agee and Barbara Rose, *Patrick Henry Bruce: American Modernist, A Catalogue Raisonné* (New York, 1979).

[2]   Ibid., 32.

[3]   Ibid., 36.

92

Arthur Dove
American (1880-1946)

Music
Oil on cardboard mounted on canvas
15¹/₂" x 11¹/₂"
Lent by Mr. and Mrs. Henry A. Ashforth, Jr. (Georgia M. Perkins, class of 1954)

Literature: Donna Cassidy, *Painting the Musical City, Jazz and Cultural Identity in American Art 1910-1940* (Washington, D.C., 1997), 81, fig. 52; Donna Cassidy, "Arthur Dove's Music Paintings of the Jazz Age," *American Art Journal* 1 (1988): 4-23 and 8, fig., 4; Barbara Haskell, *Arthur Dove* (Boston, 1975), 29; William Innes Homer, *Alfred Stieglitz and the American Avant-Garde* (Boston, 1977), 211, fig. 98; Ann Morgan, *Arthur Dove: Catalogue Raisonné* (Newark, Delaware, 1984), 114, no. 13.1; Judith Zilczer, "Synaesthesia and Popular Culture: Arthur Dove, George Gershwin, and the Rhapsody in Blue," *Art Journal* 44 (Winter 1984): 361-66 and 362, fig. 3

Arthur Garfield Dove, born in Canandaigua, New York in 1880, and raised within a prosperous and politically active family, graduated from Cornell University in 1903.[1] He abandoned future plans for law school to become a freelance illustrator in New York City, working for *Collier's*, *McCall's*, and *The Saturday Evening Post*. While studying painting in France between the late spring of 1908 and July 1909, Dove encountered European avant-garde aesthetics, particularly the cubism and Fauvism practiced by Cézanne and Matisse, as well as the Italian-born theory called futurism, which admonished painters and poets to reflect the dynamic energy and movement of contemporary life in their art.

Within a year of Dove's return from France, Alfred Stieglitz began promoting his career, first exhibiting the artist's work in a group show entitled, *Younger American Painters* (March 1910) at the Little Galleries of the Photo-Secession (commonly referred by it's Fifth Avenue address, "291"). A solo exhibition of Dove's paintings and pastels, *Arthur G. Dove First Exhibition Anywhere*, also mounted by Stieglitz at "291," followed in 1912. Outstanding among the works Dove exhibited were a series of nonrepresentational pastels, known as *The Ten Commandments*, which received some praise, but also contentious criticism, and earned Dove recognition as the first American to show nonillusionistic art publicly. Dove later explained that he had based these works on the concept of nature as a living force, rendered pictorially by organic forms within an abstract style.[2]

Music is one of about fifteen paintings and sketches on the theme of music that Dove produced throughout his career from circa 1912-13 to 1944.[3] After the *Ten Commandments* pastels, some of which were given titles associated with music, the painting discussed here is the artist's earliest known nonillusionist, musically-inspired oil painting.

Dove probably painted *Music* after seeing the famous *International Exhibition of Modern Painting*, better known as the Armory Show, held in New York in February 1913. There, Dove must have seen, studied, and discussed with his colleagues the totally abstract paintings by Francis Picabia and Wassily Kandinsky on view. Picabia, who had arrived in New York in January 1913, had come to "291" nearly every day thereafter. Donna Cassidy has commented that *Music* was Dove's response to synaesthesia—the analogy between one art form, or the faculty of its perception, and another—a theory popular among the New York avant-garde at the time. Cassidy is among the scholars that have argued persuasively the seminal importance of Francis Picabia's influence upon Dove.[4] Dove's *Music* is similar in many respects to Picabia's painting, *Dances at the Spring*, displayed at the Armory Show. Both share motifs of simplified natural forms in modulated color with repeated arcs creating visual rhythm.

Both Picabia and Marcel Duchamp, who also exhibited at the Armory Show, articulated the concept of dynamism as the characteristic of the modern age, and both artists saw the concept manifested in American Jazz, skyscrapers, and advertising.[5] *Music*, although highly abstract, contains elements that suggest skyscrapers in the upper left corner. Moreover, the repeated arcs, which swirl about in the foreground, suggest sound waves associated with the syncopated rhythm of jazz.

Critics within the Stieglitz circle, such as Paul Rosenfeld, documented the popularity of the music-painting analogy among the New York avant-garde. Rosenfeld presented music as an abstract and spiritual art form, and artists in turn, painted nonobjective,

supernal visions and called them music. Marsden Hartley and Abraham Walkowitz gave their abstract paintings musical titles. Moreover, Dove, as an amateur musician, would have been particularly receptive to the music-painting analogy. Dove learned to think subjectively and to recreate form and color through certain sensations, the vibrations of music being foremost among them.

Rebecca Lawton

[1] Dove's father served several terms as County Clerk and Dove was named for the Republican presidential and vice-presidential candidates, who won election that year.

[2] Sherrye Cohn, *Arthur Dove: Nature as Symbol* (Ann Arbor, Michigan, 1985), 7.

[3] Donna M. Cassidy, *Painting the Musical City 1910-1940* (Washington, D.C. and London, 1997), 81.

[4] Ibid., 81.

[5] Ibid., 77-79.

93

Georgia O'Keeffe
American (1887-1986)

Blue Morning Glories, New Mexico, II (1935)
Oil on canvas
12¼" x 9"
Signature: on verso, "G. O'Keeffe35"
Promised Gift of Anonymous, class of 1953

Provenance: Georgia O'Keeffe; Malvina Hoffman; by descent to her nephew, Charles Hoffman; James Maroney, New York; Estate of Peter Gilbert; Gerald Peters Gallery, Santa Fe, New Mexico

Exhibitions: *Georgia O'Keeffe, Recent Paintings*, An American Place, New York, January-February 1935, no. 14; *Georgia O'Keeffe and Her Circle*, McKissick Museum, University of South Carolina, Columbia, South Carolina, August-September 1980, no. 8; *Twenty-Eighth Annual Theta Charity Antiques Show*, Houston, September, 1980

One of the most emblematic women artists of the twentieth century, Georgia O'Keeffe was born near Sun Prairie, Wisconsin in November 1887. A childhood interest in art propelled her to study with several teachers in numerous places between 1905 and 1916, when she spent a final semester studying with Arthur Wesley Dow at Columbia University Teachers College in New York. Also in 1916, Alfred Stieglitz discovered O'Keeffe's work and thereafter exhibited her art in his various New York galleries. O'Keeffe joined Stieglitz's circle of avant-garde artists, such as Arthur Dove (see cat. no. 92), John Marin, Paul Strand, and Marsden Hartley, among others, becoming Stieglitz's protégé and companion, and in 1924, his wife. Even before her marriage, O'Keeffe had established a pattern of independence from Stieglitz that continued until his death in 1946.

O'Keeffe fashioned a variety of advanced art theories into a personal idiom. *Morning Glories*, of 1935, is a good example of her method for attaining originality based upon her perceptual experience. O'Keeffe started painting large floral subjects in 1924, the year of her marriage, exhibiting for them first time in 1925, at a group show organized by Stieglitz at the Anderson Galleries in New York. Immediately popular, the floral paintings continued her longstanding interest in simplified natural forms and rhythmic movement, but in these works the imagery, though recognizable, was no less original than her abstractions. O'Keeffe painted her flowers not in the traditional still-life fashion, as an arrangement of shapes and colors placed in a vase on a table, but as solitary, larger-than-life-sized objects presented startlingly close up. She said she wanted to paint flowers that captured people's attention.[1] Yet, as one approaches O'Keeffe's flowers, they cease to appear as flowers, instead dissolving into brushstrokes connoting nonrepresentational forms and color sensation.

O'Keeffe disagreed with the critics, who characterized her flower paintings as sexual metaphors, just as she also negated the assumption that her isolated paintings of flowers were based upon the extreme close-up photographs of flowers taken in the 1920s by Stieglitz, Paul Strand, Edward Steichen, and Edward Weston.

Early critical response to O'Keeffe's work seldom failed to take note of her gender or to view her work through Freudian analogies and as associative connections to the female body. The critic, Paul Rosenfeld, a member of Stieglitz's circle, promoted Stieglitz's early view: "Woman *Feels* the World *differently* than Man Feels it."[2] In his essay on Arthur Dove in *Port of New York*, Rosenfeld clarified the distinction between O'Keeffe's "female" art as an intuitive feeling that "the world is within herself" and Dove's "male" art, in which "he feels himself present out in [the world's] proper elements."[3] William Murrell Fisher perceived O'Keeffe's highly intuitive method of interpreting nature as "mystical" and "musical" and thus not significantly different from Dove's interpretation of nature.[4] Dove, upon viewing O'Keeffe's first abstractions, in turn told Stieglitz, "this girl is doing naturally what many of us fellows are trying to do, and failing."[5]

Rebecca Lawton

---

[1] See Abraham A. Davidson, *Early American Modernist Painting 1910-1935* (New York, 1981), 204.

[2] Quoted by Dorothy Norman in *Alfred Steiglitz: An American Seer* (New York, 1973), 137.

[3] Paul Rosenfeld, *Port of New York: Essays on Fourteen American Moderns* (New York, 1924), 170-71.

[4] Quoted by Charles C. Eldredge, *Georgia O'Keeffe: American and Modern* (New Haven and London, 1993), 177.

[5] Ibid., 176.

94

Georgia O'Keeffe
American (1887-1986)

Cottonwood No. 1 (1944)
Oil on canvas
30" x 36"
Promised Gift of Mary Pick Hines, class of 1953

Provenance: Georgia O'Keeffe; Gerald Peters Gallery, Santa, Fe, New Mexico

Trees, various kinds and painted during various seasons, were a major theme in O'Keeffe's work. She perhaps felt about trees as she did about flowers (see cat. no. 93): each motif appealed to her desire to hold the viewer's attention, to make viewers look, rather than glance, and to make viewers respond to them, as natural artifacts of mystery and wonder.

O'Keeffe introduced paintings of cottonwood trees at her annual exhibition at An American Place in early 1944 and painted them several times thereafter. Her first series of cottonwood trees—as evident in the painting under discussion here—are the most realistic of all the series. Here the cottonwood tree is placed within a representational landscape setting with green grass and blue sky.

Yet, like her flower painting, the tree is the subject, presented without additional details and elements cluttering the composition. O'Keeffe's emphasis is upon the swelling forms of the trunks and billowing branches, which she has painted through the subtle gradations of hue. O'Keeffe's simplification of form, the paring down of the design, and the hardening of contours, gave her trees a spare elegance.

In later paintings, she extrapolated and accentuated the wispy, feathery quality of the cottonwood's leaves, thereby making them appear increasingly nonillusionistic.

Rebecca Lawton

95

Isamu Noguchi
American (1904-88)

Untitled (1930)
Ink on paper
71¹/₄" x 39"
Collection of Priscilla Morgan, class of 1941

Isamu Noguchi, the sculptor and designer, was thirty-three when he returned to Asia, after having left Japan at the age of twelve to attended American schools. His financial success as a portraitist allowed him to visit Beijing for eight months in 1930-31, where he studied brush drawing with the great painter, Qi Baishi (also spelled Chi Pai Shih, meaning "Great White Mountain"). The seventy-year-old master lived in a compound "surrounded by his children and grandchildren," and Noguchi was received "with great kindness" by Qi Baishi's family.[1] In his biography, Noguchi looked fondly back at this period in his development as an artist when he made "enormous drawings with fantastic brushes and expressionist flourishes upon their incredibly beautiful paper."[2] Bruce Altshuler noted in 1994 that Noguchi's "natural facility was never more clearly displayed than in his quick mastery of the difficulties of ink-brush painting and in the large number of scrolls that he produced in such a short time. These are dramatic works, combining long, restrained lines with dynamic ink washes of great agitation. They are unique in scale and ambition among Noguchi's many drawings, which after this point would consist primarily of travel sketches and ideas for sculpture."[3]

The Noguchi scroll in this exhibition depicts a naked infant kicking his left leg in a large circular motion. (Perhaps he is even one of Qi Baishi's grandchildren, drawn while Noguchi studied at the compound.) The sensual quality of the brush work and the simplic-

ity of the rounded forms around the head and the body not only allude to contemporary Chinese painting, but also the influence of Brancusi, with whom Noguchi apprenticed in Paris just three years earlier. When he departed Brancusi's studio after six months, Noguchi had obtained a deeper respect for materials and a greater understanding of how to use the tools of a sculptor than he had learned in the United States, but he was not converted to pure abstraction, as he noted, "pure abstractions, or at least those geometrically derived, left me cold, and I was always being torn between Brancusi's admonition and my desire to make something more meaningful to myself."[4]

This joyous image may hark back to Noguchi's childhood memories of Japan, where kites and paper objects were so common. Noguchi's stay in Beijing, after such a long hiatus from Asia, allowed him to revel in Asian materials and painting traditions. They also prepared him psychologically for his subsequent trip to Japan to meet with his estranged father.

Francesca Consagra

1   Dore Ashton, *Noguchi east and west* (New York, 1992), 29.

2   Isamu Noguchi, *A Sculptor's World* (New York, 1968), 20.

3   Bruce Altshuler, *Isamu Noguchi* (New York, ca. 1994), 20.

4   Noguchi, *A Sculptor's World*, 18.

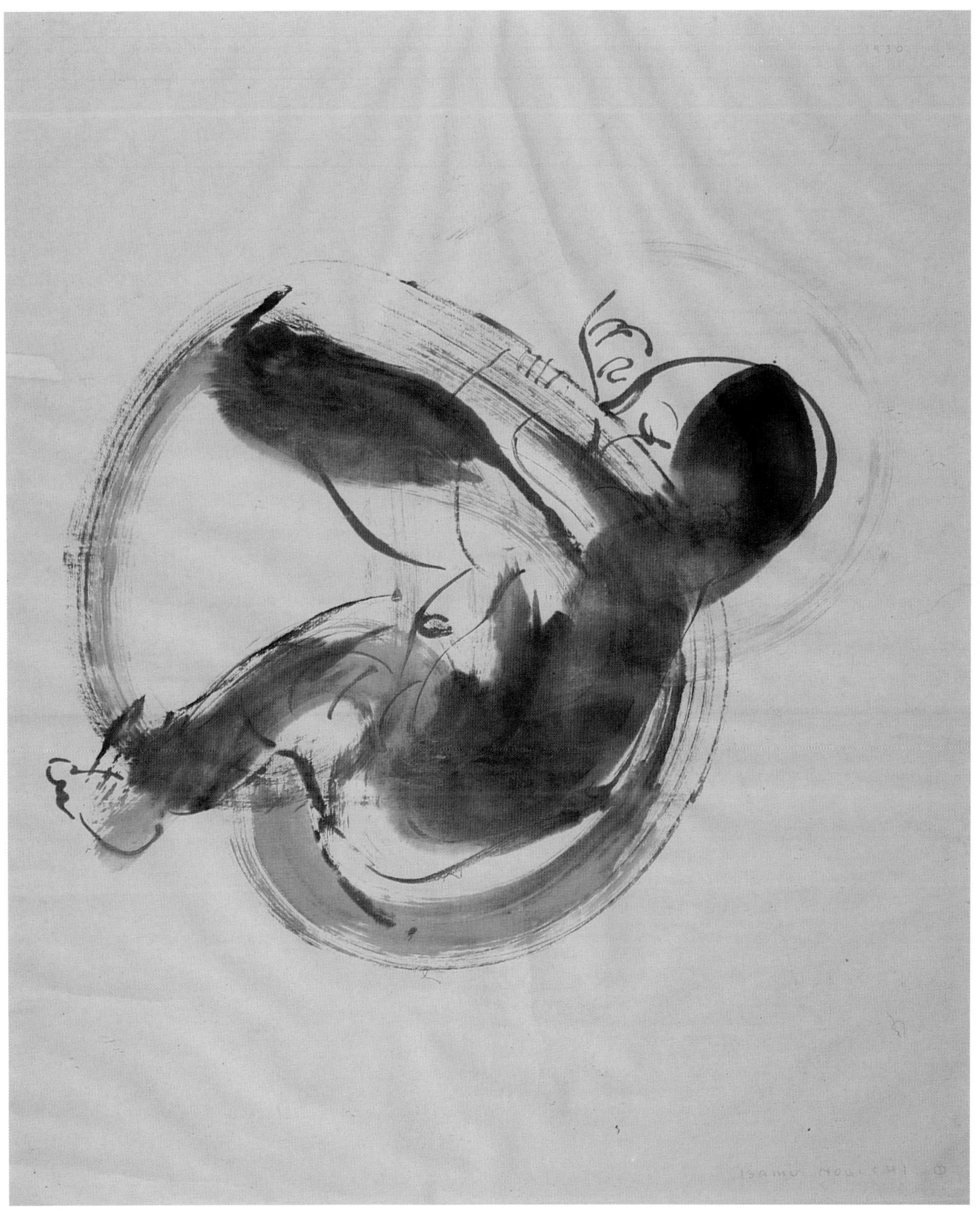

96

Isamu Noguchi
American (1904-88)

Floor Frame (1962)
Bronze
Height, 15"; width, 44"; depth, 26"
Lent by Joan and Robert Bernhard (Joan E. Mack, class of 1953)

Floor Frame was created at a time in mid-career, when Isamu Noguchi, who historically preferred working in stone over all other materials, turned to another traditional sculptural material, bronze, and began to experiment with cast rather than carved works of art. These bronzes, begun in 1944 and completed in 1963, were modestly scaled works, with some quite modest indeed, no larger than a foot square. Others, like *Floor Frame*, were of a size that suggest that the sculptor envisioned them as private rather than public works, but works designed nonetheless to define and punctuate a significant area of open space.

Noguchi's inspiration to work in bronze surely came from his study and interest in ancient Greek sculpture (he did a series of works in Greek marble during roughly the same period as the bronzes), but also from an awareness of Chinese bronzes, about which he had known since his travels to Asia on a Guggenheim grant in 1927-29. Still, according to the critic, Dore Ashton, the most important experience related to *Floor Frame* came during Noguchi's visit to Japan, at the end of World War II, and specifically to a number of Japanese gardens.

Floor Frame, a sculpture that literally lies upon and celebrates the floor, recalls the landscaped Ryoan-ji garden in Kyoto, which, created during the Muromachi period, is strongly influenced by a Zen aesthetic. Ryoan-ji consists of an open rectangular space of smoothly raked gravel and rocks. Like the rocks and gravel of Ryoan-ji, *Floor Frame* exists partly as a metaphor, and partly as itself: that is, partly as a "frame" upon the floor, and partly as an object which, simply by being placed upon the floor, draws attention not only to itself, but to the floor, and to the viewer's relation to both the sculpture and the floor. In *Floor Frame*, Noguchi demon-

strates a personal aesthetic that has much in common with traditional Japanese aesthetic values, including a love of natural material, a taste for asymmetry, a sense of humor, and, finally, a tolerance for the paradoxical or contradictory. But Noguchi was also deeply influenced here, as well, by Western modernism, with its love of pure form, pure materials, and pure abstraction.

According to Ashton:

> Much of what [Noguchi] learned visiting the old landscaped gardens [of Japan] confirmed his early intuitions of a universal order. As a sculptor he lived with a sense of environing space and questioned its nature always. His concentration on the relation of man's relation to the earth, both literally and figuratively, led him quite naturally to ponder the meanings of the Japanese vision of sculptured space. In Japanese gardens the principle of restraint reigns. Subtlety speaks....Floor Frame with its tectonic lines, broadens the reference [to floor and earth]. As early modernists discovered, the pedestal is not always eloquent. Sometimes our sense of space is heightened when our vantage point shifts from eye level to floor level.[1]

Noguchi, whose primary concern as a sculptor was always man's relation to earth, seemed to agree, for, as he stated shortly after his return from Japan, "The floor is our platform of humanity, as the Japanese well know. The floor in its entirety graces all who enter. They partake in the experience of being sculpture."[2]

Justin Spring

---

[1] Dore Ashton, *Isamu Noguchi: Bronze and Iron Sculpture* (New York, 1988), v.

[2] "Isamu Noguchi on his Sculpture," *Art News* 47 (1949), as quoted in Ashton, *Isamu Noguchi*, v.

97

David Smith
American (1906-65)

Untitled (1951)
Gouache on paper
$25^3/_4$" x $19^7/_8$"
Inscription: lower left, "ΔΣ 1951"
Lent by Belle K. Ribicoff, class of 1945

"Drawing is the most direct, closest to the true self, the most natural liberation of man—and if I may guess back to the action of very early man, it may have been the first celebration of man with his secret self—even before song....Drawings remain the life force of the artist. Especially this is true for the sculptor, who, of necessity, works in a media slow to take realization." David Smith[1]

The most original American sculptor in the decades after World War II, David Smith had gone to art school as a painter and was virtually untrained as a sculptor. His interest in freestanding sculpture dates from the early 1930s, when he first saw illustrations of the welded metal sculpture of Pablo Picasso and another Spanish sculptor, Julio González. In 1933 Smith created "almost certainly the first [welded sculpture] to be made in the USA."[2] Welding metal allowed him greater freedom than working with stone or wood, and it matched his desire to create works that spontaneously sprung from his unconscious. Smith soon produced a large body of abstract biomorphic forms remarkable for their inventiveness, diversity, and quality.

By the 1950s, he was producing between three hundred and four hundred drawings a year, among them this untitled drawing, done while on a renewed Guggenheim grant that allowed him the freedom to conceive of larger, more ambitious works in metal. This gouache was most probably not a study for a specific work, but rather created as a means to understand better the forms and elements of sculpture yet to be conceived and made. Here Smith develops some of the images already seen in his works during the late 1940s, especially those inspired by skeletal prehistoric birds, like those he sketched at the Museum of Natural History, New York, in 1948, the same year he created his famous sculpture, *Royal Bird* (Walker Art Center, Minneapolis), based on the skeletal remains of a *Hesperornis regalis*.[3] This gouache also alludes to Smith's anti-imperial political views reflected in his poems, drawings, and sculptures in the form of eagles or other birds of prey as symbols of monarchies.[4]

In 1951, Smith conflated his interest in talons and mandible-like jaws with the teeth and cutting implements of farm machinery for his first series of sculpture known as *Agricola*; so, it is no wonder that he continued to draw skeletal birds and eagles in 1951, as he began to explore the shapes of agricultural tools.

Francesca Consagra

---

[1]   David Smith, lecture given at Tulane University, New Orleans, Louisiana, 21 March 1955. For transcript of entire lecture, see Jörn Merkert, *David Smith: Sculpture and Drawings* (Munich, 1986), 154-55.

[2]   Karen Wilkin, "David Smith," in *Dictionary of Art*, ed. Jane Smith (New York, 1996), 28:876.

[3]   Edward F. Fry, *David Smith* (New York, 1969), 53.

[4]   Ibid.

98

Dmitri Hadzi
American (born 1921)

Primavera (Spring)(1958)
Bronze
Height, 81^1/$_2$"; width, 23"; depth, 14"
Lent by Frances Fergusson and Michael Moohr

A professor emeritus at Harvard University, Dimitri Hadzi was educated at Cooper Union in New York City. In 1950 he attended the Polytechnion in Athens, Greece and began what was to be a twenty-five-year period as an expatriate in Europe, primarily in Rome, where he acquired his first studio in 1951. In that city he not only discovered its excellent foundries and artisans, but also a group of innovative artists, including Marino Marini and Matta and, at the American Academy in Rome, a group of archaeologists and scholars from whom he gained a deeper appreciation about the art and history of Italy. It was in this environment in 1958 that he created one of his most lyrical and delicate sculptures cast in bronze, *Primavera.*

The title is the Italian word for "spring," and the sculpture's form might be interpreted as two elegant plant stems with abstracted blossoms tentatively touching each other, like lovers early in a courtship. The delicacy of these shafts or stems is counterbalanced by the heavily textured surface produced in the casting of the bronze. Balken notes that the surfaces of

[A]ll of Hadzi's sculpture, in which passages of bronze material remain unadulterated in their rough, original state, add to the sensuality that has always been a central feature in his work. The prescription that materials be allowed their own autonomy was one Hadzi gleaned from...Henry Moore, who admonished that 'a work of art must have a vitality of its own...independent of the object it may represent.'[1]

Primavera was made in the same year that Hadzi had his first one-man show at the Galleria Schneider in Rome and participated in several international exhibitions, including the twenty-ninth Venice Biennale. The popularity of this sculpture, done during such an important time in Hadzi's career, may be attested to by the fact that he made several castings of it, one of which is owned by the Dallas Museum of Art.

Francesca Consagra

---

[1]   Debra Bricker Balken, "The Continuity and Contradiction of Sculpture," in *Dimitri Hadzi* (New York, 1996), 86.

99

George Rickey
American (born 1907)

Two Open Trapezoids, One Up, One Down (1980)
Stainless steel
Height, 5' 6"
Promised Gift of Virginia Herrick Deknatel, class of 1929

George Rickey is America's foremost sculptor of kinetic art. His *Two Open Trapezoids, One Up, One Down* is a modestly-scaled example of the sort of sculpture that has made him famous: a work consisting of two trapezoidal forms constructed of brushed stainless steel, mounted on a single armature, so perfectly balanced in tense and delicate equilibrium that each trapezoid rotates gently and independently when touched by the merest current of air.

Two Open Trapezoids, One Up, One Down is one of a series of works created by Rickey to explore the complex movement of structures in planar orientation (other works in the series include *Two Open Rectangles, Diagonal Jointed* (1984) and *Four Open Rectangles Diagonal Jointed II* (1984). Although the work relies on the natural forces— air currents and gravity—for its movement, the sculptor's exploration is not of forms found in nature, but rather of forms, and formal relations, found in geometry: namely, the spatial relation of two essentially two-dimensional trapezoids moving independently in parallel space. In these works, Rickey demonstrates a constructivist passion for geometric forms, but he makes the work his own by indulging his personal passion for gentle, wind-generated kinesis.

Though the American-born Rickey studied art and art history through the late 1920s in Scotland, England, Germany, and in Paris (where he worked with Andre Lhote), he has created the sculpture for which he is best known only since the mid-1950s. His style is perhaps best described as an idiosyncratic blend of constructivist geometric abstraction with kinetic ideas first introduced to sculpture by Calder and (to a lesser extent) Duchamp. Still, Rickey's own personal brand of kinesis is *sui generis*; if the artist owes his inspiration for movement in these works to anyone, that person is probably Rickey's grandfather, a watch- and clockmaker intimately acquainted with the art of balancing and calibration.

Rickey has created many public commissions. But his work, which possesses a toylike delicacy celebrated through air-powered movement, is rarely monumental in scale. The larger works have been criticized by some (architects, mostly) for their relative lack of physical presence. The modest scale of this particular sculpture suggests that it is meant for private display and exhibition rather than as a public work, though its reliance on wind currents for movement again indicates that it is designed for outdoor rather than indoor display.

Justin Spring

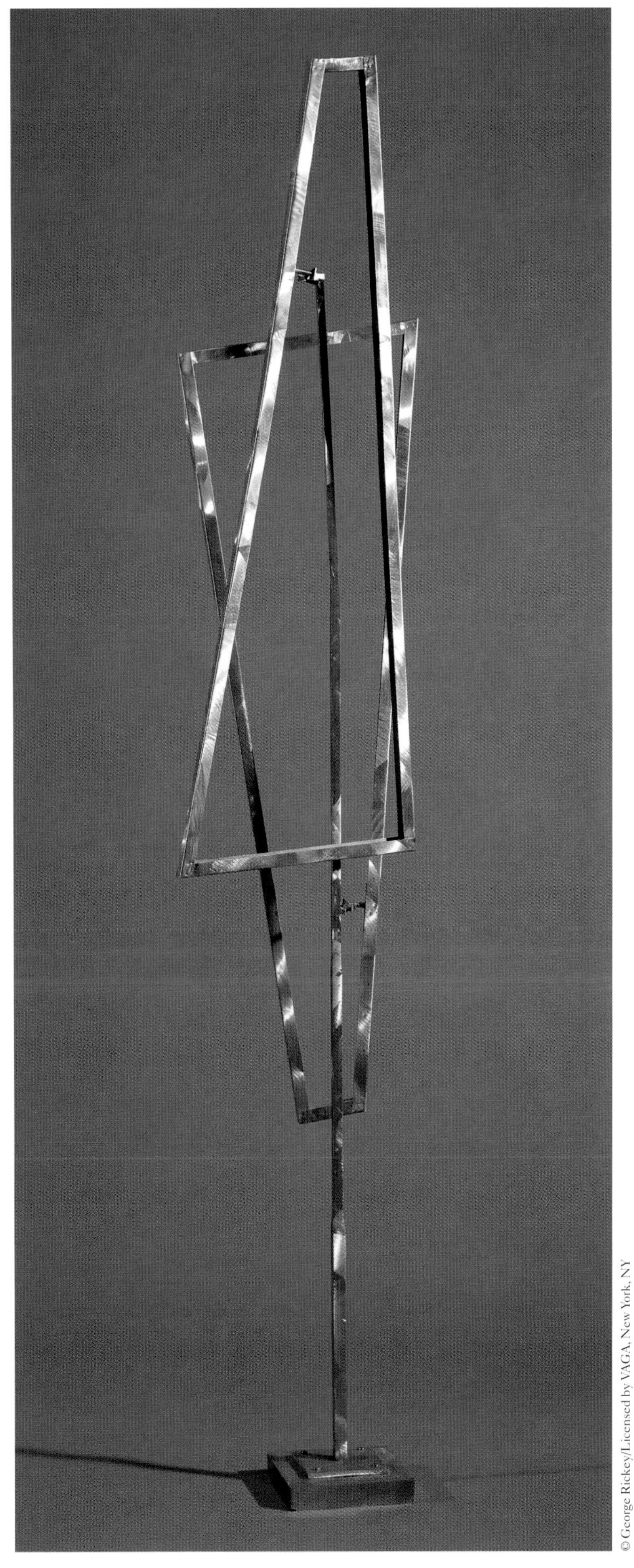

100

Ad Reinhardt
American (1913-67)

Untitled, 1951 (1951)
Gouache on paper, mounted on board
22¹/₂" x 30³/₄"
Lent by Mr. and Mrs. Henry A. Ashforth, Jr. (Georgia M. Perkins, class of 1954)

Ad Reinhardt, one of the great figures in American abstract painting, is today remembered for geometric abstraction, a style he championed both as a practitioner and theoretician, and also for his pioneering aesthetic of rejection and refusal, which later became the core of the minimalist movement of the 1960s. *Untitled, 1951* is a good example of Reinhardt's breakthrough dark-on-dark paintings of the early 1950s. In this work, Reinhardt fuses the nonobjectivity, harmony, and "overallness" of the abstract expressionist movement with the visual vocabulary of analytical cubism to create paintings of great visual subtlety. These dark-on-dark works would eventually find a logical conclusion in the "black" paintings for which Reinhardt is best remembered, paintings he would describe in the early 1960s (with typical absolutist bravado) as "the last paintings anyone can make."[1]

Reviewing the show in which this work appeared in 1952, art critic and painter, Fairfield Porter, noted,

> Chiefly concerned with what painting should not be, [Reinhardt] adheres successfully to a number of negative rules. On the positive side you see, in all but two of the canvases, horizontal brush strokes about two inches wide by about four long, in bright, drug-store colors of almost the same value that make your eyes rock. He is not the first artist to do this, nor does he do it with enough precision to make it clear whether it is intended.[2]

Porter was not alone in his exasperation with Reinhardt's rigid aesthetic and his determinedly uncommunicative paintings. Throughout Reinhardt's life, the artist maintained a contrary and oppositional stance to prevailing modes of thought, just as his paintings maintained their resolute nonobjectivity. But the difficulty of the work is in many ways its point: it is what it is, nothing more and nothing less.

Among the abstract painters of the 1940s, 50s, and 60s, Reinhardt stands alone in the consistency of his vision. Unlike the gesturalist "action painters," he always believed in a style that emphasized order, rectilinearity, and the flatness of the canvas, a determinedly nonromantic style of painting, in which the presence of the painter is minimal. A classicist, he held the artist to the highest possible moral standard, insisting that "the one standard in art is oneness and fineness, rightness and purity, abstractness and evanescence." Consequently, he embraced abstraction as the only and ultimate expression of "art-as-art," which is to say, art that serves no purpose but its own. "Abstract painting," he once remarked, "is not just another school or movement or style, but the first truly unmannered and untrammeled and unentangled, styleless, universal painting. No other art or painting is detached or empty or immaterial enough."[3]

Justin Spring

---

[1] Quoted in Lucy Lippard, *Ad Reinhardt Paintings* (New York, 1967), n.p.

[2] Fairfield Porter, "Ad Reinhardt," *ArtNews* 50 (February 1952): 41, no. 10.

[3] Quoted in Barbara Rose, ed., *Art-as-Art: The Selected Writings of Ad Reinhardt* (New York, 1975), 123.

101

Max Ernst
German (1891-1975)

The Lady Hears a Nightingale
Frottage on paper on linen
15³/₄" x 10⁵/₈"
Promised Gift of Leon M. and Marian A. Despres (Marian H. Alschuler, class of 1930)

One of a number of surrealist techniques for bringing an element of chance into the process of making a work of art, *frottage* (French for "rubbing") is a form of automatism. Pioneer surrealist, Max Ernst, claimed to have invented it on 10 August 1925, "recalling how in childhood the panel of imitation mahogany opposite my bed had served as the optical stimulant to visions of somnolence."[1] In *frottage*, random objects (pieces of wood, fossils, lace, string, etc.) are rubbed with a pencil or charcoal through a piece of paper or canvas, drawing a texture that becomes a point of departure for the artist to work back into.

By relinquishing control at the start, surrealists hoped to summon access to their subconscious minds, and thereby enter into the irrational world of the dream. For Ernst, who liked to say that he "was hatched from an egg which his mother had laid in an eagle's nest,"[2] those "visions of somnolence" have a particular science-fictionlike cast to them, demarcated as a strange intersection between biological and mechanical, human and insect, cultured and primitive forms. The entire surface of *The Lady Hears a Nightingale* seems overlaid by a wet web of drips, an organic tracery that resembles coral, moss, or some other primitive life form. The lady herself—and it is she who is created by *frottage*, composed in sections rubbed from unidentifiable objects—beckons with robotic charm.

Given this drawing's probable date of 1953, it marks the close of the American chapter, and start of the final, European phase of Ernst's career. Thus, the totemic anatomy of the figure that Ernst draws out of this *frottage* might also be seen to resemble one of the Kachina figures that he started collecting after he emigrated to New York in 1941. His interest in Zuni and Hopi material led him to explore the Southwest, where he discovered in the desert wilder-ness and heat, the landscape of his dreams. In 1946, he settled in Sedona, Arizona, where he built a house and surrounded it with monumental figures, the sculpted forebears of the lady in this drawing. The bird she listens to harks back to the title of an early painting, made during Ernst's days as a Dada artist in Germany, *Two Children Are Threatened by a Nightingale* (1924; Museum of Modern Art, New York). Named for a poem by Ernst, the painting was one of his last to be based on *collage* (pasting), a technique of composing images using found pictures cut out of magazines and other sources. In terms of his artistic development, the influence of *frottage* would become increasingly evident, as he moved from away from the illustrative nature of *collage* and into a more revelatory realm through the open-ended textures of *frottage*. "I am surprised," he wrote of the drawings thus obtained, "by the sudden intensification of my visionary capacities."[3]

This painterly, late drawing offers a peep at the grand new style that art historian, John Russell, attributed to Ernst's 1953 return to Europe, "a place where fine painting had been going on for hundreds of years." Russell saw in the new paintings, "the artist's ability to raid the unconscious mind and come back alive" and noted, "They are very much not a young man's painting, in so far as the energy within them is completely under control."[4] The following year, Ernst was awarded the Grand Prize for Painting at the Venice Biennale.

Ingrid Schaffner

---

[1]   Quoted in Max Ernst, *An Informal Life of M.E.* (New York, 1961), 7.

[2]   Ibid., 14.

[3]   Ibid., 14.

[4]   John Russell, Max Ernst: Life and Work (New York, 1967), 162.

102

William Baziotes
American (1912-63)

White Form (1959)
Watercolor
17 ¹/₂" x 23¹/₂"
Lent by Gerry Gewirtz Friedman, class of 1941

In 1950, the art critic, Weldon Kees, considered Baziotes "a hybrid among American painters, half abstractionist, half surrealist...one of the last full-blown romantics of a period in which such obsessive and loving personal allegiance to the fanciful and fantastic has almost disappeared."[1] Indeed, Baziotes was the first abstract expressionist to associate with the surrealists, meeting Kurt Seligmann in 1939 and Matta in 1940. Baziotes was especially attracted to their approach—beginning a work of art without a plan—as well as their dependence on form, rather than pure abstraction. Baziotes himself articulated this in 1947:

"Each beginning suggests something. Once I sense the suggestion, I begin to paint intuitively. The suggestion then becomes a phantom that must be caught and made real. As I work, or when the painting is finished, the subject reveals itself."[2]

During the 1950s, Baziotes took a more conservative approach to painting. He began to plan his compositions and sometimes took up to six months to finish a single painting. Apparent in *White Form* is this more calculated working method. Baziotes applied the watercolor in a delicate, soft, almost ghostly manner. He then, as if using a template, controlled these fields of translucent greens, blues, and blacks with sharp edges to create a negative space that produced two strong central forms. The end result is a serene image that carries land- and seascape overtones prevalent in his work of this period. One can almost imagine a Mediterranean townscape on the top tier of the drawing (with turrets, domes, and fortifications). The suggestion may be justified since Baziotes began to put classical references in many of his works, such as those to Pompeii and Egypt, during the 1950s—all of which may stand as testimonies to the artist's investigations into his own Mediterranean heritage.

So, while the abstract expressionists were identified more and more with action, gesture, and color-field painting during the 1950s, Baziotes became identified with a type of painting described as historical, controlled, and spectral. It was through such objectlike silhouettes, as those seen in *White Form*, that Baziotes sought to evoke, in his own words, "the mysterious that I love in painting....the stillness and the silence. I want my pictures to take effect very slowly, to obsess and to haunt."[3]

Francesca Consagra

---

[1]   Weldon Kees, *The Nation* 170 (4 February 1950): 113.

[2]   From a statement by Baziotes in *Possibilities* 1 (Winter 1947-48); quoted in International Program of the Museum of Modern Art, *The New American Painting* (New York, 1959), 20.

[3]   Quoted in Maurice Tuchman, *The New York School: Abstract Expressionism in the 40s and 50s* (London, 1971), 45.

Bazaine

103

Diego Giacometti
Swiss (1902-85)

Side Chair (ca. 1962)
Iron and leather
Height, 36⅝"
Lent by Joan and Robert Bernhard (Joan E. Mack, class of 1953)

A member of an artistic family, Diego Giacometti came into his own creativity relatively late in life, as a sculptor of furniture. Born in Stampa in 1902, Diego's father, Giovanni Giacometti, was an Impressionist painter of repute in Switzerland. His older brother, Alberto, was the internationally famous Modern sculptor and painter. It was while working as an assistant to Alberto in Paris that Diego honed the techniques that he would deploy in his own works of carved stone and cast and patinated bronze. Having spent his early youth traveling and taking temporary jobs—while working briefly for a funerary monument sculptor in Italy—he learned how to carve marble. Diego settled in Paris in 1925, where his brother was just beginning to establish himself as an artist. Submerging himself in the production of his brother's work, Diego worked so closely with Alberto that the latter often referred to Diego as his "other pair of hands." During the 1930s, the Giacometti brothers were approached by the fashionable interior decorator, Jean-Michel Franck, to design lighting and accessories. Their collaboration was so close that it became difficult to establish the hand of either brother in both design and execution of their work.

When World War II broke out, Alberto returned to Switzerland, and Diego remained in Paris taking care of the studio. In his brother's absence, he pursued some decorative commissions with the League of Advertising, a successful stint that ended on an off-note, when Diego proposed celebrating Liberation with a perfume bottle in the shape of an American jerrycan. He also took sculpture classes at the Académie Ranson. Among the first objects he made, starting in 1949, were bases and stands for sculptures and other objects. By the 1950s, as Alberto increasingly turned to painting, Diego had begun to establish a new career for himself as a furniture designer, creating tables, chairs, drawer pulls, and shelves.

The linear rectitude and hieratic style of this chair are evocative of ancient furniture, which Giacometti remembered first admiring on a trip to Egypt in 1927. Indeed, it would seem to enforce a moment of regal bearing for whomever uses it. One imagines that to sit on the cushioned seat and lean straight against the tall back, feet square on the floor, would be a transformative experience that would render one part of a sculptural vignette, in which a body is framed by a chair. Initially unique objects, the demand for Giacometti's furniture quickly warranted their production as multiples. He also received many significant commissions, including, in 1984-85, one for the Musée Picasso in Paris, for which he designed the furniture and lighting fixtures.

Ingrid Schaffner

104

Saul Steinberg
American (born 1914)

Tabletop (1974)
Mixed media
4" x 31" x 24"
Lent by John H. Friedman and Jane H. Furse

Tabletop is a curious work by a man who holds a curious place in modern art. Since the 1940s, when he became a regular contributor to *The New Yorker* and joined the Betty Parsons Gallery, Saul Steinberg has been a respected figure in both the worlds of graphic and fine arts for essentially the same body of cartoonlike works on paper. A consummate draughtsman, he has mastered techniques as far-ranging as calligraphy, cartography, and cubism, and is apt to draw on the full battery he keeps at hand in a single image. Steinberg's imagery is a mental-landscape of contemporary culture (largely American), filtered through the artist's dry, detached, and witty perceptions, which are fundamentally European. His habit of quoting other artists and styles of representation has been seen as a form of criticism of the very notion of style itself. Indeed, the artist himself regards his drawing as a form of parody or art criticism.

Steinberg's unique position seems linked to his commitment to the art of drawing. Traditionally considered a minor art, a preliminary step to making a painting or sculpture, drawing is for Steinberg an end in itself. Even his sculpture, *Tabletop*, ultimately, reads as a drawing in wood. Part of a body of work that Steinberg invented during the 1970s, *Tabletop* translates the imagery of his studio—the notebooks, pencils, rulers, erasers, rubber stamps, even the cartoon-thought bubbles that appear in his drawings—into a three-dimensional tableaux. They evolved from his casual habit of whittling paintbrushes and drawing pads out of wood and painting them to look like the real thing. Art-historically, they participate in the puzzling play of perceptions, of deciphering the representational from the real, that is perpetrated in the *trompe-l'oeil* paintings of such American painters as William Harnett, as well as to the cubist sculpture of Pablo Picasso.

More intimately, for Steinberg, these tableaux refer to those environments that have nurtured his creativity since childhood. The son of a commercial printer in Romania, Steinberg remembers that his first toys were rulers, press-type, and paper, the tools of his father's trade. As an adult, Steinberg views these same objects as his erotica. As represented in *Tabletop*, they appear to be fondled and touched, if only by the eyes. As a student in Milan, Steinberg studied architecture, and though he never practiced it, after he emigrated to America in 1942, an architect's sensibility is evident. In *Tabletop*, the overall composition reads like an urban plan, with each element as deliberately sited as a building or park, with none of the chaos that Steinberg loves to unleash in his drawings of fantastic cities, which bustle with mad architecture and diverse human, animal, and automobile traffic.

Depicting the controlled haven of his studio, the tabletop sculptures are a discrete body of Steinberg's work. The act of whittling, for him, is a form of doodling, and the square tabletop is a sheet of paper—this work easily joins the rest of his oeuvre. To be sure, Steinberg draws a black outline around each of the sculpted objects' edges, indicating that this departure continues on familiar terms.

Ingrid Schaffner

105

Anthony Caro
British (born 1924)

Slap (1976)
Steel, rusted and varnished
Height, 30"; width, 65"; depth, 53"
Promised Gift of Lissa Cabot von Wentzel, class of 1964

Literature: Dieter Blume, *Antony Caro Catalogue Raisonné, vol. 3 in Steel Sculpture 1960-1980* (Cologne, 1981), 237, no. 1132

Anthony Caro, born in 1924 in New Malden, Surrey, studied engineering at Christ's College, Cambridge, before becoming a sculptor. He studied sculpture at Farnham School of Art, the Regent Street Polytechnic, and the Royal Academy Schools in London. From 1951 to 1953, Caro worked as an assistant to Henry Moore, who was enormously influential upon his development. Caro began making land-based welded-steel abstract sculptures in 1960, after visiting the United States for the first time the previous year. Caro painted many sculptures from the sixties in bright, industrial colors, but in 1970, he began leaving his steel sculptures unpainted, using varnish or wax as a surface treatment. In 1969, Caro represented England in the Sao Paulo Bienal. The Museum of Modern Art in New York and the Tel Aviv Museum mounted major exhibitions of his work in 1975 and 1977, respectively. In 1987, Queen Elizabeth awarded Caro a knighthood.

Slap is part of a series of sculptures Caro made in the mid-1970s as a departure from his brightly colored, architectural sculptures, composed of fragments of industrial tubing, steel mesh, and girders. By comparison, *Slap*'s color, resembling a brownish, damp earth, suggests the natural world, and its shape is organic. In contrast to his earlier, open-formed sculptures, *Slap* is composed of steel elements that lean in a diagonal on top of one another. The form is essentially closed; however, open and seemingly hidden interior spaces have been created within the steel folds by the casual, perpendicular arrangement of the two main sections. *Slap* is floor-bound, a horizontal landscape that combines contradictory gestures—straight versus irregular, smooth versus rough, slim versus chunky, and light versus heavy.

Rebecca Lawton

106

Donald Judd
American (born 1928)

*Untitled (*1989)
Galvanized steel and Plexiglas
Height, 9"; width, 40"; depth, 31", each unit
Lent by Stephen Mazoh

Literature: Brydon Smith, *Donald Judd: Catalogue Raisonné of Paintings, Objects, and Wood-Blocks 1960-1974* (Ottawa, 1975), 209, no. 208

Donald Judd served in the United States Army in Korea in 1946-47, before attending the Arts Students League in New York. He graduated from Columbia University in 1953, receiving a degree in philosophy, but continued to attend the Art Students League at the same time. In 1957, Judd enrolled in Columbia University's graduate school, where he studied art history with Rudoph Wittkower and Meyer Schapiro. Judd supported his painting by writing art criticism for *ArtNews* and by working as a contributing editor to *Arts Magazine.*

In the early 1960s, Judd stopped painting and began to make freestanding objects. His first solo exhibition at the Leo Castelli Gallery, in early 1966, consisted of metal boxes, which Judd had fabricated in galvanized iron at Bernstein Brothers, a metalworking firm in New York. He suspended boxes of the exact same dimensions in vertical rows up the gallery's wall as in a "stack." Rather than arranging the boxes using the traditional, painterly means of composition, Judd relied upon mathematical progressions to determine how the boxes (or elements) related to the intervals (or empty spaces between the boxes). Judd introduced new materials, such as stainless steel, brushed and anodized aluminum, copper, and brass into his sculptures. He also worked with a variety of colors and different surfaces by using Plexiglas, enamel, and lacquer.

Throughout the sixties, Judd's sculptures became larger. He focused upon the issues of scale and space and made extensive use of repetition. Thus, his sculpture is first experienced as a distinct, single form and then becomes part of a repetition of similar forms that in turn can be taken apart. The elements interact, but are independent from each other, and neither the element nor the interval is subordinate or dominant to the other. Overall, Judd sought to eliminate the painterly dependence upon gesture as a means of communication. For Judd, truth in art was attainable only through clarity.

Judd belongs to a group of artists whose theoretical concerns for breaking down art to its essential features created the impulse toward conceptual art and minimalism. Judd's art is straightforward, like a declarative sentence. The work discussed here, made in stainless steel and blue Plexiglas on sides and front, consists of ten units (only nine are exhibited here), each 9" x 40" x 31", and originated in 1970[1], although Judd had used the forms and numerical procession in 1963.

The act of viewing Judd's large-scale wall sculptures is much like experiencing the sensation of height while standing on a bridge. At the same time that one is compelled to move toward the edge, one is also repelled by the fear of it. By introducing shiny, pristine surface color, Judd also invites viewers to sense purity by touching it, yet by touching it, one destroys its purity. The irony of the situation makes Judd's sculptures far more complicated in meaning than their apparent simplicity first implies.

Rebecca Lawton

---

[1] Brydon Smith, *Donald Judd: Catalogue Raisonné of Paintings, Objects, and Wood-Blocks 1960-1974* (Ottawa, 1975), no. 208.

107 and 108

Andy Warhol
American (1930-87)

The Shoe, from *Paisley Pink Shoe on Lavender-Stockinged Leg* (1954)
Hand-colored photo-offset print
8³/₄" x 11³/₄"
Signature: lower left, "Andy Warhol"

The Leg, from *Paisley Pink Shoe on Lavender-Stockinged Leg* (1954)
Hand-colored photo-offset print
14³/₄" x 7³/₄"
Promised Gifts of Diana Klemin, class of 1944

The son of Czechoslovak immigrants, Warhol graduated from the Carnegie Institute of Technology, Pittsburgh, with a degree in pictorial design in 1949. He then went to New York City and started freelancing as an illustrator of books and advertising campaigns. According to David Bourdon, "Andy cleverly ingratiated himself with almost anyone who was in the position to give him work. He made and gave away numerous personalized artworks....This endeared him to art directors, many of whom treasured every drawing he sent their way."[1] The warmth and appreciation that an art director at Doubleday, Diana Klemin, still feels for Warhol may be best understood in her recollection of the day in 1954, when, at lunch, he gave her this copy of *Paisley Pink Shoe on Lavender-Stockinged Leg*:

> [Andy] arrived at Doubleday around noon, carrying a brand new attaché case and a great big brown bag....We went to luncheon and sat facing each other at a small table. During lunch, he explained he had just bought this attaché case at Brooks Brothers....I just thought it amusing to see disheveled Andy carrying a swish, proper attaché case. So he opened it up and presented me with the framed shoe, dazzling in its Dr. Martin dye tints of shocking pink and lavender....I adored it framed flush in its light wood frame by Louis Shuma. Then he apologized because the case couldn't hold the second half of the [print] which he produced by digging into the brown bag. I was touched and appreciative and embarrassed because wherever we were, people didn't...dig into brown grocery bags at luncheon. Andy explained how they should be hung: the leg to the right and slightly higher than the shoe to create tension.[2]

By the end of the 1950s, Warhol was one of New York's leading illustrators, and it was this combination of wit, intimacy, and generosity that helped his rise in the commercial art world of the city.

It should be noted, too, that the shoe was an important icon for Warhol during his early career. His first freelancing job in the city was drawing women's "suit shoes," for *Glamour* in 1949.[3] He then became the designer for a successful campaign of newspaper ads for the I. Miller shoe company. His commercial work and reputation helped launch his career as an artist. The first time any of his creative works reached a national audience was through a double-page spread in *Life* that covered a group of collages of highly decorated golden shoes, each an allegorical portrait of a famous personality of the day (e.g. Zsa Zsa Gabor, Elvis Presley, and Julie Andrews), that were on display at New York's Bodley Gallery in 1957 and today considered his "most successful creations of the 1950s."[4]

Paisley Pink Shoe on Lavender-Stockinged Leg predates the golden shoe series, and is a product of one of Warhol's "coloring parties." Having his original drawings reproduced by offset printing was one of Warhol's ways to expedite his production of images. Hand-coloring them, however, took time, and he got around this by inviting friends over for "fun occasions," in which everyone contributed to the coloring of these images. Bourdon describes well the guidelines Warhol set at these parties:

> Each individual was usually assigned a particular hue—one person, for instance, brushed on the pink, the second filled in the magenta, while the third added the yellow. If the assembly line were interrupted, the proportions and sequencing of the colors might change. The more hues involved, the less likely it was that every version of the same hand-colored [print] would be identical. Andy watercolored some sheets entirely himself, but it did not bother him if he did not put his own hand to each finished work.[5]

Ms. Klemin is likewise not too concerned if the signature on the print is Warhol's: "I took it to be Andy Warhol's own handwriting at that time. I never asked. (Why should I?) I accepted the gift as a treasure and [a sign] of friendship."[6] Her copy, moreover, is unique in that it came framed in two parts, with careful hanging instructions.

Although Dr. Martin dyes fade quickly, and the colors do not have the same shock value as they had in the 1950s, *Paisley Pink Shoe on*

Lavender-Stockinged Leg still represents an important moment in Warhol's early career as an illustrator and an artist, and as a warm and beguiling collaborator with friends and art directors alike.

Francesca Consagra

---

[1]   David Bourdon, *Warhol* (New York, 1989), 34.

[2]   Diana Klemin, letter to James Mundy, 23 November 1997, 2-3, Frances Lehman Loeb Art Center, Vassar College, Poughkeepsie, New York.

[3]   Trevor Fairbrother, "Tomorrow's Man," in *Success is a Job in New York* (New York and Pittsburgh, 1989), 64.

[4]   Fairbrother, "Tomorrow's Man," 64.

[5]   Bourdon, *Warhol*, 44.

[6]   Klemin, letter to James Mundy, 23 November 1997, 4.

108

107

109

Claes Oldenburg
American, Swedish-born (born 1929)

Proposed Colossal Monument for the End of Navy Pier, Chicago: Side-View Mirror (1967)
Crayon and watercolor
7³/₄" x 10¹/₂"
Promised Gift of Leon M. and Marian H. Despres (Marian H. Alschuler, class of 1930)

Monuments start to dot the landscape of Claes Oldenburg's art in the Spring of 1965, when he returned to New York after an extended period abroad and moved into a vast studio space on East Fourteenth Street. The scale of the new studio and recent memories of traveling in Europe, and throughout America, all suggested to him an imagery of landscape. Gradually, Oldenburg worked out a way to reconcile the landscape tradition with his contemporary Pop sensibility. By placing familiar objects within a landscape he brought together both small-scale still life and large-scale landscapes. He rendered atmosphere and the use of perspective to make these objects look colossal.

Among the first colossi were the whimsical, yet prescient, proposals for two midtown Manhattan monuments: a skyscraper-scaled rabbit (not far from where *Playboy* magazine would shortly thereafter erect its bunny logo) and a Goliath-sized Good Humor ice cream bar (where the Pan Am/Metropolitan Life Building would soon bar Park Avenue). By 1967, Oldenburg's drawings were envisioning the potential for such monuments in major cities around the world, including *Proposed Colossal Monument for the End of Navy Pier, Chicago: Side-View Mirror.* Like all of Oldenburg's colossi, this one begins with a profoundly antiheroic object of everyday life, which performs one of the characteristic gestures of Pop Art. By inflating scale and cultural ambition, Pop transforms an everyday banality into a subject of celebrated esteem. A barn-sized side-view mirror demands serious appreciation. At the same time, big toys, tools, appliances, and junk food all knock elevated precepts, such as art, off their pedestals and down to street level. A huge mirror on the end of a pier would be a handy device to help docking vessels pull in and out of busy river traffic. For landlubbers, it would glitter at the city's edge, glaring its radiance over the water like a permanent, ready-made sunset or moonrise.

Drawing plays an important role in Oldenburg's art by providing a consistent means of exploration throughout an expansive practice that has, since the 1960s, embraced painting, performance art, sculpture, print-making, and monument building, as well as numerous hybrids thereof. In drawing, he had long held command of a versatile range of styles, from gestural graffiti to analytical drafting. But it was in 1965, in tandem with the genesis of the monuments, that Oldenburg arrived at his signature style. As exemplified by this drawing, it is breezy, notational, and lush with the fluidity of writing. It speaks of Oldenburg's habit of annotating his life and work through a constant stream of written and drawn notes.

Since 1976, colossal sculptures have been the artist's most absorbing production. Working collaboratively with his wife, Coosje van Bruggen, Oldenburg has realized major commissions, including a baseball bat in Chicago (1977); a matchbook in Barcelona, Spain (1992); and a garden hose in Freiborg im Breisgau, Germany (1983). These colossi realize a lifetime ambition with monumental simplicity, and further, a romantic objectivity. They are unsentimental reflections of things as they are—facts honestly faced, and yet somehow beautiful.

Ingrid Schaffner

110

Lee Bontecou
American (born 1931)

Untitled (1971)
Pastel
18" x 24"
Signature: "Lee Bontecou"
Promised Gift of Peggy Brooks, class of 1940

Literature: Carter Ratcliff, *Lee Bontecou* (Chicago, 1972)

Exhibition: *Lee Bontecou*, Museum of Contemporary Art, Chicago, Illinois, 25-27 March 1972

"My concern is to build things that express our relation to…this world—to other worlds—in terms of myself. To glimpse some of the fear, hope, ugliness, beauty and mystery that exists in us all….The individual is welcome to see and feel in them what he wishes in terms of himself." Lee Bontecou, 1960[1]

Although best known for her abstract, welded-steel framed sculptures of the early 1960s, many of the elements that Bontecou sought then remain in her more figural work dating from the early 1970s, like her series of sculptures and drawings depicting primordial fish and flora.

In the pastel exhibited here, Bontecou depicts a dense group of diverse fish, many of her own invention, moving from right to left as if following an underwater current across the ocean's depths. Bontecou explores "other worlds" filled with the fear and ugliness epitomized by those aggressive fish with razor-sharp teeth, which are juxtaposed to the beauty of the smaller ones that look like tropical reef dwellers. All glide along in a world full of dark mystery, with no sea floor or sunlight. These primordial fish come from very deep waters indeed.

At the same time that she was drawing fish, Bontecou also made a series of clear plastic sculptures of them. "The aggressiveness of these constructions," Carter Ratcliff writes, "was modified by their endless capacity for other moods; the point with the dangerous-looking fish remains the link to be made between perception and 'blind form'—a link which becomes, once made, an endlessly varied mood of activated presence (the viewer's)."[2]

Francesca Consagra

---

[1] Quoted in Dorothy Miller, *Americans 1963* (New York, 1963), 12.

[2] Carter Ratcliff, *Lee Bontecou* (Chicago, 1972), n.p.

BONTECOU 1971

111

Robert Motherwell
American (1915-91)

Burning Elegy (1991)
Lithograph
53¹/₂" x 63¹/₄"
Lent by Joan and Robert Bernhard (Joan E. Mack, class of 1953)

Robert Motherwell, one of the founders and principal exponents of abstract expressionism, is best known for the series, *Elegies to the Spanish Republic*, or the monochromatic ovoids alternating with bars that he places, usually alternatively, across the compositions of his canvases and works on paper. Motherwell explained that the motif of the *Elegy* series was originally conceived in 1948 as a tribute to the republic that perished in the Spanish Civil War, but it was never meant to be political, rather a general metaphor of "the contrast between life and death and their interrelation."[1] When Motherwell was elected to the American Academy of Arts and Letters in 1986, he spoke at the awards ceremony about his understanding of the motif:

> The black grows deeper and deeper, darker and darker. It is monstrous. It is unfathomable...only love, and in this instance paint, is able to cover the fearful void.[2]

The series comprised hundreds of paintings, prints, and drawings, and Motherwell continued to work on it until his death in 1991. He regarded his art as a never-ending process:

> All my life I've been working on the work—every canvas a sentence or paragraph of it. Each picture is only an approximation of what you want. That's the beauty of being an artist; you can never make the absolute statement, but the desire to do so as an approximation keeps you going.[3]

In his lithographs, the motif of ovoids and bars first appears in *Spanish Elegy I* in 1975[4], or the very year that Generalissimo Francisco Franco died, and Prince Juan Carlos moved to dismantle the authoritarian institutions of Franco's system and encouraged the revival of political parties in Spain. Motherwell was to employ the motif of the *Elegy* series in various other printed editions for the next fifteen years. He chose rich black printing inks that enhanced the theme of death in the series. In 1987 he also began to experiment with color. In *Blue Elegy* (1987)[5], both the bars and the ovoids are printed blue over a background of a lighter hue of the same color. Before Motherwell's death in July 1991, he made this impression of *Burning Elegy* at Tyler Graphics in Mount Kisco, New York, in which he printed the motif in its original deep black and added a smoldering yellow around its forms, only to push the white out to the corners of the print.

Francesca Consagra

---

[1] Grace Glueck, "Robert Motherwell, Master of Abstract, Dies," *New York Times* (18 July 1991): A:1, col. 5.

[2] Joseph P. Kahn, "Art giant Motherwell dies," *Boston Globe* (18 July 1991): Obituaries:1.

[3] Glueck, "Robert Motherwell," A:1, col. 5.

[4] Stephanie Terenzio and Dorothy C. Belknap, *The prints of Robert Motherwell: a catalogue raisonné 1943-1984* (New York, ca. 1984), no. 143.

[5] Terenzio and Belknap, *The prints of Robert Motherwell*, no. 347.

112

Richard Diebenkorn
American (1922-93)

Blue with Red (1987)
Color woodcut
37^1/$_2$" x 25^1/$_2$"
Lent by Norma Honig Schlesinger, class of 1952

Blue with Red is a color woodcut that belongs to Richard Diebenkorn's *Ocean Park* series, named after the section of Santa Monica where he kept his studio from 1966 until he moved north of San Francisco in 1988. This tremendously popular series, which comprises hundreds of paintings, drawings, and prints, is known for its wonderful luminosity and rich veilings of color, which help create a delicate balance of surface modulation and illusionistic depth. The *Ocean Park* series is abstract, but the work intrinsically figurative. Each of these abstractions can often be read as a conventional landscape with a tripartite division of space: foreground, middleground, and background. According to Kimmelman, each discloses the history of its making: "the works are composed of second thoughts, pentimenti, erasures, and emendations, which at their best combine to form images of remarkable elegance and poise."[1]

Although Diebenkorn sought a sense of order in his compositions, he preferred to work spontaneously, without preparatory studies. His working method changed little even when he collaborated with others, like the master printers who helped him produced no less than 106 editions of prints at the Crown Point Press in California. His first prints were made with a simple drypoint tool. He was later encouraged to try more complex intaglio techniques such as color hard-ground etching and spit bite acquaint to produce lush prints with complex color combinations. His first woodcut project with Crown Point in Japan was at the Shiundo Print Shop in Kyoto in

1983, where he worked with the wood carver, Reizo Monjyu, and the printer, Tadashi Toda. Diebenkorn was there "to guide and adjust, choose, and change" their reproductions of his designs, and likened himself to "an orchestra conductor."[2]

Blue with Red is a color woodcut that was probably issued from this same Japanese shop four years later. It reproduces *Untitled* (ca. 1987), a drawing first exhibited in 1994, a year after Diebenkorn's death.[3] The grain of the wood and the expert layering of color blocks uncannily reproduce the brush strokes and color veiling of the drawing, and offer a better understanding of its geometric scaffolding (the substructure of diagonal and horizontal lines) in the middleground, which is more veiled in blue, and thus more illegible, in the original drawing. As Glen noted, Diebenkorn's prints provided "an intimate access to his highly personal search for order and the means to express it."[4]

Francesca Consagra

[1]   Michael Kimmelman, "A Life Outside," *New York Times Magazine* (13 September 1992): 58.

[2]   Karin Breuer, *Thirty-five Years at the Crown Point Press: Making Prints, Doing Art* (Berkeley, 1997-1998), 175.

[3]   Richard Diebenkorn, *Richard Diebenkorn: Ocean Park paintings on paper, never before exhibited* (New York, 1994), no. 1.

[4]   Constance W. Glenn, "Richard Diebenkorn," in *Dictionary of Art*, ed. Jane Turner (New York, 1996), 8:870-71.

113

Robert Colescott
American (born 1925)

I Just Keep Losing (1990)
Watercolor and gouache on paper
40 x 29$^1/_2$"
Signature: lower right, "R. Colescott/90"
Inscription: lower right, "I Just Keep loosing"
Lent by Drs. Alvin and Lenore Weseley (Lenore S. Levine, class of 1954)

Colescott was born in Oakland, California in 1925, and, through his father, became acquainted with the work and personalities of the Harlem Renaissance, especially the painter, Sargent Johnson. After serving in the army during World War II, Colescott traveled to Paris to study under Fernand Leger, where he learned more about monumental figurative painting and compressed compositions. During a fellowship in Cairo, Egypt in the 1960s, he explored the formal qualities of Egyptian art, with its dependence on hieroglyphs, monumentality of scale, and decorative patterns. He then began making works of art that used satire and narrative figuration in order to present racial stereotypes that offered a critique of contemporary American culture from an African-American perspective. He infused his works with icons of popular culture. His painting style during the 1980s became more riotous and painterly. His cartoonlike figures and bright colors shocked the viewer to stop and look in a new way at old stereotypes. Colescott began to explore in his work the effects of racism on individuals as they strive for love, power, and money, rarely to achieve their expectations or potential.

I Just Keep Losing, for instance, depicts a black gambler smoking a cigarette with only a two of spades in his hand. The two hands of a white player that surround him hold an ace of diamonds and a king of hearts; the white man is clearly the winner of this game, and he remains anonymous, symbolized only by his hands and cards. Above the players are other cards played and a pair of dice with snake eyes, perhaps ghosts of games lost, floating in space as if time is going by, and the black gambler is down on his luck again. Even his necktie with a decorative pattern of green clovers is limited to the three-leafed variety; not a four-leafed clover in sight. The black player is out of luck, while the white one keeps getting the good hands. "Why," might Colescott want you to ask, "does the black man keep playing the white man's game when he's so down on his luck?"

Francesca Consagra

"I Just Keep Losing"
R Colescott
90

114

Jasper Johns
American (born 1930)

Savarin, Monotype #9 (1977-82)
Monotype with lithograph
49¹/₄" x 37³/₈"
Signature: lower right, "Jasper Johns"
Lent by Philip and Lynn Straus (Lynn R. Gross, class of 1946)

Literature: Judith Goldman, *Jasper Johns: 17 Monotypes* (West Islip, New York, 1982), no. 9

In this autobiographical work, Jasper Johns does not render a conventional portrait of himself, but rather merges several of his best-known motifs in a single image—his characteristic cross-hatchings, the use of body impressions, and his famous Savarin can filled with paint brushes—to create a surrogate self-portrait. When Johns superimposed these motifs with similar ones culled from the work of the Norwegian symbolist artist, Edvard Munch (1863-1944), he devised a powerful statement about his own fears of death and the inability to create art. Johns knew that Munch regarded himself as "a mystical profit of death, love, and art," who had recorded his long wait for the arrival of death in numerous self-portraits spanning from the 1880s to 1942.[1]

Roberta Bernstein noted that Johns, at the time he created this print, had recently turned fifty and "increasingly directed himself to examinations of human mortality."[2] Yet, his fascination with Munch's self-portraits as embodiments of this fear may have evolved as early as 1975, when Richard S. Field organized an exhibition on images of death that displayed both Johns's *Skin with O'Hara's Poem* (1970)[3] and Munch's lithographic self-portrait of 1895.[4] Indeed, Munch's self-portrait is perhaps his most symbolist: his white skull-like head emerges out of a black, richly inked background, bodiless, but framed by a skeletal hand and arm from below, and by his own name and date written in a thin white border from above.

John's first direct reference to Munch's self-portrait appeared in the lithograph *Savarin* (1977-81),[5] which carries both the Savarin can filled with paint brushes (as Johns's face) above the Munch-inspired arm imprint at the bottom border, with the initials "E.M" added. After the second version of this print, twenty-seven discarded proofs were used as the matrices for a series of monotypes in 1982.

The impression shown here illustrates how Johns revised the composition to include such allusions as an outline of a skull (Munch's) around the Savarin can and the addition of spermatozoa shapes at the top left and right, found in another important image by Munch, *Madonna, Liebendes Weib* (see cat. no. 70). No two monotypes from this group are alike, and the sense of creative power and "great spirit of adventure that inhabited these repaired images" may stand as symbols of resistance to the very theme of death that attracted Johns to Munch's work in the first place.[6]

Francesca Consagra

---

[1] Reinhold Heller, *Munch: his life and work* (Chicago, 1984), 226.

[2] Roberta Bernstein, "Seeing a Thing Can Sometimes Trigger the Mind to Make Another Thing," in Kirk Varnedoe, *Jasper Johns: a retrospective* (New York, ca. 1996), 50.

[3] Richard S. Field, *Jasper Johns: prints 1960-1970* (Philadelphia, 1975), no. 48.

[4] Gustav Schiefler, *Verzeichnis des graphischen Werks Edvard Munch bis 1906* (Berlin, 1907; reprint Oslo, 1974), no. 31; Bernstein, "Seeing a Thing," 72, no. 63..

[5] Varnedoe, *Jasper Johns*, no. 181.

[6] Riva Castelman, *Jasper Johns: a print retrospective* (New York, ca. 1986), 44.

varin
OFFEE
E.M.

115

Frank Stella
American (born 1936)

Etang d'ambach (1992)
Stainless steel
75" x 50¹/₂" x 60"
Lent by Stephen Mazoh

Frank Stella is an innovator whose ideas about art have taken several radical shifts since his *Black Paintings* were first shown in an exhibition at the Museum of Modern Art in 1959-60. He's moved from the nonobjective aesthetic of minimalism, or the monochromatic, flat canvases that denied any illusion of space or depth, to the complex spatial dynamics inspired by the masters of the Roman Baroque. His extremely colorful work extends outward from the picture plane to encompass the viewer, only to pull the viewer back into a fictional and complete environment.

During the early 1990s, Stella created a group of stainless steel and aluminum sculptures that included *Etang d'ambach*. The sculpture's spiral form, narrow at the bottom and expanding at the top, not only emerges out of Stella's fascination with the spatial theatricality of the Baroque, which had influenced his work of the preceding decade, but also with the motif of the smoke ring as a means to explore the forces of space, form, and movement in abstract compositions. Kaufman, in a recent exhibition catalogue, discusses the process that led the artist to understand better the configuration of the smoke ring moving in space:

Stella blew a ring into a black box with cameras mounted on each of its six sides, then fed the simultaneous photographs into a computer which produced a three-dimensional map of the smoke ring's structure. This unique representation of frozen motion...[serves] as an embodiment of the fluxant continuum in which Stella's abstraction operates.[1]

In his metal work of the 1990s, Stella has continued to investigate the conflation of plane and volume, flatness and depth, and the distinctions between mass and space inherent in both the smoke ring and the medium of sculpture. The titles of these sculptures themselves, often alluding to maritime or water imagery, evoke, too, the opposing forces of fluidity and stasis imparted by pieces of solid metal bent, bolted, and welded together with various degrees of space and light between each fragmented part—all of which extend outward, only to pull the viewer back into a vortex of the form.

Francesca Consagra

---

[1] Jason Edward Kaufman, *Frank Stella: Multiple Dimensions in the Nineties* (New York, 1998), n.p.

116

Catherine Murphy
American (born 1946)

Persimmon (1991)
Oil on canvas
25²/₃" x 29¹/₂"
Lent by Dixie Sheridan, class of 1965

Catherine Murphy makes extraordinary paintings of ordinary things. Her chosen subjects have long been the unremarkable sites and utilitarian objects typically encountered but easily overlooked in daily life. Her observational skills are so finely tuned that it is as if she possesses an eagle's eye and the remarkable technical ability to capture her subjects with meticulous precision. Since the late 1980s, her style has developed into an unconventional realism, in which the natural world is presented conceptually and the principles of modern abstraction appear fully integrated within a representational style.

Persimmon is a painting of lips, specifically those of a woman and presumably those of the artist herself. Murphy often uses herself as the model in her paintings, more out of necessity, given the time required for each work, than the desire to be autobiographical. Here, she has painted lips larger-than-life size and presented them startlingly close to the picture plane. The painting is thus a nearly square slice of face from the tip of the nose to the top of the chin that extends horizontally to the elusive corners of the mouth. By eliminating other facial features and collapsing the spatial depth, Murphy has created an undeniably unsettling image, at once disturbing for what is missing and yet uncannily familiar as the disconnected reflection of one's own mouth in a compact mirror. On the surface, Persimmon reads as a sort of landscape of physiognomy, with cavernous nostrils and linear ravines rising toward the summit of cosmetically-colored lips. The only clue to the unknown woman's character is presented by a mysterious area of smeared lipstick above the upper right lip.

In using lips as a subject, *Persimmon* recalls another painting of lips, Man Ray's *A l'heure de 'l'observatoire-Les Amoureux* (1932-34, Niarchos Collection). Man Ray, inspired by the lipstick impression made by his mistress's lips upon his shirt collar, created a painting of giant-sized lips floating over a landscape with an observatory, which summarized his interest in surrealism and Freudian imagery.

Persimmon, painted in 1991, and titled after the color of the lipstick Murphy happened to be wearing at the time, unintentionally became the final section of a triptych when hung with two prior, similarly spare, works, *Self-Portrait with Apple* (1989) and *Eric* (1990).[1] In recognition of the Christian iconography rooted within each work and the narrative structure created by linking the three paintings together, Murphy subsequently called this her *Garden of Eden Trilogy*. The idea to smear the lipstick came to her during the painting process, charging the work with emotional fervor and metaphorical associations. The artist has acknowledged that these works are among the "most loaded" [with meaning] she has painted thus far.[2] It is an undeniably modernist version of original sin. In *Self-Portrait with Apple*, Murphy's use of an unconventional viewpoint and perspective allows her audience to identify with Eve as she contemplates eating the apple. *Eric*, a painting of Murphy's friend, the photographer, Eric Lindbloom, shows a man with his hand covering his face, a gesture that recalls the palpable remorse of Masaccio's *Adam*.

Murphy's work lays at the crux of an uncharted intersection of naturalism with postmodernism. In paintings such as *Persimmon*, Murphy imposes a constructivist geometrical structure upon psychologically-charged realism to slip between coolly-rendered fact and raw emotion.

Rebecca Lawton

---

[1] Catherine Murphy, interview with Rebecca Lawton, 10 September 1998. See Gerrit Henry, "The Figurative Field," *Art in America* 82 (January 1994): 82-87, for a discussion of the *Garden of Eden Trilogy*.

[2] Catherine Murphy, interview with Rebecca Lawton, 10 September 1998.

117

Ross Bleckner
American (born 1949)

Untitled (1984)
Oil on canvas
48" x 40"
Collection of John Post Lee, class of 1981, and Karin Bravin, New York

Raised in New York and educated at the California Institute of Arts in the early 1970s, Ross Bleckner was one of the first artists to exhibit at the Mary Boone Gallery in New York, one of the most influential venues of the eighties, a period of tremendous growth in the contemporary art market. Initially influenced by late minimalism and the constructivist tradition, Bleckner exhibited a series of stripe paintings in 1981, which formed a commentary on the scale of abstract expressionism and the formal qualities of minimalism, as well as more than a passing reference to Op Art. Light began to form an increasingly important component in his art beginning in 1983, both technically and as a symbol, often emanating from or reflecting off a recognizable object. In these paintings, the backgrounds grow increasingly dark, composed of many glazes of paint in a technical manner stemming from Renaissance practice. From the mid-1980s, Bleckner's art concerned itself more with issues of loss, remembrance, and other emotions stemming from the incipient AIDS epidemic. The association of elements of his previous iconography, such as birds and light, with the soul took on a more pessimistic relevance at this time. In addition, flowers, urns, trophies, and chandeliers begin to appear, emerging from black backgrounds fueling the intensity of mourning together, with titles such as *Memoriam*, *One Day Fever*, *Hospital Room*, and *Deathlessness*.

In all paintings, however, Bleckner's absolute commitment to and love of painting comes through sincerely, an increasingly rare occurrence in late-twentieth-century painting.

The Lee/Bravin painting of 1984 came from an exhibition at Boone's gallery that featured other works replete with this memorial iconography, such as that from the same show included in the recent Bleckner retrospective at the Guggenheim Museum in New York, lent from the collection of Barbara and Eugene Schwartz[1], where an urn, strongly illuminated from within, hovers under what appears to be a Eucharistic wafer. In this painting, a bold chandelier, shaped like those one would see in an Eastern Orthodox basilica or synagogue, casts a ghostly glimmer on small fragments of cloth. The atmosphere of the painting seems thick with the smoke of incense in the church or the lingering dust of the abandoned ballroom, a somewhat typical paradox by an artist whose life-affirming personality is seemingly, at times, at odds with his painting.

James Mundy, class of 1974

---

[1] Lisa Dennison, *Ross Bleckner* (New York, 1995), no. 16.

118

Enzo Cucchi
Italian (born 1950)

Dei ed eroi (God and heroes) (1983)
India ink and collage on paper
25" x 19 1/4"
Lent by Mary Sharp Cronson, class of 1947

Provenance: Sperone Westwater, New York, 1983

Literature: Ursula Perucchi-Petri, *Cucchi: Drawings 1975-1989* (New York, 1990), 25, 375 (no. 100), ill. p. 141

Exhibitions: Sperone Westwater, New York 5-26 March 1983; *Enzo Cucchi*, Centre Georges Pompidou Musée National d'Art Moderne, Paris, 3 June-24 August 1986, 45; *Enzo Cucchi*, Solomon R. Guggenheim Museum, New York 1986, no. 84; *Enzo Cucchi: La Disegna, Zeichnungen 1975 bis 1988*, Kunsthaus Zurich; Louisiana Museum, Humlebaek; Kunstmuseum, Düsseldorf; Haus am Waldsee, Berlin, 9 September 1988-30 April 1989, 155, no. 100

Enzo Cucchi is, together with Francesco Clemente, Sandro Chia, and Mimo Paladino, part of the young generation of Italian neo-expressionist artists who made a strong impact on the art world in the 1980s. Born in the Marches, he continues to work in Rome and Ancona.

The drawing, *Dei ed Eroi* (God and heroes) is one of a series of six drawings that accompanied his poem, *La Scimmia* (The simian), completed in 1983.[1] Almost all are presently in private collections in the United States. All six are variants on a stylized self-portrait of the artist squeezed between elongated house forms, surrounded by small skulls. The house is an elemental symbol in Cucchi's art, suggesting not only refuge but also an area inhabited by mystery and the imagination.[2] In the case of the Cronson drawing, the head is seemingly squashed between the two houses, while the dark river of skulls flows out, evocative of the line from *La Scimmia*, "A dismal place, a sewer; I have found it together with the thoughts of painters."[3]

James Mundy, class of 1974

---

[1] Ursula Perucchi-Petri, *Cucchi: Drawings 1975-1989* (New York, 1990), nos. 99-104.

[2] Perucchi-Petri, *Cucchi: Drawings*, 19.

[3] Enzo Cucchi, *La Scimmia* (New York, 1983), portfolio.

119

Roger Brown
American (1941-97)

Night Scene (ca. 1968)
Oil on canvas
24¹/₂" x 24¹/₂"
Lent by Leon M. and Marian H. Despres (Marian H. Alschuler, class of 1930)

Provenance: Purchased from the exhibition, *The False Image*, Hyde Park Art Center, Hyde Park, Illinois, 1968

Although born and raised in Alabama, Roger Brown achieved recognition as one of the key figures among the so-called Chicago Imagists from the mid-1960s. Other members of the group were Jim Nutt, Gladys Nilsson, Karl Wirsum, Ed Paschke, Phil Hanson, Ray Yoshida, and Barbara Rossi. Most of these artists received at least some of their training at the school of the Art Institute of Chicago. They were later brought together by Don Baum, director of the Hyde Park Art Center, in exhibitions entitled, *The Hairy Who* and *The Non-Plussed Some*, where Brown's painting was first exhibited. What cemented the group together was an aesthetic rooted in surrealism, of which there were several prominent Chicago collections, laced with a healthy, rebellious iconoclasm quite influenced by the ephemera of popular culture, comic books, psychedelia, and California funk art. Many in the group were also influenced by the art of "outsiders," those who were (unlike themselves) self-taught, illiterate, insane, or incarcerated.

Roger Brown's painting was always idiosyncratic in its restraint among the more bombastic and aggressive paintings of Nutt and Paschke. Against a background of anonymous and repetitive schematic renderings of tract houses, skyscrapers, or rural land-scapes, Brown often set scenes of mayhem, social unrest, natural disasters, and turmoil in a deadpan manner, suggesting a banality of chaos that could form a wallpaper design as easily as it could summon feelings of alienation and futility.

The lyrical arrangements of weapons, crimes, or flames in pleasing patterns made Brown's social commentary all the more trenchant. In *Night Scene*, a city street lit by street lights, casts two pedestrians, a woman and a portly man, in silhouette in the middleground, while in the left foreground, across from a filling station, the blond head of a woman protrudes through a broken window. Obviously, a crime has been committed and Brown renders it as a film-noire moment rendered by a cartoonist. While the buildings are schematized and the figures rendered generic, like the outsider artist, Brown takes care to include details such as the bell hose at the gas station, or to arrange the broken glass fragments on the sidewalk so that none overlap. On the other hand, in spite of the naive rendering of the objects, the tenor and themes within the image suggest the darker side of an American icon such as Edward Hopper's *Nighthawks* (1942, Art Institute of Chicago), suggesting in a deadpan fashion what might have happened next.

James Mundy, class of 1974

120

Ellen Gallagher
American (born 1965)

Untitled (1995)
Oil, pencil, and paper on canvas; mounted on wood
Height, 24" x 24"
The Greenberg Rohatyn Collection, New York, N.Y. (Jeanne Greenberg, class of 1989)

Ellen Gallagher's *Untitled* prompts engagement on two levels. From a distance, the work—which incorporates both painting and drawing—appears nonreferential, minimal, and cool. Consisting of five rows of sheets of primary-school composition paper glued to a canvas and linked by painted brown dots that connect the faded blue lines of the off-white pulpy paper, its structure recalls a spare but elegant patchwork quilt. Superimposed across the bottom of the piece, two rows of organic-looking shapes seemingly add a dash of earth tones and an element of design to the otherwise restrained work. Like the paper school children learn to write on, *Untitled*, from afar, suggests structure and order.

Close up, however, the painting reveals another side of itself. Upon intimate inspection, the two rows of organic-looking shapes that partially traverse the lower section of the piece are transformed into human body parts. They are no longer seen as a series of circles and amoebalike forms, but instead as multiple sets of bulging eyes and thick brown lips. Recurrent in Gallagher's paintings of the late 1990s, these facial features are meant to evoke the history of blackface minstrelsy in America.[1]

Minstrelsy, the first national form of stage performance in the U.S., was particularly popular in northern cities before and after the Civil War.[2] Largely consisting of white actors who used makeup, gestures, props, and language to portray black Americans for white audiences, this type of entertainment created and perpetuated stereotypes of African-American people that both endorsed the practice of slavery in the South and excused the reality of race-based inequities in the North.

By deploying bug eyes and fleshy lips as symbols of blackface minstrelsy and positioning them on top of the ethereal primer paper, Ellen Gallagher blends the history of performance with the history of art. She pulls viewers in with delicate abstraction and an evocation of childhood to remind us of our indelicate and developing cultural history.

Lisa Gail Collins, Visiting Assistant Professor,
Departments of Art and Africana Studies, Vassar College

[1]   Erika Muhammad, "Ellen Gallagher's Head Trip," *Ms.* 9:2 (September-October 1998): 84-85.

[2]   Robert C. Toll, "Minstrels/Minstrelsy," in *Encyclopedia of African-American Culture and History*, ed. Jack Salzman et al. (New York, 1996), 1810-12.

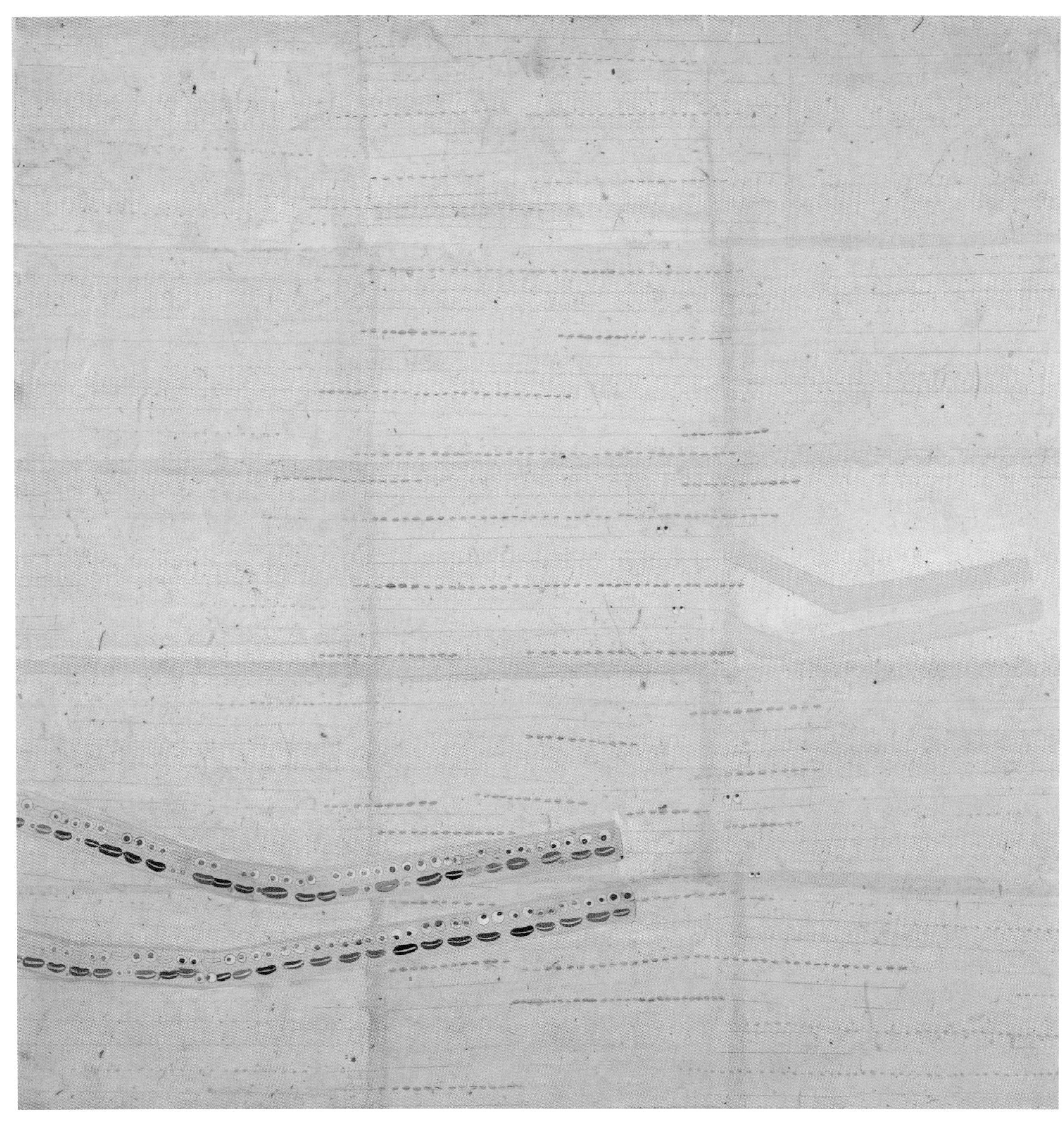

121 and 122

David Hammons
American (born 1943)

Head (1997)
Hair and stone
Height, 11"; width, 12"; depth, 5"

Rock Fan (1997)
Fabric and stone
Height, 12"; width, 18"; depth, 7"
The Greenberg Rohatyn Collection, New York, N.Y. (Jeanne Greenberg, class of 1989)

A recipient of a MacArthur Foundation Fellowship in 1991, David Hammons has gained renown as a conceptual artist whose work frequently evokes urban African-American life. Typically, Hammons shuns traditional art materials; instead, he often gathers discarded objects from the streets of New York City. Chicken wings, rib bones, liquor bottles, shorn hair, greasy brown bags, and bottle caps have all served as materials for his art over the last two decades. These found objects are not only without economic value, they are also closely linked to black people. For Hammons, this intimate human connection—the fact that people's lips, mouths, heads, and hands have touched these items—imbues them with a special energy and resonance. "I like the energy of used things. I like my objects to have spirit already in them," he has explained.[1]

Hair, in particular, carries a forceful charge. Hammons began to explore this natural fiber after seeing an African object that incorporated hair in a Chicago museum in the 1970s. After working intently with barbershop-floor remains in the late 1970s and early 1980s, Hammons was pressed to temporarily avoid this powerful material. Regarding this experience, he says, "I was actually going insane working with that hair so I had to stop. That's just how potent it is. You've got tons of peoples' spirits in your hands when you work with that stuff."[2]

In his 1997 sculptural object, *Head*, Hammons returned to his long-standing interest in black hair as well as its site. By crowning a gray stone with hair clippings, he enlivens an oval rock and renames it as the locus of knowledge. This new naming, however, also suggests the inanimate of the animate, for the rock, although sporting a designer hairdo, is entirely impenetrable.

Cultural theorist, Manthia Diawara, notes that Hammons's talent lies partly in his "titles that enact comically and literally what they designate."[3] *Rock Fan* of 1997 is another example of this pronounced skill. It also reveals Hammons's playful interest in both verbal and visual associations. In this mixed-media work, a piece of fabric, splayed like a fan, rests on top of a round stone. Positioned as if the showy cloth were trying to consume the dull rock, the assemblage both visualizes its title and mocks the hungry exchange that takes place between star and fan.

Interested in exploring charged materials, verbal naming, and visual punning, David Hammons's sculptural objects provoke and jest with viewers. As Diawara explains, "Hammons' work teases us because it is what it is: just an image with a floating irony."[4]

Lisa Gail Collins,
Visiting Assistant Professor,
Departments of Art and Africana Studies, Vassar College

---

[1] Quoted in Kellie Jones, "David Hammons: Exit Art Installation, 1989," *New Observations* 97 (September-October 1993): 35.

[2] Kellie Jones, "David Hammons," in *Discourses: Conversations in Postmodern Art and Culture*, ed. Russell Ferguson et al. (Cambridge, Massachusetts), 211.

[3] Manthia Diawara, "Make It Funky: The Art of David Hammons," *Artforum* 36, no. 9 (May 1998): 126.

[4] Diawara, "Make It Funky," 126.

121

122

123

Chéri Samba
Congolese (born 1956)

Condemnation Sans Judgement, 1989 (Condemnation without judgment)(1990)
Oil on canvas, with glitter
59" x 77"
Signature: on recto, "Chéri Samba"
Collection of Evan and Mary Tawil, New York (Evan Tawil, class of 1989)

Provenance: Annina Nosei Gallery, New York City, April 1991

Literature: Holland Cotter, "Chéri Samba at Annina Nosei," *Art in America* 78, no. 10 (October 1990): 206-07; Jean-Pierre Jacquesmin, *Chéri Samba: Le Paintre Populaire Du Zaire* (Oostende, Belgium, 1990), 59; B. Gunther, *Chéri Samba* (Chicago, 1990), 5; Chéri Samba, "Memories of an African: Chéri Samba," in *Raw: High Culture for Low Brows* 2, no. 3 (New York, 1991): 18-19; *Atheneum (Quarterly of the Wadsworth Atheneum)* (Winter 1991-92): 12

Exhibitions: *Chéri Samba*, Institute of Contemporary Art, London, 1990; *Chéri Samba*, Annina Nosei Gallery, New York City, 1990; *Chéri Samba*, Museum of Contemporary Art, Chicago, 1991; *Chéri Samba, Matrix 117*, Wadsworth Atheneum, Hartford, Connecticut, 1992

The art of Chéri Samba gained fame in the West after its presentation in the Pompidou Centre's 1989 exhibition, *Magiciens de la Terre*. A brilliant social satirist with a biting wit, Chéri Samba is a self-taught artist, former sign painter, and comic strip illustrator, with a big following in Kinshasa, Congo, where he has spent most of his working life. In 1982, Chéri Samba first visited France, invited by *Actuel* magazine, and painted a mural in its Paris office. Since then, and especially after exposure from the Pompidou show, Chéri Samba has became one of the most internationally known of all contemporary African artists.

Samba's hyper-realistic paintings combine text and image to make their message clear. Vivid, high contrast colors are sometimes accented with a flourish of glitter, as here, in the rim of the sunglasses. This painting addresses the broad theme of the extreme imbalance of wealth that exists in the postcolonial world, with Africa and Africans most often left holding the short end of the stick. As illustrated here, this situation exacerbates human relations within Africa. In this painting, the narrative begins with a young, hardworking African man, packing his bag. Determined to buy a new house for himself, he prepares to return home before spending all that he has earned while abroad. Then, upon his arrival in his home country, just off the airplane, he is greeted more with open hands than open arms. Later, as he sleeps, jealous arms reach to strangle him. In the final image, tears stream down his cheeks, while dark sunglasses, emblem of modernity, hide the full expression of his sorrow. Here, the dark glasses might also be read as a symbol of the young man's attempt at self-containment, shielding him from the poverty of the world that surrounds him.

While Samba gives this young man's situation a soap-operalike expression, the dilemma outlined in this painting is one faced by many Africans today, and has great resonance. In the final text, in French and Lingala, Samba admonishes people to recognize that it is not up to one but up to everyone to solve the social problems caused by the imbalanced distribution of wealth in today's world. Further, the text states, free handouts are not the solution. In this painting, as in other works, Samba takes fire at both the West and at Africa. As Manthia Diawara describes Chéri Samba, he is "the Amos Tutuola of African art—the stereotype that strikes back. His reclaiming of the stereotype of Africa in the modern imagination is one clue to his success."[1]

Lubangi Muniania and Carol Thompson,
Adjunct Instructor, Department of Art, Vassar College

---

[1] Manthia Diawara, "Chéri Samba," *Artforum* 336, no. 3 (November 1997): 108.

IL EST VRAI QUE L'ARGENT EST DIFFICILE A GAGNER. J'AI FAIT BEAUCOUP DE TEMPS ICI A L'ETRANGER MAIS JE N'AI PAS GAGNÉ GRAND CHOSE. MIEUX DE RENTRER CHEZ MOI AVANT QUE JE FINISSE LE PEU QUE J'AI GAGNÉ. MAIS... MBOKA YANGO PE NAZOKENDE, MINDONDO TROP. JE NE SAIS PAS SI LES MEMBRES DE SO·PE·KA / AC·DO·FA· EXISTENT TOUJOURS
FRANCHEMENT, NA MBOKA TOYEBI VALEUR YA MBONGO TE. PO DU 1er AU 31, KAKA KOSENGA—SENGA—SENGA. CETTE FOIS-CI LES FLATTEUR VONT M'ENVOULOIR.
JE NE FERAI PLUS L'ERREUR YA KOKABA MBONGO PAMBA-PAMBA. J'ACCEPTERAI AUSSI LA SOUFFRANCE DE MARCHER TOUT LE TEMPS A PIED JUSQU'A NOUVEL ORDRE.
LOPANGO ELEKI BILOKO NION-SO. IL ME FAUT UNE PARCELLE SINON JE SERAI TOUT LE TEMPS LOCATAIRE
—·—
COMITE LOCAL DES QUEMANDEURS
UN COMITÉ DECENTRALISÉ QUI A COMME DEVISE: SO·PE·KA·
SOMBELA NGAI-PESA NGAI-KABELA NGAI
L'ASSOCIATION FLATTEURS A·B·L AVEC BUT LUCRATIF
VOUS SOUHAITE LE BIENVENU. N'OUBLIEZ PAS NOTRE DEVISE: AC·DO·FA·
ACHETES MOI—DONNES MOI—FAIS MOI CADEAU. UNE FOIS TU DONNES A QUELCUN, IL FAUT LE FAIRE CHAQUE FOIS SINON TU ES MAL VU. SOKI OKABELI MOTO MBALA MOKO, KABELAKA YE KAKA, SOKI TE, OZUAMI MABE
LOKOLA NAMONI YO, NASEPELI J'ESPERE QUE TOUS MES PROBLE-MES SERONT RESOLUS. PESA NGA MBONGO. WAPI MASANGA NA NGAI
EST-CE QUE BINO BOKOKI KOKABELA NGAI TE? MIKOLO NIONSO, KAKA BINO BOSENGAKA, BOYOKAKA SONI TE? LAISSEZ-MOI TRANQUIL JE N'AI PAS GRAND CHOSE
JE T'AI DEMANDÉ DE L'ARGENT, DES BAS, DES CHAUSSETTES, DES CHAUSSURES, PARFUM ET SURTOUT MASANGA OYO OPROMETAKA NGAI AVANT QUE OVOYAGER, TU REFUSES A ME LES DONNER. OKOMI MABOKO MAKASI. MEURS AUJOURD'HUI QUE DEMAIN ON T'ENTERRE.
OKOYA KOLIA NDEKO NA YO PAMBA. IL Y A LA CRISE MONDIALE ET TOUT LE MONDE EN PARLE. L'ARGENT EST DEVENU TRÈS DIFFICILE. FRANCO AYEMBA: «TOZALAKA KOYOKA SON LELO TOKOMI MOYIMI. LIKAMBO EZALI NA MOSALA? TIKA KO CONDAMNER MONINGA NA YO SANS QUE OJUGER YE. BISONONGO, OZALI KOYOKA PAS.
LA FLATTERIE EST UN DEFAUT. POUR FINIR LA CRISE MONDIALE, IL NE FAUT JAMAIS COMPTER SUR LES EFFORTS D'UNE SEULE PERSONNE. MAINTENANT LES GENS AIMENT LA FACILITE MAIS ILS OUBLIENT LE TRAVAIL. ILS NE FONT QUE DERANGER LES AUTRES. KOKABA YANGO PE EKOMA MYSTIQUE. BA NKOKO BALOBA: «MOTO BOLIAKA NA YE, KAKA YE WANA MONGUNA NA YO. FLATTEUR ANDIMA KA NA YE MOTO TE. OKABA, OKABA TE, EZALI SE NDENGE MOKO. TANGO OKUEYI AKOLAMUSA YO TE, KAKA YE MOTO AKOSEKA YO
CONDAMNATION SANS JUGEMENT
Chéri Samba

124

Nahum B. Zenil
Mexican (born 1947)

Santo de mi devoción (Saint of my devotion) (1982)
Mixed media
$38^1/_2$" x $27^1/_4$"
Signature: "Nahum B. Zenil 82"
Lent by Bannon McHenry, class of 1952

Exhibition: *Pase Usted*, Museo del Arte Carrillo Gil, San Angel, Mexico, 1982

Nahum Zenil was born in 1947 in the state of Veracruz, a child of lower-middle-class parents in rural circumstances. He attended the Escuela Nacional de Maestros in Mexico City, the national teachers' school, whence he graduated in 1964. While he received instruction in the late 1960s at the Esceula Nacional de Pintura y Escultura, his art retains an aura of the primitive simplicity of the autodidact. His subject matter is almost entirely self-imagery over the past twenty years. He poses as his artistic and personal dilemma how to articulate his existence as a homosexual in contemporary Mexican society. The consistent return to self-portraiture and the folk art references in his work remind many viewers of the art of Frida Kahlo, one of the best-known Mexican artists outside of Mexico.

Another theme common to both artists is the emphasis on spirituality related to physical and psychological pain. In *Santo de mi devoción* (Saint of my devotion) the artist portrays himself half-length in a business suit and tie, placed before and overlaid with flames. The painting resides within a shadow box framed with a traditional Spanish Baroque molding. Along the narrow margin, between the glass of the frame and the painting, he has arranged a dozen votive candles. A garland of paper roses surround the border above the candles. In this way, the artist triggers the visual vocabulary of the traditional devotional image of Hispanic Catholicism, while portraying himself as the martyred focus of his own religion, perhaps even a sacrificial victim to the intolerance of the established church to his choice of lifestyle.

James Mundy, class of 1974

125

Julia Margaret Cameron
British (1815-79)

Portrait of Cecilia Tennyson (ca. 1869)
Albumen photograph
12" x 9³/₄"
Collection of Evan and Mary Tawil, New York (Evan Tawil, class of 1989)

Provenance: Bonni Benrubi, New York

Julia Margaret Cameron lived most of her life in Calcutta, India, having been born and raised there within a socially prominent and intellectually gifted, albeit considerably unconventional, family of Anglo-French extraction. As wife of Charles Hay Cameron, a jurist on the Indian Law Commission and later president of the Calcutta Council of Education, she remained in India until his retirement in 1848. After moving to England, the Camerons eventually settled at Freshwater on the Isle of Wight for economic reasons, but also to be close to their friend, Alfred Lord Tennyson, England's poet laureate, whom Julia Cameron idolized.

At the age of forty-eight, Cameron began making photographs with a sliding-box camera she had received as a Christmas present in 1863. The fortuitous gift, chosen by her daughter to amuse and engage her, inspired her to use the relatively new medium of photography to achieve professional status and monetary reward. With her prodigious literary and artistic knowledge, Cameron endeavored to express ideal beauty and truth—concepts more commonly associated with the "high arts" of poetry, painting, and sculpture—through photography. To prove that photography could attain the emotive power comparable to the high arts, she departed from the conventional Victorian photographic theory that required recording the world in sharp detail. Though her career lasted just fifteen years, Cameron produced over three thousand images and created a legacy as one of the most innovative and original photographers of the nineteenth century.

Cameron's rapid progress in learning to use the camera had as much to do with her energy, intellect, and willingness to experiment, as it did with the technical advice and criticism she sought and received from Oscar Gustave Rejlander and David Wilke Wynfield, both experienced photographers; the artist, George Frederick Watts, and, in particular, the eminent scientist, Sir John Herschel, who had invented the cyanotype process in 1840.

Cameron achieved critical recognition early in her career for her expressive portraits of famous men, such as Tennyson, Thomas Carlyle, and Charles Darwin, in part because her photographs found a responsive audience eager to see images of the most heroic figures of the day, but also because her unprecedented manner of photographing her sitters at close range, making their heads appear large and dramatic, shocked viewers. Cameron's intent was artistic, not scientific. Her record of the physical appearance of things was more a question of evoking beauty through poetic expression than through detail.

The portrait of Cecilia Tennyson is a striking example of Cameron's formal and aesthetic concerns. A rare portrait, Cecilia is treated in the uncomplicated and direct manner typical of Cameron's idealized portrait types, in which the sitter is photographed fully frontal against a dark, indistinguishable background. The camera is placed close to her to reduce the depth of field, and the lighting is held at a low level. Cameron often focused the lens sharply upon the sitter's eyes, as she does in this portrait, which caused other characteristics to blur and thus fuse softly into the background. Cameron's desire to make her sitter's hair appear abundant and unfettered—thoroughly at odds with the Victorian tradition of restrained coiffure for women—accentuated the idea of evanescence and recalls the Pre-Raphaelite emphasis upon luxuriant hair. Further, this technique allowed Cameron to achieve an element of ambiguity in the sitter's expression, making it difficult for viewers to assess with certainty the sitter's mood.

Cameron has draped Cecilia in dark, rather than bright white, fabric, a technique she often employed to prevent light from reflecting off the clothing. Here, she has characteristically avoided extraneous detail; the only added element to the portrait is a bouquet of vines and wildflowers that appears to have been hastily gathered and placed into Cecilia's hands.

Cecilia Tennyson, named after the poet's sister, was one of four daughters of his youngest and perhaps most eccentric brother, Horatio. In the late 1860s, Horatio, whose wife had died prematurely, brought his children to live at Freshwater under the supervision of the poet's wife, Emily. Cameron may have pressed Cecilia to sit for her (as she did many of the children at Freshwater, who had time for lengthy modeling sessions), because Cameron sensed within Cecilia the potential to express a young girl's solemnity as both ideal and natural states.

Rebecca Lawton

Alvin Langdon Coburn
British, American-born (1882-1966)

St. Paul's Cathedral from Ludgate Circus (1904)
Photogravure
16" x 12"
Promised Gift of Frances Fergusson and Michael Moohr

Alvin Langdon Coburn was an exponent of pictorialism in photography, as exemplified by this image of St. Paul's Cathedral in London. Light appears to dissolve the very substance of the architecture, which blends with the smoldering atmosphere. Passages between dark and light areas are equally ambiguous. Is it any wonder that Coburn admired the *Impressionistic Nocturnes* of James McNeil Whistler? Without sharp corners or transitions, such exquisite tonalism was also an expression of Coburn's interest in the potential for abstraction in photography. He experimented extensively, manipulating both the camera and his prints, replacing the lens with a pinhole in a card, and scumbling the platinum plate with a gum bichromate coating. In 1917 he originated the "vortograph," a photographic corollary to the Vorticist paintings and sculptures produced by England's cubist movement. These kaleidoscopic images, produced by attaching mirrors to the camera lens, are considered among the first purely abstract photographs ever made.

This particular image is one of only six photographs that Coburn printed as large-scale photogravures. A smaller version appeared in his published folio volume, *London*, of 1909. This image, made in 1904, forms a link to a fascinating collaboration between the photographer and Henry James. In 1906, the author invited Coburn to create frontispieces for each of the volumes in an edition of his complete works. The choice of photography was an unusual form of illustration at the time. And though James maintained that the photographs would be considered discreet works in their own right, he asserted for himself a role in their creation. By specifying the subjects, angles, and moods he wanted Coburn to capture, James would, in the words of art historian, Ralph Bogardus, play "director" to Coburn as "cameraman."[1] Of the over twenty images produced during the two-year project, for which Coburn traveled extensively in Europe and America, a distant view of the dome of St. Paul's was the only shot that James did not call.[2] Coburn

presented it himself as the perfect image for volume five, where it appears as the frontispiece for *The Princess Casamassima.*

At the start of the collaboration, Coburn was already a prominent, and much mentored, young photographer. Born in Boston in 1882, Coburn's introduction to photography came by way of a relative, F. Holland Day, who enjoyed photographing himself as Jesus in set tableaux. Day took Coburn with him to London in 1899 to help organize an exhibition entitled, *The New School of American Pictorial Photography*, in which their work was featured. In London, Coburn met the American photographer, Edward Steichen, a protégé of Alfred Stieglitz.

After returning to New York, Coburn became, in 1903, at the behest of Stieglitz, a founding member of the Photo-Secession, dedicated to raising photography's cultural value from a documentary form to a fine-arts medium. The group advocated that photographic images conceived with formal integrity and printed with a high regard for darkroom craftsmanship could be cherished as paintings were. A 1904 volume of Stieglitz's journal, *Camera Work*, featured Coburn's work. Coburn's popular success, however, was as a portraitist, photographing *Men of Mark*, as his 1913 book is titled. Like Americans James and Whistler, Coburn made Britain his preferred domicile. He became a British citizen in 1931, making this portrait of Saint Paul's a prescient tribute to his elected home.

Ingrid Schaffner

---

[1] Ralph Bogardus, *Pictures and Texts: Henry James, A. L. Coburn and New Ways of Seeing in Literary Culture* (Ann Arbor, Michigan, 1984).

[2] While other artists might have found James meddlesome, Coburn regarded it as a creative treasure hunt to realize the pictures his colleague had in mind. He wrote admiringly, "Although not literally a photographer, I believe Henry James must have had sensitive plates in his brain, on which to record his impressions." Quoted in Helmut and Alison Gernsheim, eds., *Alvin Langdon Coburn: Photographer, An Autobiography* (New York, 1966), 58.

127

E. J. Bellocq
American (1873-1949)

Storyville Portraits, Two Images (ca. 1912)
Gelatin silver print; gold chloride toning on printing-out paper, printed by Lee Friedlander
Each 9¹/₂" x 7¹/₂"
Lent by Drs. Alvin and Lenore Weseley (Lenore S. Levine, class of 1954)

By dying in obscurity, Eugene J. Bellocq inadvertently assured that information about his life and career as a commercial photographer in New Orleans first be subjected to speculation. The much-mythologized version of his life cast him as a Toulouse-Lautrec-like figure, an outsider, a gnome of a man with an oddly-shaped head, who frequented New Orleans's jaunty Storyville district and befriended the prostitutes, who worked in its bordellos. (The famous red-light district was created by New Orleans City Council-man, Sidney Story, in 1879. His theory of containment for vice was based upon the European model.)

Research has revealed that Bellocq was born of French descent in 1873, to a middle class Catholic Creole family, that his father worked as a bookkeeper, and that his brother became an ordained priest, who brought him photography clients from the Catholic diocese. Bellocq's career as a photographer began as a hobby and evolved into a commercial business. He took photographs of prosaic events such as high school graduations, documenting the shipbuilding industry for the Foundation Company, and working on assignment for various magazines and newspapers. It is possible that his record of New Orleans's prostitutes was a commercial assignment, but John Szarkowski believes that the pictures themselves suggest that they were not done on commission, but rather as a personal project.[1]

The two photographs under discussion here offer considerable insight into Bellocq's intentions. In both images, the subject is seated at center within a domestic setting. Each woman appears relaxed, in one she smiles and toasts the photographer with a drink, in the other, a casually-seated woman stares gently back at him. It appears as if these women have posed for Bellocq in their personal environment, surrounded by beloved mementos and meaningful pieces of bric à brac. Although not all Bellocq's sitters are clothed, in these two photographs, the women are: one woman wears an undergarment, provocatively arranged below her shoulders, and the other is dressed in a shawl, draped around her like a toga. Their vibrant stockings make bold statements against the lively-pat-terned wallpaper and carpeting. Pictures of nude women, albeit barely visible, also decorate the walls, providing a stark contrast between erotic imagery intended for salacious purposes and Bellocq's portraits.

Very few of Bellocq's Storyville photographs approximate pornography, in fact they appear as something completely at odds with it. Bellocq's women have the understated composure of real (not fantasy) women. In most of his photographs there is an implicit understanding that these women, some dressed elegantly, some playing with their dogs, some exposing their figures, had a great deal to say about how Bellocq photographed them. It is as if Bellocq might have taken their photographs for them, as a favor to them. The two photographs under discussion here present the women in clear and concise terms. These are simple, straightfor-ward images of two women, who are undoubtedly prostitutes, but he saw them nonetheless as human beings.

The photographer, Lee Friedlander, discovered Bellocq's deterio-rating glass-plate negatives in 1958, developed them on printing-out paper, and helped mount an exhibition of them at the Museum of Modern Art in 1970.

Bellocq photographs have thus taken on the role of historical documents. They reveal a great deal about legal prostitution at the turn of the century in general and the role of women within the profession in particular. Bellocq may have recognized the value of his photographs for posterity. This perhaps may explain why he appears to have done nothing to promote his Storyville photo-graphs during his lifetime, and may also answer the question why he did not destroy the glass-plate negatives before he died.

Rebecca Lawton

---

[1] John Szarkowski, *Storyville Portraits* (New York, 1970), 12.

128

Man Ray
American (1890-1976)

Jean Cocteau with Gloves (ca. 1924)
Silver print photograph
11" x 8¹/₂"
Collection of Evan and Mary Tawil, New York (Evan Tawil, class of 1989)

Literature: Julie Saul, ed., *The Mirror and The Mask, A Photo-biography* (Boston, 1992), 20, plate 6

Born Emmanuel Rudinitzky in Philadelphia in 1890, Man Ray became a seminal figure in twentieth-century art and photography. His inventive mind worked equally well in painting, photography, and filmmaking. His interest in photography, which began as a practical solution to obtaining good-quality photographs of his art, evolved into a revolutionary approach to the medium. He quickly mastered photography and prevailed upon the camera as a tool to process his creativity. As a central figure within the New York avant-garde of the teens, Man Ray developed close friendships with the French artists, Marcel Duchamp and Francis Picabia, who welcomed him to help them launch New York's fledgling Dada movement. The American leader of modernism, Alfred Stieglitz, inspired his interest in photography.

Man Ray's arrival in Paris at the end of July 1921, as "the American Dadaist," coincided with the waning of the Dada movement there. He established a photography business to support himself. Initially, Man Ray's photography was strictly commercial, with income produced by photographing Picabia's paintings and—through Picabia's first wife—Paul Poiret's couture fashions. Sometime between October 1921 and January 1922, Picabia introduced Man Ray to Jean Cocteau (1889-1963), considered then the most famous and popular figure within Parisian society. Cocteau's polymorphous talent included writing poetry, prose, plays, librettos, and music; directing films and ballets; and making drawings and graphic art, all of which both elevated and enlivened his status within the art world of Montparnasse, where Man Ray had settled in early December 1921. The fortuitous introduction to Cocteau launched Man Ray's career as a portrait photographer.[1]

Man Ray first photographed Cocteau at the apartment Cocteau shared with his widowed mother at 10 rue d'Anjou. Man Ray made at least two photographs of Cocteau on the occasion. One captured Cocteau looking through an empty picture frame and another portrayed him in profile looking at a model ship. The success of the first portraits encouraged further business from Cocteau's friends, all habitués of the café, *Le Boeuf sur le Toit*. According to Cocteau, the café's customers were "the best people in Paris, from all spheres of life....The prettiest women, poets, musicians, business-men, publishers—everybody met at the *Boeuf*."[2] The café became Man Ray's hangout and a showcase for his photographs. Cocteau continued his patronage with commissions, such as a portrait of Proust on his deathbed (taken in November 1922), and further portraits of himself.

Man Ray made the photograph of Cocteau under discussion here around 1924, two years after they had met. In style, it differs dramatically from the earlier, straightforward photograph of Cocteau looking out of the empty picture frame. It has the somber, nuanced quality popularized by the pictorialists, who aimed towards an artistic effect in all their photography and an evocation of personality in portraiture. Cocteau appears idealized and romanticized, as if photographed through haze. Far from looking staid in his proper attire, Cocteau appears as pensive, youthful, and beautiful. Unlike many photographs of Cocteau, which focused upon his elegant hands with their long, tapered fingers, here his hands are covered in woolen gloves. It is Cocteau's thin lip, which accentuates his sensuality, that expresses subdued discontent. Man Ray also took a second, far less beguiling, photograph of Cocteau at this session.[3]

After having produced such a witty, conceptual photograph of Cocteau posing within a picture frame, it seems surprising that Man Ray chose to use the nearly outmoded pictorialist style for this photograph. Perhaps it says as much about the subject as it does about the photographer's concern at the time for attracting new clients, who might prefer to see themselves as Cocteau, elegant and reflective. Yet, both the gloved hand and the soft focus, which makes Cocteau appear photographed through a finely-meshed scrim, serve to obscure his true nature and identity as a homosexual and opium addict.

With photographs of Cocteau numbering in the hundreds, it is easy to assume, especially in a post-Warholian world, that Cocteau was famous simply for being famous. Dozens of photographers—Berenice Abbott (see cat. no. 133), Cecil Beaton, Robert Doisneau, and George Platt Lynes among them—captured his life in a variety of poses, provoking Cocteau's biographer, Francis Steegmuller, to comment that, "the magnitude of his talent was constantly called on to counterbalance his posturing."[4] Man Ray made some of the most compelling portraits of Cocteau, whose early recognition of Man Ray's talent as an artist and photographer, he said, had "delivered painting anew."[5]

Rebecca Lawton

[1]   Billy Klüver and Julie Martin, "Man Ray, Paris," in Merry Foresta, *Perpetual Motif: The Art of Man Ray* (New York, 1989), 108.

[2]   Quoted in Foresta, *Perpetual Motif*, 106.

[3]   See Man Ray, *Man Ray Photographs* (Paris, 1982), pl. 327.

[4]   Francis Steegmuller, "Cocteau on Camera: A Biographical Sketch," in *Jean Cocteau: The Mirror and the Mask, A Photo-biography*, ed. Julie Saul (Boston, 1992), 11.

[5]   Cocteau's remark first appeared in "Lettre ouverte à Man Ray, photographe américan," *Les feuilles libres* (April-May 1922), here quoted in Foresta, *Perpetual Motif*, 118.

129

Margaret Bourke-White
American (1904-71)

Smokestacks, Otis Steel Co., Cleveland 1927 and 1928 (1927)
Vintage gelatin silver print with hand-inked border
$13^5/_8$" x $9^1/_2$"
Promised Gift of Anne Hoene Hoy, class of 1963

Literature: Vicki Goldberg, *Bourke-White* (New York, 1988), 36

Smokestacks, Otis Steel Co, Cleveland, 1927 and 1928 is one of a series of photographs taken by Margaret Bourke-White early in her career as part of a corporate public-relations campaign, a fact she was later hesitant to admit. Bourke-White's first photographs date from her freshman year at Columbia College in 1922; this image, and others in the series, were taken a mere five years later, and would launch the young Bourke-White on a career as one of America's most successful industrial photographers. Bourke-White was paid well for her work: she received $100 per image, which at the time was a high price indeed for the work of an unknown photographer.[1] Bourke-White would later abandon the relatively straightforward style exemplified by this photograph to experiment with abstract compositions inspired by the films of Sergei Eisenstein. Later still, Bourke-White would leave the field of industrial photography altogether, this time for photojournalism. Even so, *Smokestacks, Otis Steel Co, Cleveland, 1927 and 1928* stands as an early triumph of Bourke-White's art.

Margaret Bourke-White had long been interested in machinery and factories; her father, an engineer and inventor, had inspired her reverence for all things mechanical. Bourke-White would observe within a few years of creating these images that "the heart of life today is in the great industrial activities of the country."[2] She would surely have placed this photograph, biographically, in what she described as "the rapturous period when I was when I was discovering the beauty of industrial shapes."[3]

Formally, this exterior photograph of the soot-blackened Otis Steel mill, taken in the depths of winter, bears a strong resemblance to the industrial imagery of artist and printmaker, Joseph Pennell, who was in fact the only fine artist Bourke-White ever credited as

an influence on her photography. The image may also owe a debt, or at least shows a general similarity, to contemporaneous works by Charles Sheeler and Louis Lozowick. But the moody quality of the work suggests a strain of romanticism more readily identifiable in the work of Pennell than of Sheeler or Lozowick. Bourke-White's sensitive awareness to wintry light, combined with a sensual appreciation of the deep, sooty blacks of the steel mill and gauzy trails of steam, give this impressive industrial complex an air both dynamic and infernal. Her ability to capture a mood, combined with her sensitivity to textural contrasts and awareness of strong tonal range, raises an otherwise commonplace documentary photograph to the level of art.

Photography critic and biographer, Vicki Goldberg, has noted of this series, and of Bourke-White's industrial photography in general, that they "tend to the theatrical, even the rhetorical. [Bourke-White's] devotion to technology was certainly up-to-date, but her romantic viewpoint, more popular at the time than the cool, clean objective photography of Sheeler and the leading Europeans, might be considered less purely 'Modern.' Yet it was precisely this romantic aspect...that was responsible for her great success at *Fortune* [Magazine]...[where Bourke-White's] imagery set the general tone for industrial photography in America for years."[4]

Justin Spring

---

[1] Vicki Goldberg, *Margaret Bourke-White: A Biography* (New York, 1986), 86.

[2] Ibid., 8.

[3] Ibid., 11.

[4] Ibid.

130

Max Alpert
Russian (1899-1980)

The Dneprostroy Dam Under Construction (1928)
Gelatin silver print
11$\frac{1}{2}$" x 18$\frac{3}{4}$"
Lent by Joyce and Michael Axelrod (Joyce Jacobson, class of 1961)

Born in Odessa, Max Alpert fought in the ranks of the Red Army in 1917-24. After completing his training as a photographer in 1924, he started to work as photographer-correspondent for *Rabochaya Gazeta* (Workers' newspaper). During 1929-31, he was photo-correspondent of *Pravda* (Truth). In 1931, together with the photographers, Arkadi Shaikhet and Solomon Tules, and the editor, L. Mezhericher, he created one of the first *fotocherki* (picture-stories), *24 Hours in the Life of the Filippov Family*. It contained seventy-eight photographs and became part of an exhibition sent by the Soviet Union to Vienna, Prague, and Berlin. In the same year, a German illustrated magazine, *Arbeiter Illustrierte Zeitung,* published a number of prints of the story, and so proved the effective impact of photography as a form of propaganda. From 1931, Alpert worked on the picture magazine, *SSSR na Stroyke* (USSR in construction), which was set up at the instigation of Maxim Gorky, with the aim of propagating knowledge of the USSR abroad. In the twenties and thirties, Alpert photographed important industrial building sites that were springing up throughout the country during the First Five-Year Plan. During World War II, he was a TASS correspondent. After the war, he worked as reporter for *Sovinformbiro* (Soviet information office) and the Novosti agency. His work, which was comprehensive and included a wide range of themes, depicted more than fifty years of the development of the Soviet Union.

The Dneprostroy Dam Under Construction demonstrates how, at a particular point in Russian history, the construction of public works and the aesthetics of constructivism intersected to create a concrete and avant-garde imagery of social optimism. As first theorized in 1917, constructivism in its so-called laboratory phase was a boldly nonrepresentational art of light, transparency, and mechanized movement—as conceptually and visually radical as the new exploitation-free society it called to order. When the Revolutionary Party came to power in 1921 over a country ruined by civil war, many within the avant-garde turned from abstraction to create more tangible images, known as production art, for the proletariat. Aleksandr Rodchenko, for example, designed advertisements,

theater decor, and costumes all upon constructivist principles, which in turn informed his grasp of modern trends in European photography, as seen in his own innovative camera work. It's the prevalence of those experimental ideals and their impact that can be seen in this work by the self-taught photographer, Max Alpert.

Although not a member of the avant-garde, Alpert has clearly appropriated their adventurous approach to picture making. The rakish angle of the dam slices the composition into dynamic sections that form an equation for Soviet prosperity. On one side water churns, on the other a city rises. The future, which the dam, upon completion, will deliver, swoops forward into the present, a path as surely taken as the road that sweeps across the rim of the dam and rushes to engulf the viewer. Taken in 1928, *The Dneprostroy Dam Under Construction* marks the inaugural years of Joseph Stalin's First Five-Year Plan of forced industrialization and collectivization of agriculture. A member of ROPF, the Russian Association of Proletarian Photo-Reporters, Alpert was one of many, including Rodchenko, assigned the task of documenting the Plan's progress, as part of its official propaganda, through photography.

During the 1930s, when socialist realism became the singular style of Soviet art, Alpert continued to work successfully as a photo-journalist. For inasmuch as the 1928 photograph suggests the impact of constructivism and European modernism in general, it also displays important differences. Compared to the radical simplicity and symmetries of Rodchenko's 1929 propaganda photographs on themes of electrification, Alpert's spectacular image appears vaguely Baroque and romantically sublime. Throughout his career, Alpert received steady official recognition, including awards and commissions for his work. His specialty remained celebratory views, such as this one, of industrial subjects that would increasingly reflect the pictorial values of the painters of the AKhR, the Association of Artists of the Revolution, the official art for showing the triumphs of socialism.

Ingrid Schaffner and Steven Kasher

131

Alexander Rodchenko
Russian (1891-1956)

The Vakhtan Timber Mill (1931)
Gelatin silver print
$9^1/_2$"" x $6^5/_{16}$"
Promised Gift of Joyce and Michael Axelrod (Joyce Jacobson, class of 1961)

Alexander Rodchenko worked with the Russian constructivist movement from 1917 to 1919, and it was there that he decided that artists must leave their studios and, to quote the constructivist leader, Tatlin, "go into the factory, where the real body of life is made." Rodchenko, like Tatlin, was a politically committed artist, devoted to creating useful objects whose form would be perfectly suited to their function. He felt a special affinity for photography because it was a technological medium, and thus allied to the promising world of the future. Starting in 1921, Rodchenko gave up painting and sculpture to create posters, books, textiles, theater sets, and (perhaps most importantly) a highly innovative and idiosyncratic form of photography and photomontage. *The Vakhtan Timber Mill* is a good example of his exceptionally dynamic style as a photographer.

By 1929, Rodchenko was convinced that Russia needed "a new aesthetics, able to express in photography the aspirations and pathos of our new socialist reality." Photography was crucial to that aesthetic, for, to his mind, photography more than any other medium had actively shaped the Communist vision of the world. As leader of "The October Group" of photographers, Rodchenko created a wide variety of photographs, including photographs and photomontages created specifically for the state, which were used in a wide variety of propagandist endeavors, usually celebrating Russia's vast natural and mineral wealth, or the creation of new factories, buildings, and collectivized farms.

The Vakhtan Timber Mill, a photograph of a worker sorting wooden planks, is a 1931 propaganda photograph celebrating the efforts of the average Soviet worker in Stalin's Rapid Industrialization Program. The image is most noteworthy for Rodchenko's signature use of dynamic perspective. The freshly-sawn planks seem to zoom from the top left-hand corner and continue straight through the center of the frame, stopped only by the efforts of the hard-working laborer. Rodchenko, meanwhile, photographs the laborer from above, so that we look down onto his back; the worker's legs and feet are steeply foreshortened in the process. The result is an impersonal image of exceptional thrust and perspectival displacement. In this way, Rodchenko's disorienting aesthetic celebrates, in as literal and impersonal a manner as possible, the vigor and dynamism of the new Soviet Russia.

Justin Spring

132

Emmanuel Evzerikhin
Russian (1911-1984)

Construction of the Moscow Subway (1936-37)
Gelatin silver print
15$^1/_2$" x 10$^3/_4$"
Lent by Joyce and Michael Axelrod (Joyce Jacobson, class of 1961)

Although little is known in the West about the photographer Emmanuel Evzerikhin, it is interesting to explore this image within the contemporary context of Soviet photography. In 1932, Joseph Stalin declared an official end to the avant-garde by denouncing it an expression of bourgeois formalism. Up to this point, the constructivists, Russia's modernists, had enjoyed tremendous freedom and authority, allying their radical art with the goals of a new society. As part of Stalin's First Five-Year Plan of forced industrialization and collectivization of agriculture, which began in 1928, artists such as Aleksandr Rodchenko had created expressive propaganda based on progressive abstract principles. But when the Plan was completed one year ahead of schedule, Stalin, proclaiming the cultural revolution a success, called for the disbanding of all artistic groups in accordance with the formation of one totalitarian Artists Union. Within two years, the official art of the Soviet Union was socialist realism, the style and aims of which are exemplified by this photograph.

Compared to Max Alpert's *The Dneprostroy Dam Under Construction* (1928; see cat. no. 130), this image appears composed as if to suppress any formal adventurousness. The inherent drama of the tunnel—its rushing perspective—is deliberately stopped by the statically framed image and posed figures in order to clearly show the tasks at hand, of which *Construction of the Moscow Subway* is only one. The larger project is one that occupies both the anonymous men and the photographer, who commemorates their labor. Both are working to bring a vast, impoverished, and technologically backwards Soviet Union into the modern world, a place where cameras were as essential as subways and wristwatches. According to The People's Commissar of Education, Anatoly Lunacharsky,

"Just as every progressive comrade should have a watch, so he must know how to use a photographic camera. It is important to us to introduce the benefits of photography to the very midst of the masses."[1] For Lunacharsky those benefits were part of the special task of the pictures themselves, which he described as "not merely a chemically treated plate—but a profound act of social and psychological creation."[2]

In other words, the official aim of Soviet photography was to create a picture of a potential reality. Given the state of the Russian economy during the 1930s, the men in this photograph by Evzerikhin are probably working under slavelike circumstances—if they are not actual prisoners—of which the photograph offers no signs. But anyone who saw this image—which was most likely published in a newspaper or posted as a bulletin—would have appreciated those circumstances. Unlike in American documentary photography of the 1930s, there was no expectation that the photograph would expose illusions of prosperity. Inasmuch as the Soviet viewer was participating with the photographer in "a profound act of social and psychological creation" the socialist realist photograph was an easily legible prompt for building pride in progress, which Soviets collectively labored to realize.

Ingrid Schaffner

---

[1]   Quoted in Sergei Gitman and Valery Stigneev, "Photographers in Russia, Unite Yourselves," *Art Journal* 34 (Summer 1994): 29.

[2]   Quoted in Jo Anna Isaak, "Reflections of Resistance," in *Feminism and Contemporary Art* (London and New York, 1996), 126.

133

Berenice Abbott
American (1898-1991)

Duke Town House, 4 East 78th Street (1938)
Vintage gelatin silver print
$7^5/_8$" x $9^1/_2$"
Inscription: on mount, "E. 78th St. No. 1"
Promised Gift of Anne Hoene Hoy, class of 1963

Provenance: New York Public Library

Literature: Bonnie Yochelson, *Berenice Abbott: Changing New York* (New York, 1997), 386, pl. 4

Berenice Abbott had an extraordinary career as a photographer. Born 17 July 1898 in Springfield, Ohio and raised in Cleveland, Abbott possessed a rebellious streak and curious nature that propelled her move to New York City at the age of twenty. There, she lived in Greenwich Village among the avant-garde, who had also gravitated to the neighborhood's bohemian character. She found an outlet for her artistic inclinations through sculpture and a channel for her wanderlust by leaving New York for Paris in the spring of 1921.

Her career as a photographer began in Paris as a darkroom assistant for the American expatriate artist, Man Ray, whose portrait business was thriving (see cat. no. 128). He provided Abbott with technical experience and access to important people, who came to his studio to have their portraits taken and subsequently to her own studio. By the time Abbott returned to New York in January 1929, she had acquired considerable status within the international art and fashion worlds.

The French photographer, Eugène Atget (1857-1927), had an enormous influence upon Abbott's development as a photographer. Although Atget died shortly after Abbott met him, she was able to acquire a large body of his documentary work on Paris and its environs—1,400 glass plate negatives and 7,800 prints—through financial help from friends. Of equal importance, Abbott learned to see the world photographically through his method of documenting it with restraint and understated elegance.

The photograph under discussion here, *Duke Town House, 4 East 78th Street*, belongs to Abbott's epic project to "mak[e] a documentary interpretation of New York City in photographs" which she titled, *Changing New York*, and published as a book in 1939.[1] It was in large measure Atget's influence, but also Abbott's own willful nature, which fueled her ambition—she herself called it passion—

to document the entire city. Despite several years of searching for sponsorship, she began to realize the fulfillment of her goal when the Works Progress Administration's Federal Art Project (WPA/FAP), which hired her as a photographer in 1935, allowed her to pursue the project under its aegis.

Abbott photographed the mansion of tobacco tycoon, James B. Duke, on 20 January 1938. The photograph is among Abbott's most successful images from the project, contrasting the faded opulence of the age of conspicuous consumption, as evidenced in the French-inspired Duke *"chateau"* with the new modern style suggested by the sleek canopy of the fifteen-story apartment building across the street. The photograph reveals Abbott's eye for dynamic compositions, with sharp diagonal lines crossing the vertical lines of the windows. The entrances to the buildings trenchantly underscore the stark contrast Abbott intended to elucidate in her photographs. The slender iron rods supporting the canopy of the apartment house oppose the massive ionic limestone pillars of the mansion. Here too, is Abbott's ability to be realistic and objective with the camera, while actually evoking a highly expressive response from her photography. The mansion, where the world's richest girl—Duke's daughter, Doris,—lived, appears vacant and hauntingly silent, while the building at 969 78th Street suggests activity with the ubiquitous doorman standing at attention, ready to assist the newly rich with the comforts of apartment living.

The Duke mansion is the only image documenting "millionaire's row" above East 59th Street that Abbott included in *Changing New York*. The mansion became New York University's Institute of Fine Arts in 1958.

Rebecca Lawton

---

[1] Bonnie Yochelson, *Berenice Abbott: Changing New York* (New York, 1997), 15.

969

134

Ralph Steiner
American (1899-1986)

Clotheslines, 1925 (printed by Steiner, 1980)
Gelatin silver print
5" x 4"
Promised Gift of Anne Hoene Hoy, class of 1963

Ralph Steiner's *Clotheslines, 1925* was taken when Steiner, aged twenty-six and but a few years out of Dartmouth College, was working as a freelance magazine and advertising photographer in New York. Within a year of taking this photograph, Steiner would have his first photographic exhibition at the J. B. Neumann Print Gallery in New York. This exhibition would be the first step in a wide-ranging artistic career that would eventually include documentary film-making, Hollywood cinematography, and, in later years, a teaching position at Sarah Lawrence College.

Clotheslines, 1925 records a typical urban sight, clotheslines strung across a residential courtyard. Steiner finds a delicate beauty in the way these lines (and an occasional undergarment) crisply capture and hold the light against a background of tonal gloom. The delicate play of these silvery lines imbue the somber and workaday scene with a lyrical, calligraphic delicacy that is both pleasant and surprising. Some of the lines seem to describe, abstractly, a series of smiling or laughing mouths.

Steiner's awareness, in this photograph, of the importance of rich, dark tones to create a strong visual impression may have evolved, at least in part, out of his work in 1922-23 for the photogravure plant that had once printed Alfred Steiglitz's journal, *Camera Work*.

Steiner was certainly well aware of Steiglitz's *Camera Work*, and of Steiglitz's aesthetic judgments on photography. But Stieglitz was not his only influence; in fact, Steiner's greatest inspiration here comes from Paul Strand, the photographer Steiglitz once referred to as "brutally direct, pure and devoid of trickery." Like Strand, Steiner has found rare and surprising beauty in an unposed and unmanipulated subject. *Clotheslines, 1925* is an image that—fresh, immediate, and spontaneous—finds the exceptional in the everyday.

Though by 1932 Steiner's involvement with The Group Theater signaled a shift in his primary interest from photography to documentary filmmaking and, eventually, cinematography, Steiner's photographic work would be included in group exhibitions in the Museum of Modern Art in 1937, 1939, 1949, and 1969; his photographic work would also be featured in a group show at the Whitney Museum of American Art in 1974.

This version of *Clotheslines, 1925* is a gelatin silver print created by Ralph Steiner fifty-five years after the image was first photographed.

Justin Spring

135

Imogen Cunningham
American (1883-1976)

The Unmade Bed (1957)
Gelatin silver print
9¹/₂" x 10"
Promised Gift of Marian Phelps Pawlick, class of 1948

Imogen Cunningham's photographic career spanned nearly the entire twentieth century. Born in 1883, she began photographing in 1901, and continued until her death in 1976. Self-taught, Cunningham learned how to use a camera and to make prints through a course offered by the International Correspondence School. She learned the technique for platinum printing by studying with Edward S. Curtis. Her early work, influenced by the Pre-Raphaelite painter and poet, Dante Gabriel Rossetti, and by the leader of the English Arts & Crafts Movement, William Morris, has much in common with the allegorical photography of Julia Margaret Cameron (see cat. no. 125). Like Cameron, Cunningham directed friends dressed in costumes to pose as actors in fairy-tale settings, many of which were inspired by Rossetti's poems and Morris's verse. Her photographs were exceedingly romantic and emotional.

In the 1930s, Cunningham joined the f/64 Group, a loose, convivial association of like-mined photographers living along the West Coast. The f/64 Group challenged the perception that for a photograph to be art it had to mimic painting as the pictorialist photographers had done through the technique of modifying the negative to achieve painterly effects. Members of the f/64 Group, such as Edward Weston, Ansel Adams, and Willard Van Dyke, among others, promoted an antipictorialist aesthetic that advocated using the camera (specifically, a large-format view camera and a small lens aperture of f/64), to probe the exterior appearance of things. Their aim—to present reality as precisely as possible— involved intensive focusing upon their subject with uncompromising clarity, which in turn would create art as an expression of the natural or organic order of the world. The f/64 Group's insistence upon straight photography, with its stark, crisply captured imagery, became a cornerstone of modern photography and the foundation for future generations of street photographers.

The purist doctrine Cunningham practiced throughout the remainder of her career and taught to dozens of photography students was not, strictly speaking, that of the f/64 Group. She allowed cropping and increasingly made use of the element of chance, which could happen either during shooting or development of the contact print.

The Unmade Bed is among Cunningham's most celebrated photographs. In an interview, the photographer said, "I've sold more copies of that [image] than any other print."[1] According to Cunningham, the photograph was made originally as a joke, and she frequently gave a print of it as a wedding present to friends, "as a warning to the new husband."[2] Cunningham made the photograph after being told by a friend (who was studying photography with Dorothea Lange at the San Francisco Art Institute), that Lange has issued a class assignment to "make a meaningful photograph of [their] environment without people."[3] Cunningham, inspired to respond to Lange's challenge, dropped a few of her hair pins on her bed, developed the print and mailed it to Lange. Enchanted with the image, Lange asked Cunningham to make her a print. At the last class, held in Lange's house, *The Unmade Bed*, hung on the wall as a focal point for discussion.

Rebecca Lawton

---

[1]   Margery Mann, "Imogen Cunningham: An Excerpt (1966)" in Amy Rule, ed., *Imogen Cunningham Selected Texts and Bibliography* (Boston, 1992), 112.

[2]   Margery Mann, *Imogen Cunningham Photographs* (Seattle, Washington, 1970), n.p.

[3]   Ibid.

136

Henri Cartier-Bresson
French (born 1908)

Picnic on the Marne (1938)
Gelatin silver print
9¹/₄" x 14"
Signature: signed in ink and embossed copyright credit stamp in the margin
Promised Gift of Marian Phelps Pawlick, class of 1948

Alternately entitled, *Au Bord de la Marne* (By the edge of the Marne) and *Dimanche Au Bord de la Marne* (Sunday by the edge of the Marne), this relatively early Cartier-Bresson photograph, taken on the outskirts of Paris, shows two working-class couples enjoying a picnic lunch on the uncomfortably steep, weedy banks of the River Marne. The day is hazy, the river glassy; the meal is almost over, with dirty plates and utensils abandoned and an empty wine bottle fallen on its side. A fat woman, her back to the photographer, contemplates a chicken bone, while a well-fed man, his hat perched jauntily on his head, pours himself another drink.

Cartier-Bresson's photograph, which plays with the traditional French idea of the *fête champêtre* (particularly calling to mind Renoir's *Luncheon of the Boating Party* (1881, Phillips Collection, Washington, D.C.) and Seurat's *A Sunday Afternoon on the Island of La Grande Jatte* (1884-86, Art Institute of Chicago) portrays a brief moment of leisure in the lives of the working poor. Unlike the wealthy or middle-class folk celebrated by Manet or Seurat, however, these people have no boat of their own, and very little in the way of cosmopolitan style; still, they are enjoying their meal.

The image is beautifully composed. The photographer is looking down at these people, just as, in life, they are probably looked down upon by others for their lower-class status. Yet they are happily oblivious to such observation. The tone among the picnickers is rather one of quiet satisfaction: the man with the tipsy hat is enjoying his wine, the fat woman is focusing on a dainty morsel; the other couple, surrounded by picnic paraphernalia, is quietly contemplating the view. Two boats, moored just out of reach, suggest the distant possibility of nautical pleasure and adventure. The day's dull weather adds a melancholy note.

Cartier-Bresson, who was born into a wealthy family, originally studied painting with Jacques-Emil Blanche and, later, Andre Lhote, and so gained an early awareness of the importance of solid and telling pictorial composition, a quality that has distinguished his photography throughout his career. His aim in photography has always been to capture *le moment juste* (the decisive moment), which is to say, the moment that captures his subject in its quintessence. In capturing that moment, Cartier-Bresson also distinguished himself for stylish and elegant formal organization of his images. For him, photography was an instant of both the recognition of a significant fact, and a rigorously organized formal perception that expressed the meaning of the fact.

At the time he took this photograph, Cartier-Bresson had only recently returned to France from a series of overseas travels, including an extended visit to America, where aside from working as a freelance photographer and having a first exhibition at the influential Julien Levy Gallery, he briefly studied filmmaking with Paul Strand. Two years after taking this photograph, Cartier-Bresson was imprisoned by the occupying forces, but gained freedom in 1943, and afterwards covered the French liberation. He worked as a freelance photographer from the late 1940s to 1966, providing photographs for magazines and newspapers including *Life*, and was a founding member of the Magnum photo agency. Today he is perhaps the most famous, celebrated, and beloved photographer in the world.

Justin Spring

137

Alfred Eisenstädt
German (1898-1995)

Five Monks Walking in Cobblestone Street, 1947 (1947)
Gelatin silver print
10³/₄" x 9"
Lent by Hilda Bijur, class of 1940

Alfred Eisenstädt was born in 1898 in Dirschau, West Prussia, and grew up in Berlin. He was well-established in Berlin as a photojournalist as the Nazis rose to power. Being Jewish, he decided to leave Germany in 1935, but he returned there until the opening days of World War II on assignment as a press photographer, and many of his most famous photographs include images of Hitler and his top ministers of the Third Reich. For the rest of Eisenstädt's life, New York would be his home, but this most peripatetic of photojournalists was constantly on the move, and his camera has recorded significant events worldwide. Today he is considered by many to be the father of modern photojournalism.

During his career as a top photographer for *Life*, Eisenstädt would have ninety-two cover photographs and over 2,500 assignments. His most celebrated photographs were usually of heads of state, prominent social figures, or celebrities; his ability to capture a telling expression or gesture was unparalleled. During and after the war, however, he also specialized in subjects of general human interest, and in 1947 he visited the devastated landscapes of Italy and Japan. When Eisenstädt turned his gaze on everyday life, as in *Five Monks Walking in Cobblestone Street, 1947*, the results were often quite touching observations of everyday life, in this case on a street in the picturesque town of Siena, Italy.

Eisenstädt has been a late arrival into the pantheon of celebrated photographers, for his work is strongly journalistic. His eye was really more for character than for composition or style, and his specialty was really for being in the right place at the right time. Eisenstädt had few pretensions about what he was doing; in fact, he maintained a lifelong humility about the artistic content of his photographic efforts, deflecting praise with wit.

Justin Spring

138

Manuel Alvarez Bravo
Mexican (born 1902)

Angel del Temblor (Angel of the earthquake) (1957)
Gelatin silver print
$6^{1}/_{2}''$ x $9^{1}/_{2}''$
Lent by Ann L. Balis Morse, class of 1959

Manuel Alvarez Bravo was born in Mexico City in 1902. He attended Catholic schools in Tlalpan from 1908 to 1914 and during that time witnessed the revolution that began in 1910 and subsequently ushered in nearly a decade of civil war. In the early 1920s, Alvarez Bravo became increasingly interested in photography. The German photographer, Hugo Brehme, who took picturesque views of Mexico, provided technical training in the darkroom and encouraged his career. Alvarez Bravo bought his first camera in 1924, and within two years took first prize in a competition held in Oaxaca. Moving to Mexico City in 1927, Alvarez Bravo continued to photograph and established an art gallery in his home, in which he exhibited works by key members of Mexico's cultural renaissance, including Rufino Tamayo, José Clemente Orozco, Diego Rivera, and Frida Kahlo, among others. In 1929, he and Italian photographer, Tina Modotti, introduced Alvarez Bravo to Rivera. Alvarez Bravo subsequently joined Rivera at the Academia San Carlos, where he held the directorship. Throughout the decade of the 1930s, he formed associations with a number of influential photographers such as Edward Weston, Paul Strand, and Henri Cartier-Bresson (see cat. no. 136), as well as the French poet, André Breton, who as leader of the surrealists, invited him to participate in their exhibition in Mexico City in 1938. During this fertile period, Alvarez Bravo developed a distinctive, personal style with roots in surrealism and Mexico's indigenous folk culture. His photographs addressed the humanist ideals of the revolution and the metaphysical qualities integral to the medium of photography.

Nissan Perez, among other critics, has commented upon the complex iconography of Alvarez Bravo's imagery, categorizing the photographer's fusion of Christian and pre-Hispanic mythology as "hermetic, inaccessible and incomprehensible to the non-Mexi-can."[1] Regardless, Alvarez Bravo's work can be appreciated on purely formal and technical levels. He is a consummate master of the tonal possibilities of black and white and is able to use light to achieve a poetic sensibility and sensuousness in the variety of shapes and textures.

Angel del Temblor is one of the photographs Alvarez Bravo took during the aftermath of the 1957 quake that severely damaged Mexico City. Its subject, a piece of fractured sculpture, was once the figure of an angel, a gift from France that had been placed upon a pedestal in the Avenue of Reform.[2] Alvarez Bravo has endowed it with the motifs most commonly associated with his work—religion, death and mortality, and a highly conscious formalism. The photographer's ability to handle light allows the sculpture to appear both surreal and substantially sensuous. His great achievement is in making the sculpture's inexorable deterioration and crumbling decay —the graphic evidence of its violent destruction—a part of its beauty. While the angel erodes, its beatific expression appears nonetheless intact and points to the photographer's complex combination of traditional Christian symbolism with pre-Columbian cultural artifacts. Rivera made the cogent assessment that Alvarez Bravo's photography "is Mexican by cause, form, and content, anguish is omnipresent and the atmosphere is supersaturated with irony."[3]

Rebecca Lawton

[1]   Nissan N. Perez, "Visions of the Imaginary, Dreams of the Intangible," in *Revelaciones: The Art of Manuel Alvarez Bravo* (San Diego, California, 1990), 14.

[2]   Ian Jeffrey, "Dreams Visions Metaphors," in *The Photographs of Manuel Alvarez Bravo* (Jerusalem, Israel, 1983), 22.

[3]   Frederick Kaufman, *Manuel Alvarez Bravo: Photographs and Memories* (New York, 1997), 68.

139

Ray Metzker
American (born 1931)

Philadelphia (1968) (1968)
Gelatin silver print
7" x 10"
Promised Gift of Anne Hoene Hoy, class of 1963

Ray Metzker's *Philadelphia (1968)* is part of a series of photographs that the artist has described as combining "abstract design with a wealth of everyday information."[1] The everyday information included in this particular image, which employs techniques of photomanipulation and photomontage, concerns the Philadelphia streetscape: pavements, vistas, signage, trolley windows, and, of course, people, either standing in doorways, waiting to cross a street, or else simply walking. The overall sense in the image is one of dynamic movement countered by the heavy, decrepit atmosphere of the Philadelphia inner city on a hazy summer day.

Though taken during 1968, the year in which Metzker was chiefly preoccupied with two series of Jersey Shore photographs, *Couplets: Atlantic City* and *Sand Creatures*, *Philadelphia (1968)* is a much more complex and abstract composition than any work in those series, and unrelated, as well, in terms of subject matter. It is much more closely related to Metzker's *Composite* series, which had been exhibited at the Museum of Modern Art the year before. But *Philadelphia (1968)* also bears a relation to the earlier abstract photographic compositions of others, including Harry Callahan (with whom he studied), Margaret Bourke-White, and Laszlo Moholy-Nagy.

Metzker had moved to Philadelphia to teach at the Philadelphia College of Art in the spring of 1962, but his initial response to the city was negative. As he recalled, "Philadelphia wasn't a very exciting city to come to…Europe [had] had so much romance, so much to look at. In 1962, the core of Philadelphia was rotting. South Street was a cesspool of poverty, and it repelled me."[2] Metzker's ambivalence to his new environment may have been a factor in his decision to pursue formal innovation; so too was his job as a teacher at the Philadelphia College of Art, where, as he later recalled, "I was stressing the experimental aspects of photography."[3] Then again, a tension exists throughout Metzger's oeuvre between formalist and documentary concerns.

The *Composite* series evolved at a time when Metzker began to doubt the viability of the single-frame photographs with which he had established his reputation. As Metzker later recalled, "Simultaneity was a key factor [for the new series]—ongoing, continuous interaction of one element or form with another. My need was to integrate the variety of experience, to fashion a form that pulled diverse parts together without stripping the parts of their vitality."[4] There is a musical aspect to these works as well: "Percussion, the playing of one beat against the next, began to translate into the photographs."[5]

Philadelphia (1968) chronicles the active process of looking, by a formally sophisticated, modernist photographer who feels that "a photograph that freezes everything seems a misconception."[6]

Justin Spring

[1] Interview with Ray Metzker; quoted in Anne Wilkes Tucker, *Unknown Territories: Photographs by Ray K. Metzker* (New York, 1984), 122.

[2] Ibid.

[3] Ibid.

[4] Ibid., 123.

[5] Ibid.

[6] Ray Metzker, quoted in *Archives of American Art Journal* 31, no. 3 (1991): 39.

140

Irving Penn
American (born 1917)

Paper Cup with Shadow, New York, 1975 (1975)
Platinum palladium print
22" x 14¹⁄₂"
Lent by Thomas Krasne Levine, class of 1982

Irving Penn's commercial photography projects have long shown a quiet interest in detritus: the fashion and celebrity photographs for which he is best known have frequently featured an ironic leitmotif of disposed, cast-off, or half-consumed materials, including cocktails, meals, cigarettes, newspapers and magazines. They have also consistently featured such archetypal symbols of mortal decay as mice, flies, beetles, stains, and moldering walls. In part, Penn has included these elements out of an awareness that these items create a substantial contrast to the fresh and newly-made consumer items his photographs usually celebrate; but in part, his choice has been an aesthetic one, for fashion photography is itself an evanescent medium, and the majority of work created in the service of fashion is as disposable as the flattened piece of garbage described in *Paper Cup with Shadow, New York, 1975.*

During the 1970s, Penn broke away from fashion and celebrity photography to make everyday detritus a central subject, first with his *Cigarettes* series, then the *Street Material* series, and finally with a series entitled *Recent Still Lifes. Paper Cup with Shadow, New York, 1975,* which belongs to the *Street Materials* series, is a platinum palladium image of a soiled and flattened white cardboard cup, photographed against a stark white background. Curator John Szarkowski of the Museum of Modern Art has suggested that much of the work in the series looks as if it has been retrieved from the gutter, perhaps "in the wake of a street roller."[1]

Penn's fascination with garbage may be seen as a tacit acknowledgment that so much of what we prize in our culture (in part because of fashion photography like his own) is bound to be consumed and discarded within a very short period of time. The other side of the consumption fantasy—objects that have been purchased, consumed and then discarded or abandoned—therefore possess a disturbing, ghostlike resonance for him.

Still, it would be wrong to suggest that Penn's interest in the discarded paper cup suggests an element of criticism, protest, or even sentimental attachment. The deadpan irony of this photograph suggest Penn's philosophical relation to the Pop Art aesthetic, which celebrates the glamour industry and consumerism, is a fact of everyday life.

Penn's preoccupations in *Paper Cup with Shadow, New York, 1975* are purely, almost disturbingly, formal. As with the rest of the *Street Materials* series, the picture is "graphic in conception and uncompromisingly flat."[2] Furthermore, the platinum palladium printing method gives Penn's simple, frontal photograph an extraordinary clarity and detail. The clarity and detail are in themselves somewhat confusing, however, for they implicitly raise the question of why the subject should be the recipient of such close and attentive examination. Penn's use of the platinum palladium process is distinctive. As Szarkowski has observed,

> By the early seventies, after long, meticulous, and expensive experiment, Penn had perfected his command of this demanding alternative to the prevalent silver print. Because of its costliness and complexity, and because of its irrelevance to work intended for magazine reproduction, the process had been widely neglected for half a century....The platinum-palladium process is prized for the richness and delicacy of its tonal scale, and thus for its ability to make the nicest of photographic distinctions...it is perhaps not too much to say that in Penn's prints the descriptive resources of the photographic gray scale have never been more fully exploited.[3]

In light of Penn's use of this expensive and difficult technique, particularly in light of the choice of subject matter, *Paper Cup with Shadow, New York, 1975* is probably best described as an extravagant *jeu d'esprit* by a photographer whose creative endeavors in the service of the art and fashion have raised his work to an extraordinarily high level of technical achievement.

Justin Spring

---

1 John Szarkowski, *Irving Penn* (New York, 1984), 39.

2 Szarkowski, *Irving Penn*, 39.

3 Szarkowski, *Irving Penn*, 38.

141

Joel-Peter Witkin
American (born 1939)

Olympia (1974)
Gelatin silver print
$4^1/_2$" x $7^1/_2$"
Lent by Isabelle and Jerome E. Hyman (Isabelle Miller, class of 1951)

Joel-Peter Witkin was born in Brooklyn, New York in 1939. A triplet at birth, only he and his brother, Jerome, survived. Jerome became a painter; Joel-Peter discovered cameras and, at his mother's instigation, signed up for a photography class. She worked for a company that made lights for photography studios and her employer was giving a class in photography.[1] By the mid-1950s, Witkin was thoroughly immersed in photography and learning to photograph primarily by reading books. At the time, he took photographs of carnival freaks at Coney Island for Jerome to use as references for his paintings. Jerome's biographer, Sherry Chayat, has noted similarities between the brothers' work, linking each to an interest in the macabre and seeing in both brothers' art "a tweaking of reality. Each seems drawn simultaneously toward the mystical and the iconoclastic...."[2] In 1961, Joel-Peter enlisted in the United States Army, working as a staff photographer and witnessing the invasion at the Bay of Pigs.

Both Witkins mine the Old Masters, especially Rembrandt and German expressionist artists, such as Käthe Kollwitz, for imagery. Jerome's paintings from the 1970s are, like Joel-Peter's photographs from the same period, full of art-historical references. The photograph, *Olympia* of 1974 is just such an example.

As an explicit reference to Edouard Manet's *Olympia* (1863, Musée d'Orsay, Paris), with—to quote Chayat—"a tweaking of reality," Witkin joins a number of artists provoked to respond to Manet with their own versions of his masterpiece,[3] including Cézanne, Gauguin, Picasso, Sebastián Junyer-Vidal, and the Pop artist, Larry Rivers.

Witkin's whimsical version retained the major motif of the reclining nude, but varied minor ones, such as the servant, and dispensed with the cat altogether. He replaced the black maidservant with a male, somewhat similarly posed as Manet's—standing behind the bed holding a bouquet of flowers, but shows him nude, with the bouquet covering his genitals. By cropping the figure at the neck, Witkin deprived the audience from seeing the servant's facial expression. Further, Witkin has toned the figure so as to leave open the question of his race.

Witkin's *Olympia* shares certain physical features with Manet's model, a known courtesan named Victorine Meurent, but unlike Victorine, the model here is known only to the photographer and in the late twentieth century not so easily typed as a prostitute; with both figures unclothed, Witkin offers multiple interpretations. Yet, like Victorine, Witkin's *Olympia* blatantly stares out at the viewer, wearing a black ribbon at her neck, a bracelet on her arm and slippers on her feet, all of which accentuate her nudity. Also like Victorine, the model plants her clawlike hand firmly over her pubic area. Aside from their hair, the most prominent feature not shared by the two women is the size of their breasts; those of Witkin's model appear considerably larger.

Witkin may have been drawn to remake *Olympia* as a photograph because Manet's brilliant use of white and ivory tones and the strong dark contrasts suggested a rich graphic translation in silver nitrate. The idea to recreate *Olympia* may have been inspired also by Theodore Reff's article on the sources for Manet's paintings, which cites the artist's interest in erotic photography.[4]

Manet's *Olympia* attained notoriety immediately upon its unveiling at the Paris Salon in 1865. It was offensive and scandalous to the public, described with derision and resentment by critics, but endlessly fascinating to many artists, who were captivated by Manet's choice of a contemporary subject. Witkin's departure from propriety by pursuing subject matter considered taboo has earned him similar notoriety and contributed to his recognition. Yet, his *Olympia* is rather tame when compared to the far more provocative photographs he made in the decades that followed it. These photographs, which have elicited violent public reaction and revulsion, also remind us that art's capacity to shock and disturb has not lessened over time.

Rebecca Lawton

---

[1] Sherry Chayet, *Life Lessons: The Art of Jerome Witkin* (Syracuse, N.Y., 1984), 11.

[2] Ibid., 4.

[3] For analysis of Manet's *Olympia*, see Theodore Reff, *Manet: Olympia* (New York, 1977), passim; Francis Cachin et al., *Manet 1832-1883* (New York, 1983), esp. 174-83.

[4] See Theodore Reff, "Manet Sources: A Critical Evaluation," *Artforum* 8 (September 1969): 40-48.

142

William Clift
American (born 1944)

Shadow, Streams, Mt.-St.-Michel, France (1982; printed 1990)
Gelatin silver print
4⅝" x 5⅞"
Signature: "William Clift" on border
Lent by Ann L. Balis Morse, class of 1959

Provenance: William Clift to owner, 1991

Literature: William Clift, *The Photographs of William Clift 1956-1992* (New York, 1993), cover illus.

Exhibitions: *The Photographs of William Clift 1956-1992*, The Equitable Gallery, New York, 12 March-12 June 1993

William Clift, born in Boston in 1944, became interested in photography at a young age, organizing his first darkroom in 1954. Three years later, he took a photography workshop directed by Paul Caponigro (see cat. no. 143). Clift worked as a commercial photographer in Boston and specialized in architectural photography before moving to Santa Fe, New Mexico in 1971. During the seventies and eighties, he received prestigious awards, such as National Endowment for the Arts Photography Fellowships 1972 and 1979, and Guggenheim Fellowships in 1974 and 1980. Joseph Seagram and Sons, A. T. & T., and the Reader's Digest Association, are among the corporations that commissioned Clift to do photographic projects. From 1963 to the present, Clift's photographs have been included in several notable survey exhibitions, such as *Mirrors and Windows, American Photography Since 1960* (Museum of Modern Art, 1978) and *American Photography in the 1970's* (The Art Institute of Chicago, 1979); he has participated in numerous group shows and has been given solo exhibitions, the latest of which occurred at the Frances Lehman Loeb Art Center in July-September, 1995.

Like many photographers, in particular his teacher, Paul Caponigro, Clift has defined his subject matter. After moving to Santa Fe, he began to photograph the Western landscape, and a commission from Reader's Digest in 1984 initiated another ongoing landscape project, a series of photographs of the Hudson River Valley. Clift also established two further bodies of work, *Family Pictures* and a project to photograph the Benedictine Abby at Mont-Saint-Michel (hereafter, Mt.-St.-Michel), off the coast of Brittany, France. A large retrospective of his work held in 1993, at the Equitable Gallery in New York City, brought together these various themes, which have engaged Clift over the years.

Clift first traveled to Mt.-St.-Michel in 1977. He made a second trip in 1981-82, and a third trip in 1997. The photograph under discussion here, although taken in 1982, was not printed until 1989, demonstrating "once again that early enthusiasm or, on the other hand, dismissals, often miss the mark."[1]

The Mt.-St.-Michel photographs share many of the same aesthetic concerns as his Western landscapes. Both bodies of work are part of an ongoing, sustained visual study. Clift's initial interest is in the act of description. As his title for this photograph indicates, the work considered here is a photograph about shadow, water, and a specific, monumental place, Mt.-St.-Michel. It is also an example of his use of the camera's lens to engineer the flatness of the picture plane, and an example of his treatment of light to make shadow and landscape act as delicate, transparent layers lying on top of one another. His impressive command of his medium allows for a cogent formal expression and ability to render textures, but belies his interest in exploring photography as a philosopher does language and logic. His photographs are exquisitely made, printed by the photographer to his exacting standards. The lyrical quality of his photographs, as evident in the tonal gradations of black and white, and the radiance of light, requires them to be held by the eye, as objects worthy of contemplation.

The photograph of Mt.-St.-Michel discussed here, reveals Clift's interest in using the exterior appearance of things to suggest deeper meaning. The choice of a Gothic monument as a subject cannot have been an arbitrary one. Rather, Clift's exploration of what a Gothic cathedral represents offers the opportunity to examine how his own philosophical attitude toward photography relates to Gothic architecture.

Clift partakes of the Medieval concept of *splendor veritatis* in presenting Mt.-St.-Michel not as an illusion, but as a revelation.[2] The cathedral, as the symbol of the kingdom of God on earth, transcended all of its physical dimensions. It is the place where heaven and earth merge. When silhouetted against the sky, or in this instance, perceived as a shadow, the Gothic cathedral's pointy shapes and sharp projections appear to dissolve in the upward (or outward) sweep of the eye. Photography, like Gothic architecture, exploits the possibilities of light, the most natural phenomena, and embodies it as a metaphysical experience. Mt.-St.-Michel, because of its location, is seen both as an ever-changing silhouette that ebbs and flows according to the tides surrounding the island, and as a vision, a supernatural manifestation of the senses.

Rebecca Lawton

1   William Clift, "Regarding Shadow, Streams, Mont Saint Michel, France, 1982," written statement, 20 January 1989, in the possession of Ann Balis Morse.

2   See Otto von Simson, *The Gothic Cathedral, Origins of Gothic Architecture and the Medieval Concept of Order* (Princeton, New Jersey, 1962), xvii and passim.

143

Paul Caponigro
American (born 1932)

Pan Ascending, Kerry, Ireland (1993)
Gelatin silver print
18³/₄" x 14"
Signature: lower right, below image, "Paul Caponigro"
Lent by Ann L. Balis Morse, class of 1959

Provenance: Schmidt Bingham Gallery; Candace Perich Gallery; current owner since 1997

Exhibitions: *Paul Caponigro New Silver Prints 1958-1996*, Schmidt Bingham Gallery, New York, April 1996; *Paul Caponigro Masterworks*, Candace Perich Gallery, Katonah, New York, 22 February-26 March 1997

Born in 1932 in Boston, Caponigro developed a talent and fondness for music that led to a year of study at the College of Music at Boston University. His long-standing enthusiasm for photography began to play a more important role in his life when Alfredo Fondacaro accepted him as private piano student. Fondacaro had a seminal influence upon Caponigro's philosophical growth, allowing him to discover the places where visual and auditory stimuli intersect, a location known to Caponigro as the "state of heart."[1]

Caponigro credits his captivation with a bar of soap, while serving in the Army's Signal Corps in the mid-1950s, as a formative experience in his development as a photographer.[2] While looking at a deteriorating bar of kitchen soap, he recognized that a camera could record what is obvious, the external appearance of things, but a photograph could reflect his vision, transcending fact by evoking stronger, deeper associations, particularly to the metaphysical world. Thus, Caponigro developed a vast technical knowledge of photography to better express his faculties of perception and intuition. With a matchless intensity and sense of purpose, Caponigro has approached photography as a craftsman; his relentless desire to master material and technique has been commensurate with his ceaseless investigation of his subject matter.

Caponigro's exposure to the work of photographers dedicated to the fine art photography, such as Imogen Cunningham (see cat. no. 135), Ansel Adams, and especially Minor White, with whom he studied intermittently between 1957 and 1959, became the foundation for his personal expression. What has evolved and matured through decades of commitment to the act of looking at nature, is a concentrated and unwavering ardor for his subject matter—rocks, trees, flowers, and fauna. The photographer's years of silent and solitary labor at his craft have produced an assiduous refinement of his vision and an exquisite inquiry into the tonal possibilities of the medium of silver nitrate.

Caponigro's admiration for work of the artist, Morris Graves, with its mystical pictorial content, inspired the photographer's similar concern for human history and man's relationship to nature. The photograph under discussion here, *Pan Ascending, Kerry Ireland*, is evidence of Caponigro's preoccupation with the theme of ancient meaning. The photograph is about the passage of time, and it reflects the attention and affection Caponigro gives to his subjects, here a rock wall in a timeless battle with the forces of nature and a decomposing carcass of a calf embedded in sand, a graceful and eloquent statement.

In *Pan Ascending, Kerry Ireland*, Caponigro shot only the calf's hind quarters. Writing about the image, he noted, "When I saw the negative and the 1st [sic] proof print, I realized that the impulse had unconsciously welled up from within to touch and release my own interest in Irish Fairy Tales and mythology."[3] The Greek god, Pan, called Vidar in Norse mythology, is a representative of incorruptible nature. Surnamed the Silent God, Vidor lives in an impenetrable forest, where the sounds of manmade civilization are never heard. "Vidor is the imperishable, wild, original nature, the eternal matter, which reveals its force to, but is not comprehended by man; a force which man sees and reveres, without venturing an explanation."[4]

Caponigro first visited Ireland in 1966 on a Guggenheim Fellowship. Drawn to the ancient stone architectural sites, the subject was an instinctive progression from his earlier study for meaning in the formal arrangements of rocks. Treating each photograph as a personal statement, the photographer uses what is unseen to evoke what is unsaid. Caponigro's photographs are triggers for universal feelings common to all mankind.

Rebecca Lawton

---

[1]   Paul Caponigro, *The Wise Silence Photographs* (Boston, 1985), 28.

[2]   Ibid.

[3]   Paul Caponigro to Ann Morse, letter dated 2 February 1998.

[4]   R. B. Anderson, *Norse Mythology* (Chicago, 1888), 339.

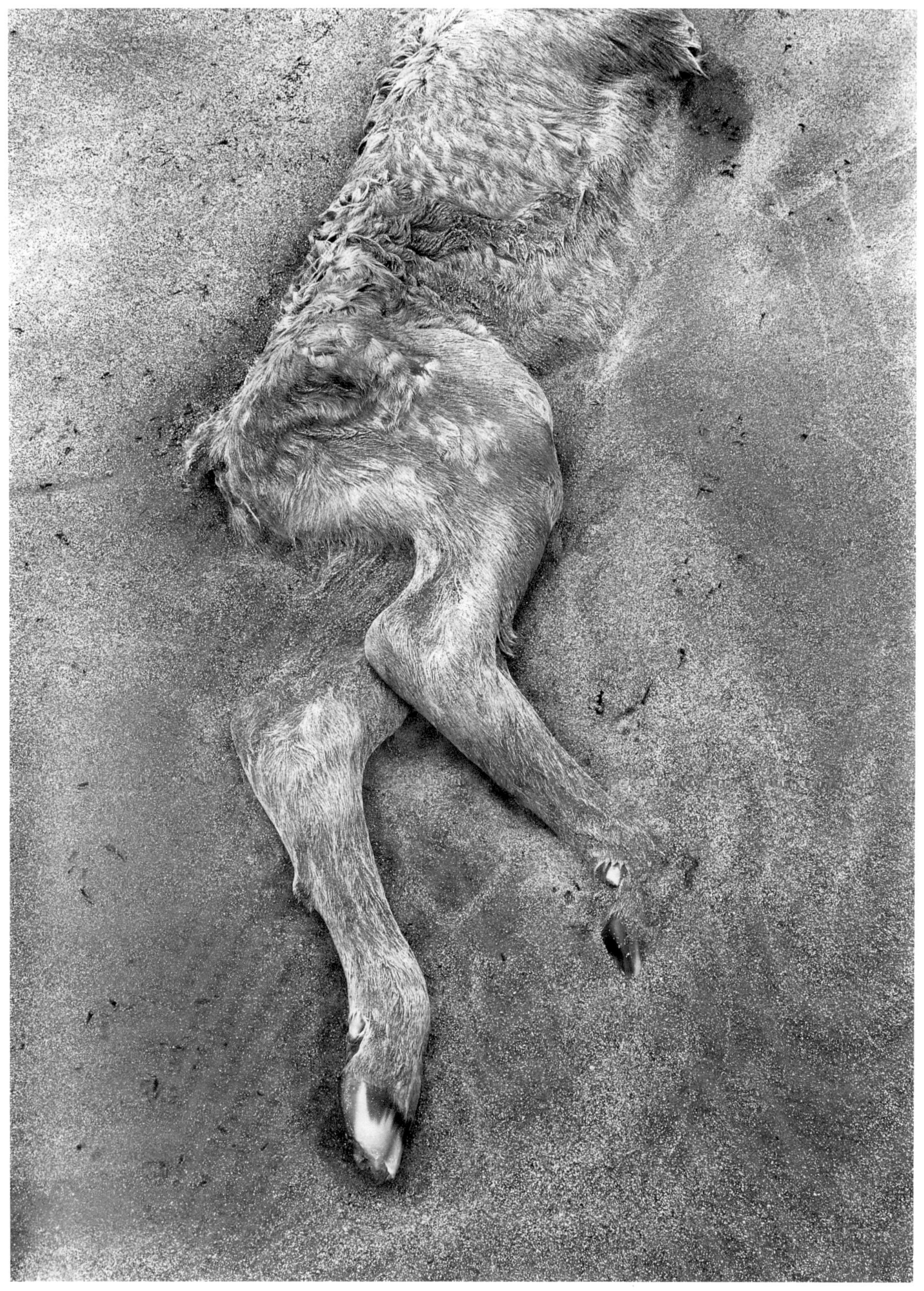

317

144

Richard Misrach
American (born 1949)

Swimmers, Pyramid Lake Indian Reservation, Nevada (1987)
Color coupler print
20" x 24"
Lent by Thomas Krasne Levine, class of 1982

Throughout his career as a photographer, Richard Misrach has made the modern-day desert a subject of his work, for he feels that the desert, and America's treatment of its desert, is an important symbol of the (scarred) American psyche.

From the earliest, America has systematically engaged in the scarring, poisoning, exploitation, and destruction of the American desert, most notably in the atomic testing which began at Los Alamos during World War II. Nonetheless, the desert not only endures; it looms large in the collective imagination (in part due to the success of Hollywood Westerns) as a place of freedom, expansiveness, and austere natural beauty, in short, as a symbol of the American wilderness. Misrach consequently sees the desert not as an empty wasteland, but a place full of resonant beauty, and of important (and contradictory) symbols. As a result, his photographs, which brilliantly record the desert's extraordinary atmosphere and light, also unflinchingly record scenes of manmade (and often government-ordered) destruction, exploitation, ugliness, and death.

Since 1983, Misrach's continuing explorations of the American desert have been organized into what he describes as *Cantos*, a term borrowed from Ezra Pound's long poetical work of the same name. Misrach feels that his work, like Pound's poetry, is (in Misrach's words) "free-associative," but nonetheless the combined images add up to a larger, coherent whole. Misrach was well along in the *Canto* series when he began the series from which this photograph comes, which he later entitled *Cantos: [Prologue]*.

The series began when Misrach noticed cultural and physical similarities between the American desert and the deserts of antiquity, and to notice as well that many early settlers of the western United States had named a number of geographic locations and natural formations after biblical sites. He soon began photographing sites in the United States that bore a relation, natural or titular, to sites in the Middle East. In 1989, he traveled to the Middle East, where he soon noted "the West's impact on the contemporary Middle East," including urban sprawl, ecological spoilage, and Western-style advertising. The two bodies of work (the pictures of the American West and the pictures of the Middle East) were subsequently combined in ironic juxtaposition in *Cantos: [Prologue]*.

Justin Spring

145

Hiroshi Sugimoto
Japanese (born 1948)

English Channel, Weston Cliff (1994)
Gelatin silver print
20" x 24"
The Greenberg Rohatyn Collection, New York, N.Y. (Jeanne Greenberg, class of 1989)

"The Seascapes are split into two images, an image of the sea and one of the sky. Both have been in motion since their creation."
Hiroshi Sugimoto[1]

English Channel, Weston Cliff is part of one of the three original series that Hiroshi Sugimoto first conceptualized during the mid-1970s, *Dioramas*, *Theaters*, and *Seascapes*, categories which, for him, respectively address themes of science, culture, and religion. Having studied politics and sociology in Tokyo during the late 1960s, Sugimoto turned to art when he moved to Los Angeles in 1972, where he applied himself to learning photography at a local college. His extracurricular activities included an in-depth analysis of the effects on his own system of a variety of chemical halluci-nates. The period, Sugimoto remembers, was one of intense creativity and stimulating thinking, out of which the idea for the three series emerged suddenly and fully-formed shortly after he relocated to New York in 1974. He began with the *Theaters*, images taken while a film is projected, of movie screens suffused with light to the point of brilliant blankness; then came the *Dioramas* of natural history and wax-museum tableaux—still life in the ex-treme. Work on the contemplatively stark *Seascapes* began in the early 1980s. Today he continues to develop all three series, each involving travel to new locations. He has photographed the Yellow, Marmar, Ligurian, Ionian, and Red Seas, among others, during the day and at night, but always with the horizon line bifurcating the picture plane at dead center. This division is significant for Sugimoto:

> Usually Japanese people like to see Mount Fuji. For me, it was important to see the ocean, the big ocean....[As a series, this image] had to do with the idea of ancient man, facing the sea and giving a

name to it. Naming things has something to do with human aware-ness, with the separation of the entire world from you. Language has to do with the need to communicate with a world that is separated from yourself, the separation between inner and outer world would be less clear without language. So with the *Seascapes* I was thinking about the most ancient human impressions. The time when the first man named the world around him, the sea.[2]

In writing on Sugimoto's work, critics have referred to the Japanese terms *ukiyo-e* ("the floating world" of Edo-period graphics) and *shashin* ("transforming the real," which is Japanese for "photogra-phy"). For his own part, Sugimoto invokes the European tradition of Northern Renaissance painting. He admires the art of Jan van Eyck, Petrus Christus, and Rogier van der Weyden for its pristine realism and high degree of craft, both of which he sees as related to early photographic tradition. These are also aspects of his own work, with its refined detail and technique. There is all the fascination of a miniature in observing each wavelet peaking with almost hallucinatory clarity upon the English Channel in a photo-graph taken with Sugimoto's single piece of equipment, "a wooden camera, like a 19th-century style box."[3] In early photography one also finds Sugimoto's palette. Eschewing color, he only prints in black-and-white, "an abstraction from the real world [that] gives people a more realistic impression."[4]

Ingrid Schaffner

---

[1] Quoted in Thomas Kellein, "Interview with Hiroshi Sugimoto," in *Time Exposed* (London and New York, 1995), 89-95.

[2] Ibid.

[3] Ibid.

[4] Ibid.

146

Sally Mann
American (born 1951)

Dead Duck, 1988 (printed 1990)
Gelatin silver print
8" x 10"
Lent by Ann L. Balis Morse, class of 1959

Sally Mann has emerged in recent years as a celebrated but controversial figure in American photography, for her beautiful and mysterious images of her family and home that often feature disturbingly suggestive images of her children, who frequently appear nude. Advocates on behalf of child-victims of sexual, physical, and psychological abuse, finding Mann's imagery deliberately provocative, have called for its censorship, but others have found in Mann's work a rare honesty and fiercely independent-minded appreciation of natural physical beauty.

Mann herself is ambivalent about the use of her nude children in staged tableaux that have violent, incestuous, or otherwise sexual overtones. She has written openly of her own childhood, noting her doctor-father's "unapologetic self-indulgence"[1] and his creation of sexually provocative sculptural objects with which he decorated the family home. Mann survived that childhood with a strong sense that "reputation is something that people with character can do without,"[2] and an awareness that her own family values, while not necessarily those of her neighbors, are ones with which she feels entirely comfortable. She has, in fact, continued in her father's footsteps, remaining in the place where she grew up in southwestern Virginia, and raising a family of her own, exposing them, in the meantime, to situations other parents would not.

Of her photographs, Mann has observed:

> [My children] have been involved in the creative process since infancy....We are spinning a story of what it is to grow up. It is a complicated story and sometimes we try to take on the grand themes: anger, love, death, sensuality, and beauty. But we tell it all without fear and without shame.[3]

Dead Duck, though it contains no child nudity, does indeed have an element of the sensational about it. In the image, Mann's daughter,

Jessie, wearing an adult's sweater, stands with her face stuck through a wire fence, her arms folded before her in a way that suggests that the sweater might double as a straitjacket. On the fencepost to her right, in a metal cone designed to minimize its death-struggle, a duck, its throat slashed, bleeds into a plastic bucket. The duck's incarceration in the tin cone mimics the child's incarceration in the sweater; the duck's head sticking through the bottom of the cone mimic's the child's head sticking through the fence. But the child stares directly and impassively into the camera as if absolutely nothing is wrong—and apparently nothing is, for (according to Mann) her child's witnessing the death of a duck in this manner is a fact of everyday life on the family farm.

Dead Duck was a difficult photo to create. As Sally Mann recalled to the owner of this photograph, Ann Balis Morse, class of 1959,

> [It] took more tries than most. The first time we took it, the duck had just received its death sentence. Jessie simply stepped into the scene...its throat was slit, the blood dripped into the bucket, and I snapped the picture...[But] I didn't like [the image]...so...we tried the picture again. Jessie had begun to dislike the death scene so I hoped the second try would be better.
>
> It wasn't, so we tried again. This time [our friends] agreed to simply freeze the duck and the blood...[so] that's a frozen duck in your picture.[4]

Justin Spring

---

[1] Sally Mann, *Sally Mann: Immediate Family* (New York, 1992), n.p.

[2] Ibid.

[3] Ibid.

[4] Sally Mann to Ann Balis Morse, undated, collection Vassar College Archive, courtesy Ann Balis Morse.

147

John Coplans

American, British-born (born 1920)

Self-Portrait, Torso, 1984 (1984)
Gelatin silver print
20" x 16"
Lent by Sue Peirce Hartshorn, class of 1962

Provenance: Pace/ MacGill Gallery, New York

With the exhibition, *A Body of Work*, in 1988, John Coplans, then sixty-eight years old, earned extensive public recognition for his photography.[1] Prior to establishing his career as a photographer, Coplans had occupied several others within the art world: painter, scholar, museum director and curator, author and critic. In 1962, he help found *Artforum*, a magazine dedicated to publishing critical opinion. Twenty-two years later, in 1980, he began to devote his full attention to photography.

Coplans's own nude body became his preferred subject in 1978, at the time he held the directorship of the Akron Art Museum. Photography was then a nightly hobby, an intuitive, solitary exercise performed at the end of his work day. He also did street photography and portraiture, yet found photographing his body a more compelling subject. Coplans uses the camera as a drawing implement, "...I ramble over myself. I'm concerned with frontality, size, scale, edge, tension, drawing."[2] His art is an exercise in formality and photography is about perception. Garry Winogrand's cogent remark, "I photograph to find out what something looks like photographed," applies equally to Coplans's method of using the camera to see what it has already seen.[3]

Coplans photographs his body without his head and with the help of several assistants. His photographs, therefore, lack identity, but remain self-portraits in that they evoke associations to the photographer's past. Moreover, by presenting the nude body dispassionately as a document, Coplans makes his body unequivocally non-erotic. The human figure devoid of sexuality or prurient interest is free to become something else. Whether grotesque or comical, the body can be used as a reference to the past —to time or memory, or as a point of departure to the past through Jungian associations. For example, Coplans associates the photograph in this exhibition, *Self-Portrait, Torso, 1984* to "a seventeenth-century drawing of a face."[4] The photographer has explained, "I [don't] know how it happens, but when I pose for one of these photographs, I become immersed in the past. It is akin to Alice falling through the looking glass. I use no props....I make very few images no more than about 9 a year average."[5]

Rebecca Lawton

---

[1]   *A Body of Work* was shown at the Museum of Modern Art in New York in spring 1988, selected from an exhibition originally organized by Sandra S. Phillips at the San Francisco Museum of Modern Art.

[2]   Christopher Lyon, "Seeing from Inside: John Coplans on A Body of Work," *Museum of Modern Art Members Quarterly* (Spring 1988): n.p.

[3]   Garry Winogrand; quoted in Janet Malcolm, "Certainties and Possibilities," in *Diana and Nikon* (Boston, 1980), 37.

[4]   Ibid.

[5]   John Coplans, "My Chronology," in *John Coplans: A Self-Portrait 1984-1997* (New York, 1998), n.p.

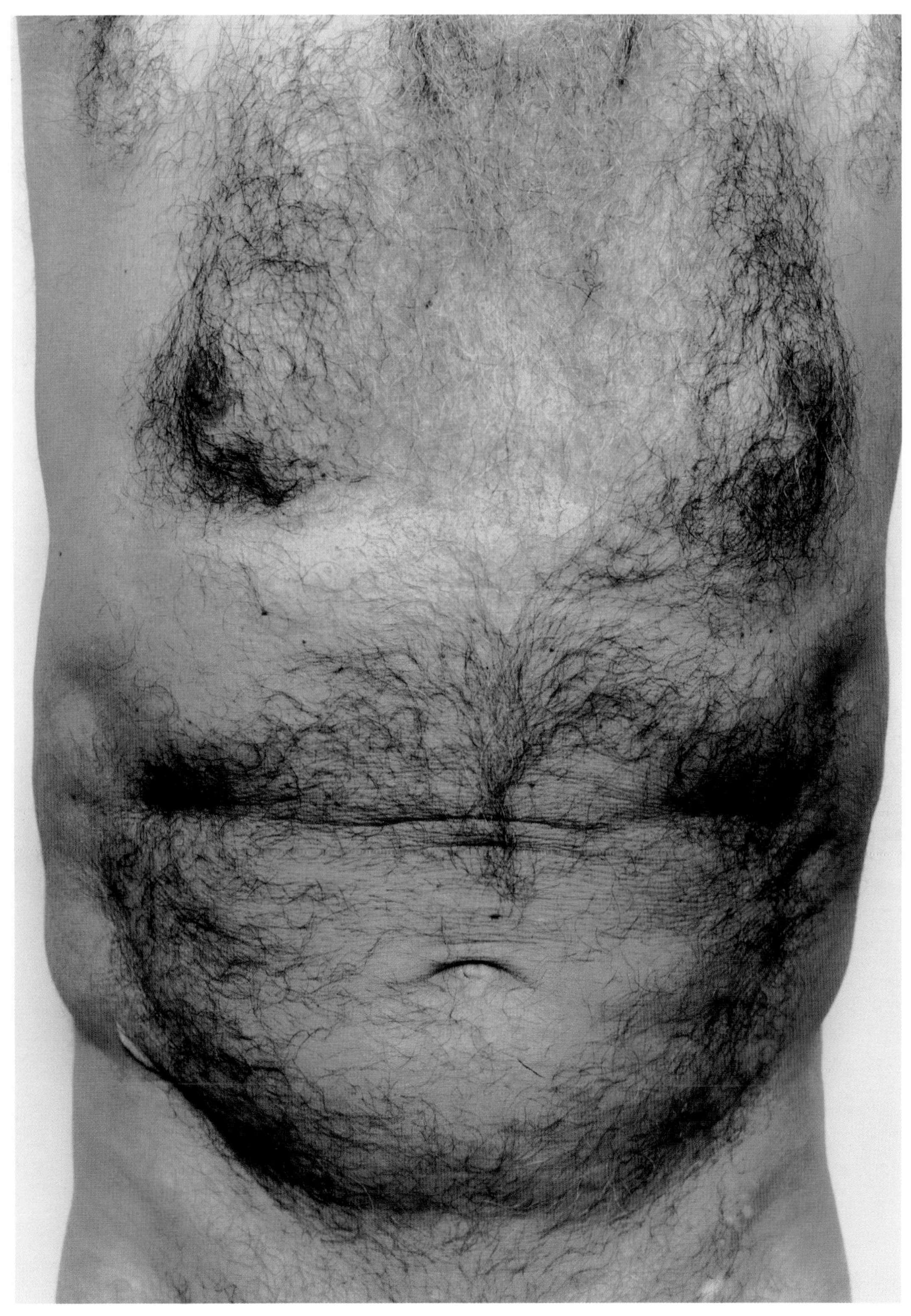

Index of Artists

PHOTOGRAPHY CREDITS

Dean Beasom, XYSTUS Studios, cat. nos.: 63, 77.
Douglas Baz, cat. nos.: 15, 19, 20, 29, 30, 36, 38, 40, 42, 53, 76, 82, 85, 86, 89, 97, 98, 99, 105, 106, 126, 147.
Ben Blackwell Photography, cat. no.: 112.
Peter Brenner Photography, cat. nos.: 140, 144.
Ali Elai-Camerarts Studio, cat. no.: 45.
Greg Heins, cat. no.: 43.
©Justin Kerr 1997, cat. nos.: 5, 6, 8.
Courtesy of Lennon, Weinberg, Inc., cat. no.: 116.
Robert Lorenzson, cat. nos.: 4, 7, 9, 11, 16, 17, 18, 21, 22, 23, 24, 27, 34, 39, 41, 50, 55, 58, 68, 69, 74, 81, 83, 87, 88, 91, 95, 96, 102, 103, 104, 107, 108, 110, 111, 113, 114, 118, 127, 133, 134, 137, 139.
Dan Morse, Firefly Studios, cat. no.: 51.
Tom Powel, cat. nos.: 120, 121, 122, 145.
©P. S. Ritterman, cat. nos.: 130, 131, 132.
Phillipp Scholz Rittermann, cat. nos.: 10, 14, 25, 28.
©Steven Sloman, 1992, cat. no.: 115.
Oren Slor, cat. no.: 117.
Jerry Thompson, cat. nos.: 138, 142, 143.
Michael Tropea Photography, cat. nos.: 101, 109, 119.
Dorothy Zeidman, cat. no.: 73.